PLEASING GOD

by Knowing and Doing His Will

William P. Bunnell, MD

DEDICATION

Dagny

Elijah

Silas

Isaiah

Micah

Reuben

Will

Jake

Matthew

And everyone who desires to know and do the will of God.

KEYWORD LIST

CHRISTIAN LIVING

GOD'S WILL

PLEASING GOD

BIBLICAL IMPERATIVES

BIBLICAL LITERACY

DECISION-MAKING

TOPICAL BIBLE STUDY

Contents

KEYWORD LIST   iv

LIST OF TOPICS   vi

PREFACE   viii

INTRODUCTION   x

TOPICS   19

EPILOGUE   295

DISCUSSION QUESTIONS   299

ACKNOWLEDGMENTS   369

APPENDIX A: Bible Translations   371

APPENDIX B: Websites   372

APPENDIX C: Books of the Bible and Abbreviations   373

ABOUT THE AUTHOR   375

LIST OF TOPICS

ACCOUNTABILITY

ADULTERY

ALIENS

ANGER

ANXIETY

APOLOGETICS

ATTITUDE

AUTHORITY

BAPTISM

BLASPHEMY

BLESSING

BODY

CHARACTER

CHARITY

CHILDREN

CHOICES

CHRISTIAN COMMUNITY

CHURCH

COMMUNION

COMPASSION

CONFESSION

CONFIDENCE

CONTENTMENT

DEVIL

DEVOTION

DISABLED PERSONS

DISCIPLESHIP

DISCIPLINE

DIVORCE

DOUBT

DRUNKENNESS

EMPLOYEES

ENEMIES

ENVY

EVIL

FAITH

FAITHFULNESS

FAMILY

FASTING

FEAR

FEAR GOD

FORGIVENESS

FREEDOM

GENEROSITY

GENTLENESS

GOD HATES...

GOD LOVES...

GOLDEN RULE

GOSPEL

GOSSIP

GOVERNMENT

GREATEST COMMANDS

GREED

HATE

HOLINESS

HOLY SPIRIT

HONESTY

HOPE

HUMILITY

HYPOCRISY

IDOLS

JOY

JUDGMENT

JUSTICE

KNOWLEDGE

LIFESTYLE

LOVE

MARGINAL ISSUES

MARRIAGE

MATURITY

MEDITATION

MERCY

MISSION

MOTIVATION

MURDER

NEIGHBOR

OATH/VOW

OBEDIENCE

ONE ANOTHER

PATIENCE

PEACE

PERSECUTION

PERSEVERANCE

PLEASING GOD

POVERTY

PRAISE

PRAYER

PRIDE

PRIORITIES

PRISONERS

PURITY

RECONCILIATION

REMINDERS

REPENTANCE

RESPECT

REST

REVENGE

SABBATH

SACRIFICE

SALVATION

SANCTIFICATION

SCRIPTURE

SERVICE

SEXUALITY

SIN

SLANDER

SOLITUDE

SPEECH

SPIRITUAL GIFTS

SPIRITUAL WARFARE

SUBMISSION

SUFFERING

TEACHING

TEMPTATION

THANKSGIVING

THEFT

TIME

TRUST

TRUTH

UNITY

WAITING

WEALTH

WILL OF GOD

WISDOM

WITNESS

WORK

WORKS

WORLDLINESS

WORSHIP

YOU ARE…

PREFACE

WITHOUT FAITH, IT IS IMPOSSIBLE TO PLEASE GOD

Writer of Hebrews

Hebrews 11:6

CAREFULLY DETERMINE WHAT PLEASES THE LORD

Apostle Paul

Ephesians 5:10

ONLY THOSE WHO PLEASE GOD BY KNOWING AND DOING HIS WILL CAN ENTER THE KINGDOM OF HEAVEN

Jesus Christ

Matthew 7:21

YOU MUST NOT ONLY KNOW, BUT DO THE WILL OF GOD

Apostle James

James 1:22

THE PERSON WHO DOES THE WILL OF GOD WILL LIVE FOREVER

Apostle John

1 John 2:17

INTRODUCTION

I FIRST BECAME AWARE OF the concept of "God's will" as a young teenager and came to understand that one of the most important challenges of the Christian life was to learn about God's will, and then to do it. I'm at the other end of life now. Over the years, I have spent significant time reading and studying the Bible, listened to many talented pastors and teachers, worked hard at my profession, and accumulated many life experiences which I attempted to understand in light of the Christian worldview. Along the way, I made many decisions—some good and others not—in my attempt to live in a way that is consistent with God's will.

I recently had an unexpected block of time away from work during which I read through the entire Bible in a short time. While I was reading through the historical books of the Old Testament, it suddenly became apparent to me that the epitaph for each of the kings of Israel described him as one that "pleased God" or "did not please the Lord." This pronouncement was always based on whether or not the king followed both general and specific instructions given by God. The rest of Scripture is similarly clear: to live a life pleasing to God means following his instructions. In order to do so, it is imperative that we know what these instructions are and how they apply to twenty-first-century Christian belief and behavior.

I have a renewed interest in the subject of God's will after trying to live it for several decades because I now see that my original understanding of it was incomplete. It is my specific intent in writing this book to help you understand the concept and specifics of "God's will" and to know how to live your life in a way that is pleasing to him. Dear Lord, may it be so!

This is a different kind of book. Please read the entire introduction and you will better understand the basis, layout, and how you might find it most helpful.

WHAT IS THE WILL OF GOD?

Finding the will of God for my life was a significant goal of mine as a young Christian. My understanding of "God's will" at that time was focused primarily on what I saw as my major life choices: Where should I go to college? What should be my major? Should I marry and whom? Which job opportunity should I take? Where should I live? Later on, as mid-career choices arose, my thinking had not changed much. Should I accept a job offer across the country, far away from friends and family? Should I accept a major increase in responsibility? I treated each of these major decisions as an intense spiritual exercise. I searched the Bible for guidance and attempted to apply promising passages,[1] prayed for wisdom and guidance, and sought counsel from the Holy Spirit and from friends. Even though each of these efforts was an important part of the decision process, none provided a specific answer for questions like "shall I move to California?" It was disconcerting to realize that most of the guidance for such big decisions was subjective.

I believe now that I had the wrong model for understanding God's will. "God's will" seemed to be a specific but secret intention of God for me, and it was my challenge to find out what that intention was. A good mental image for this view is a maze. God's will is at the center, and I am to start on the outside and try to find my way to the center. There are many decision points and many different paths to take on this journey, but most are dead ends. Finding the center of God's will proved to be more difficult than I expected. If God had a specific will for me regarding specific choices I was to make, and if I was to be in the center of his will, why should that place be so difficult to find?

God's will for you and me is no mystery, nor is a maze a good way to think about it. At its heart, God's will is a call to faith in him and his Son, Jesus Christ, which places us in a loving relationship with himself. This faith, regardless of how small, is absolutely essential in order to please him. **"Without faith, it is impossible to please God."**[2] Genuine faith is more than mere belief. It is the confident assurance in what we hope for and a conviction about things we cannot now see.[3] It is the key to knowing and understanding God's will and the motivation to do it.[4,5] A life of faith is what is ultimately pleasing to God. You might think of this book as filling in the details of such a life.

It is very appropriate to think of your life and relationship with God as something that pleases him. To please simply means "to give gratification, joy or pleasure to someone" or "to give someone a gift that they find aesthetically appealing or attractive." What a beautiful description of a life lived as God intends.

The idea of pleasing God may conjure difficult associations for some. Negative feelings associated with demanding or abusive parents, an unreasonable boss, an unfortunate life experience, or unfulfilled dreams and aspirations may unconsciously be projected on to your understanding of God, transforming him into a capricious or vindictive tyrant who is impossible to please.

While understandable, this picture of God is not consistent with the biblical descriptions of him as a loving Heavenly Father, full of grace and compassion and wanting the best for his children. A more appropriate analogy would be that of new parents taking great delight in the first sounds their baby makes, the first smile, the first steps, the first words, the toddler antics, the cute remarks, and so on as the child grows and matures. This happy young child is anxious to please his/her parents because they all live in a loving relationship that brings them joy. These parents have ideas about what they want their child to be and do, and likewise God has plans for what he wants you and me to be and do. This is a good illustration and definition of God's will for us. Like the young child who wants to please his/ her parents, pleasing God for us results in a joyful relationship with a loving Heavenly Father and is never a dreadful obligation.

In its simplest and most general terms, God's will is what he desires or intends for us to be and to do. We learn about the specifics of his expectations in the Bible where they are expressed as imperative statements. These commands are occasionally given as a list (for example, the Ten Commandments[6]), but they are often imbedded in narrative stories that provide important context and enhance our understanding of their meaning.[7]

In the New Testament, Jesus is recorded on multiple occasions affirming the two greatest commandments ever given, which he said summarized all others: "Love God with all your heart, soul, mind and strength, and love your neighbor as much as you love yourself."[8-10] He later added one more intended specifically for his followers: "Love one another."[11]

The imperative statements of Scripture are a very clear and specific expression of God's will, that is, what he wants us to be and do. In fact, these commands are the only objective statements of God's will that we have. They are timeless moral imperatives that primarily have to do with our belief, character, behavior, relationships, and worship. They are the details of God's blueprint for your life.

A blueprint is a good model and illustration for thinking about God's will. This is a detailed written description of a designer's vision for a final product. It includes specific instructions for construction, type of materials to be used, related services to be included, and so on. It defines the project, sets goals and boundaries, and establishes the standard by which progress is to be evaluated. When followed, it reassures during the chaos of construction that the final product will be as the designer originally intended. In a very similar way, the biblical imperatives are like the lines on a blueprint. They are very specific expressions of God's will and plan for building a life that is pleasing to him.

It will be helpful at this point to distinguish between three types of imperative statements found in the Bible. The first are clearly situational directives to specific people in specific historical circumstances and therefore of no interest for this work. (for example, Jonah told by God to go to Nineveh).[12]

The second type of imperative is ceremonial, describing commands given by God to Moses for the new nation of Israel (a theocracy) to govern worship and religious practices. These ceremonies along with the rules for sacrifice, observance of feast days, and dietary restrictions marked the Jews as God's chosen people and helped keep their focus on him. Jesus made it very clear that he came to earth to fulfill the purpose of these laws by offering himself as the ultimate and perfect sacrifice for sin.[13-17] Christians are no longer bound by these ceremonial laws for this reason.[18]

The most important imperative statements in the Bible for us are moral in nature. They reflect the nature and character of God and as such are holy, just, and unchanging. They express God's will for our own character and interpersonal relationships. They have to do with the possibility of hurting or helping ourselves or others. They deal with principles of right and wrong. We recognize the relevance and value of these laws by using reason, conscience and common sense. Because such laws are based on the unchanging nature of God, all moral laws become timeless moral imperatives for each of us. We are instructed to imitate God.[19] The Bible is authoritative on these issues.[20]

However, many issues and life decisions are non-moral, meaning they do not involve moral principles (for example, buying a new house, or choosing whether to accept a different job), and on these the Bible has little to say. The appropriateness and quality of such choices are based on other factors such as wisdom, opportunity, circumstances, convenience and preference. Since there is no specific guidance in Scripture for making non-moral choices, we can infer that God leaves these kinds of choices up to us. He gives us wisdom, good judgment and the freedom and ability to plan for our future and make good choices.[21-23]

DECISION-MAKING AND THE WILL OF GOD

How then does a sincere Christian seeking to know the will of God for their own life make important non-moral decisions? Although that discussion is beyond the scope of this work, learning how to answer the question is crucial for many of life's major choices. To that end, many wise Christians have recommended taking the following factors into consideration and generally in the following order of importance.

1. Is there any direct Scriptural imperative relevant to this decision?

2. Is the Holy Spirit leading you in any specific way as you pray about this decision?

3. Have you obtained the counsel of wise friends and advisors?

4. Do your abilities and personal desires lead you in any particular direction?

5. Do your circumstances lead you in a certain direction?

Taking such an approach to decision-making about non-moral issues will help you avoid making bad choices and direct you on a path that God will bless. If you ask, he will give you wisdom and guidance to work out the details of your choices. In the process, you will find yourself drawn closer to God and enjoying increased fellowship with your friends and advisors.

WHY I WROTE THIS BOOK

I hope to show in the following pages that God has been very specific about how to please him and that doing so is the key to a happy and fulfilling life.

While reading through the Bible, I came to a deeper realization of the importance and relevance of the imperative statements or commands found there. They constitute much more than just a list of "do's and don'ts." They communicate God's definitive will for what he wants us to be and do. They present a coherent picture of the nature and character of God which he wants us to imitate.[24] They deserve our special attention if it is our intention to please God.

What started as a realization became a calling and a fulfilling mission for my life in semi-retirement. I recognized the potential for helping others understand God's will and this goal became highly motivating for me to complete the work.

My goal has been to collect all the biblical imperatives I could find, organize them by topic, and write them out in a topical format that anyone can easily access, understand, and apply. I hope to encourage personal discovery in these matters and enthusiasm for becoming a person of character who pleases God.

My goal is not to "share my heart" or what I think about these issues. It is the heart of God I wish to share, his loving intentions for people everywhere, and the character traits he has chosen for display in those who follow his Son, Jesus Christ.

Unfortunately, biblical illiteracy is prevalent within the Christian community. Many people have never been taught basic biblical content, and many more have never taken time to discover and apply biblical truth to their lives. There are also significant misunderstandings of what the "will of God" means and how it should affect our daily lives. This book represents my contribution to helping address this problem. Knowing and doing the will of God should be a top priority for everyone who chooses to follow Jesus. I pray this book will help you with the "knowing." The "doing" is left up to you.

HOW I WROTE THIS BOOK

Other than this introduction and a short epilogue at the end, this book does not contain my words or ideas. I have collected them from the Bible and arranged and referenced them by topic for easy access and verification. In addition to the imperative statements, I have included additional references that provide biblical commentary on the subject. I have not included any personal or otherwise secondary commentary on these imperative statements. Every sentence is extracted from its primary source, the Bible, and is referenced by superscript to that source. This feature allows you to verify that what I have compiled accurately represents what God intends for you to understand.

This project developed over time. My initial goal was to collect and organize only imperative statements from the Bible. However, I quickly came to the uncomfortable realization that I was just compiling a list of "do's and don'ts." I also soon noticed that nearly all of the imperative statements were accompanied by another statement explaining its reason and importance. (for example, "honor your parents" because you will have a longer life[25]). Sometimes these "indicative" statements directly accompany the command and at other times they are found elsewhere in the Bible. These explanations greatly enrich our understanding of the imperatives and it seemed logical and appropriate to include them in this work.[26-28] Although I never intended to write a more complete discussion of any topic beyond the obvious imperatives, I have since included references that provide additional explanations in the Bible's own words about many topics.

Some statements in the Bible imply or infer imperatives. Inference"is based on evidence and reasoning from available facts rather than on an explicit statement. Although lacking the same firmness of a direct imperative, I have included some statements of this type. I have not used conjecture, which is opinion only and is not based on factual evidence.

There are many topics in the Bible which you might expect to be included here but are not. These apparent omissions are because, in keeping with my goals, I did not find direct imperative statements on the subject despite ample biblical coverage of the topic.

While reading through the Bible, I began marking references that contained imperative statements about moral issues. Later on, I went back page by page, collected the marked references, and entered them into Microsoft Excel, tagging each with a topic label (for example, "love"). After I had completed this step, I then collected all the references within a specific topic and arranged them by subtopics which became paragraphs (love for God, love for others, love for fellow Christians). The reference statements were then arranged to create free-flowing sentences. I carefully referenced every sentence I wrote to its biblical source. I used a computer program (Accordance, Oaktree Software) to compare multiple translations of the Bible and to choose the wording which fit most seamlessly into its new context.

My initial goal was to make every statement an exact copy of the words used in any one of the readily available translations. This proved impractical. Some of my sentences contain words from more than one translation to express the intent and some others combine the thoughts of several references into one statement. This method of writing required minor changes of words and connectors to facilitate smooth reading. It also allowed substitution of words in some cases which seemed to better express the original meaning in current vernacular or because of their new context (for example, substituting "surgeon's scalpel" for "two-edged sword"). It also became impractical to note which translation was used and I abandoned the attempt. A list of translations consulted can be found in Appendix A.

Finding imperative statements in the Bible and categorizing them by topic was easy. Finding and adding the explanatory statements was usually not difficult. Adding verses that imply or infer imperatives required more thoughtful consideration. Arranging verses within topics to flow into meaningful paragraphs and sentences without introducing or changing meaning was the most demanding and time-consuming part of the process. Choosing modern words and idioms to express ancient truths was a very satisfying challenge.

PRESUPPOSITIONS

Every author has relevant presuppositions, and I want you to know mine. Based on what I have read in the Bible, I understand that a personal and powerful God exists and that he created the universe out of nothing and intelligent human beings for the purpose of fellowship with him. He wishes to communicate with us and has done so by revealing his general characteristics in the wonders of creation[29] and specifically by sending his Son, Jesus Christ, into the world to fully represent and speak for him.[30] The prophets of the Old Testament spoke and wrote down the words of God. The disciples of Jesus were firsthand witnesses to what he said and did and recorded these details in the Gospels. The remainder of the New Testament was written by the apostles of Jesus, all of whom spent time with him, except for Paul, who received a special revelation from God. All of these writings have been miraculously preserved for us in the Bible which is the primary means of our receiving communication from God.

I understand that God has specific intentions and expectations for our character and behavior, belief, worship, and treatment of others, and that these are expressly communicated through the imperative statements of the Bible. All Scripture is inspired by God and is authoritative in these matters.[31] It is a revelation from God and did not originate in the human mind or imagination.[32,33] It contains all that we need to know for salvation and living a life that pleases him.[34] The Scriptures inform and transform our minds and our behavior. They are a revelation from God about his nature and his will for us. They contain the most compelling and the only objective statements of God's will available to us.

Generally speaking, the meaning of Scripture is clear, especially in the critical areas of belief and behavior. Some statements stand on their own ("do not tell a lie"[35]), and some require multiple references to fully understand them ("you must be born again"[36]). Additions and subtractions to what has been written in Scripture are forbidden.[37-40]

Context is of critical importance for the correct and proper interpretation of any communication. Every imperative statement presented here is extracted from its biblical context or story and you will not get that context from reading just what is written here. That is the primary reason for connecting almost every sentence by superscript to its specific reference in the Bible. You will want to read these references in their full narrative context to more fully understand why the imperatives are important and also to be sure that what I have written accurately conveys the intent of Scripture. Check them out!

DISCLAIMERS

This book is not intended to be an abbreviated or rewritten version of the Bible. It is also not intended to be a substitute for reading whole sections of the Bible at one time, which is necessary in order to fully understand the importance of its imperatives. It is also not intended to be a comprehensive discussion of any one topic but is primarily limited to imperative statements. It is intended to be a step toward biblical literacy; a reminder of how much of God's will affects daily life, actions, and attitudes; and an encouragement to live life in ways that please God.

EDITORIAL DECISIONS

Situational commands are usually obvious and not included. Specific commandments regarding the construction of Noah's ark or Solomon's temple obviously have no moral significance. Jesus and the apostles Peter and Paul each declared the Old Testament dietary and ceremonial laws non-binding on Christians and so they are not included.[41-44] Faith in Jesus Christ, not adherence to the Law of Moses is the new requirement for pleasing God.[45,46]

I have made the text gender neutral. Use of the masculine was common in ancient writings and was intended to be inclusive, as in "mankind." Both men and women are created in the image of God, have equal standing before him, are equally bound by his commands, and equally accountable to him.

I have included a few topics that are only descriptive and not strictly imperative because they are such a powerful and definitive expression of what seriously pleases or displeases God. The expression "God loves…" appears many times throughout Scripture and begs special attention. Likewise, "God hates…" instantly raises brilliant red flags and should instill the fear of God in all of us.

I have made every effort to avoid any distortion of the true meaning of the Scripture and accept full responsibility with regret for any errors I have made.

HOW TO USE THIS BOOK

The book is intended as a workbook for personal or group study and discussion. It is not necessarily a cover-to-cover read. Each topic stands alone and is not dependent on any others. This helps explain why you will find some repetition as you move from topic to topic. The topics are presented in alphabetical order. A complete list appears at the front of the book. Pick a topic of interest and go directly to it.

The narrative portion of each topic appears on the right- facing page and should be read and considered first. The objective is to see all the relevant imperatives on a specific topic collected in one place and to gain a good understanding of what God expects of us in that area.

The superscripts after nearly every sentence correspond with the biblical references from which the statement is taken and which are listed on the left facing page for each topic, except for this introduction where they are listed at the end. I have deliberately omitted the text of the references so readers will not be distracted by trying to compare words against the text of this book. Instead, the references are provided so that you can easily locate them and read the words directly within their biblical context.

I have developed a list of study questions for each topic suitable for group discussion and personal application. They are located at the back of the book and are in alphabetical order. These open-ended questions bring up specific aspects of each topic as well as pertinent side issues and are designed to stimulate discussion and further personal study.

You will find a short epilogue followed by appendices at the end of the book.

WHO SHOULD READ THIS BOOK

The will of God is a topic of major importance to all ages and stages of social and spiritual development. You will likely find this book helpful if:

- You are wondering what it would mean to follow Jesus Christ.

- You are wondering what kind of person or life would please God.

- You are new in your life of faith.

- You have questions about the will of God.

- You have never learned much about the Bible.

- You are a mature Christian trying to understand God's will.

- You are a parent instructing your children in God's ways.

- You are a teaching or discussion-group leader.

RESOURCES

I consulted numerous translations of the Bible to find specific wording most appropriate for this presentation. As a young person, I memorized and learned from the King James Bible and found it was often my "native language" in remembering concepts and specific wording. I have used the New International Version most of my adult life and have several marked-up copies. I have also made frequent reference to the New Living Translation and The Message. Use of multiple translations ensured that I had a correct understanding of the meaning of each passage and helped in choosing my wording.

Accordance Bible Software (AccordanceBible.com) is a powerful computer program available for both PC and Mac. It is easy to use and very fast, with searches for specific words or references appearing in milliseconds. Numerous Bible translations are available, and a single keystroke instantly moves from one to another. An extensive library of reference materials is literally at your fingertips and can be purchased in modules appropriate for beginners or advanced scholars. I consulted many of these resources to help explain unfamiliar passages of Scripture.

The Narrated Bible, by F. LaGard Smith was instrumental in starting this project and is a great learning tool. This New International Version (NIV) translation is arranged in chronological order. The historical episodes are told only once (for example, history of Israel, life of Christ) with marginal notes indicating where there are multiple references to the same incident. The text is divided into sections with a short "narration" at the beginning of each which explains the significance of what you are about to read. A small icon marks out 365 days (without dates) which is helpful in pacing your reading.

Modern technology provides many helpful resources for study and understanding the Bible in general and God's will specifically. The internet provides access to many websites produced by reliable Christian sources. They often appear at or near the top of the search list and offer in-depth discussions on almost any topic you might imagine. Wikipedia can be a good place to start for an overview of a given topic. I found it useful to place the words "Christian view of…" ahead of my search term (See appendix B for a list of helpful Internet resources.).

MY PRAYER

My prayer at the beginning of every writing session went something as follows:

Dear Lord, Please grant that:

> every step of this process be guided by your Holy Spirit,
>
> every observation made while reading your Word,
>
> every meaning derived from every reference,
>
> every subject category into which it is placed,
>
> every paragraph and sentence written,
>
> every keystroke made,
>
> all be a true and accurate representation of your good and perfect will.

And may every reader be drawn closer to you, gain a more complete knowledge of your nature and character, and a firmer determination to please you by knowing and doing your will.

My prayer as I conclude the project mirrors that of King David: "May the words I have written and the meditation of my heart be pleasing in your sight, O Lord, my Rock and my Redeemer.

INTRODUCTION

1	Heb. 11:6	22	James 1:5	43	1 Tim. 4:4
2	Heb. 11:1	23	James 3:17	44	Rom. 14:17
3	James 2:20	24	Eph. 5:1	45	Rom. 10:4
4	James 2:26	25	Ex. 20:12	46	Gal. 2:16
5	Ex. 20:1	26	Col. 2:2		
6	John 15:4	27	Col. 1:10		
7	Matt. 22:37	28	Matt. 7:21		
8	Mark 12:30	29	Rom. 1:20		
9	Luke 10:27	30	Col. 2:9		
10	John 13:34	31	2 Tim. 3:16		
11	Jer. 29:11	32	2 Peter 1:20		
12	Jonah 1:2	33	2 Peter 1:21		
13	Matt. 5:17	34	John 20:31		
14	Heb. 9:12	35	Ex. 20:16		
15	Heb. 9:13	36	John 3:3		
16	Heb. 9:14	37	Deut. 4:2		
17	Heb. 9:15	38	Deut. 12:32		
18	Rom. 10:4	39	Rev. 22:18		
19	Eph. 5:1	40	Rev. 22:19		
20	2 Tim. 3:16	41	Mark 7:18		
21	Ps. 32:8	42	Acts 10:15		

TOPICS

ACCOUNTABILITY

1	Heb. 9:27		34	1 Cor. 12:24
2	Rom. 14:12		35	1 Cor. 12:25
3	Rom. 3:19		36	1 Cor. 12:26
4	1 Peter 4:5		37	Eph. 4:25
5	Heb. 4:13		38	Rom. 12:16
6	1 Peter 1:17		39	Rom. 15:5
7	2 Cor. 5:9		40	James 1:19
8	2 Cor. 5:10		41	1 Thess. 5:14
9	Ezek. 3:17		42	Heb. 10:24
10	Ezek. 3:18		43	1 Thess. 5:11
11	Ezek. 3:19		44	Col. 3:16
12	Ezek. 3:20		45	Heb. 10:25
13	Ezek. 3:21		46	Col. 3:15
14	Matt. 7:1		47	Gal. 6:7
15	Heb. 3:13		48	Gal. 6:8
16	1 John 5:16			
17	James 5:19			
18	James 5:20			
19	Gal. 6:1			
20	1 Cor. 10:12			
21	John 15:17			
22	1 Peter 1:22			
23	Rom. 12:10			
24	1 John 4:21			
25	Gal. 6:2			
26	Rom. 14:13			
27	1 Cor. 12:27			
28	1 Cor. 12:18			
29	1 Cor. 12:19			
30	1 Cor. 12:20			
31	1 Cor. 12:21			
32	1 Cor. 12:22			
33	1 Cor. 12:23			

ACCOUNTABILITY

You are destined to die, and after that you will have to face judgment.[1] You will have to give a personal account of your life to God.[2] The whole world is accountable to him and he will be the judge of everyone.[3,4] Nothing in all creation can be hidden from his sight.[5] Live in reverent fear of him because he does not show favoritism.[6]

Make it your goal to please God because you will have to appear before him to give an account of the things you have done in life, whether good or bad.[7,8]

You must watch out for others in your community. You must warn an ungodly person or one who has turned away from a righteous life of the coming judgment. You are not accountable for the other person's response.[9-13] Do not judge others - they are not accountable to you.[14]

You must warn each other every day of the coming judgment so that no one will be deceived by sin and become hardened against God.[15] Pray especially for a Christian brother or sister who is committing a sin or has wandered away from the truth of the gospel.[16,17] You can be sure that if they turn back, you have brought about forgiveness and saved them from death.[18] Restore them to your fellowship gently and watch out for yourself so that you do not fall in temptation.[19,20]

Love one another with genuine affection and in a caring and sincere way.[21-23] This is a visible demonstration that you love God.[24] Carry each other's burdens; in this way you fulfill the law of Christ.[25] Do not let your lifestyle be a stumbling-block to others.[26]

You are a part of Christ's body (the Church) and accountable to all the other parts.[27] This spiritual body is like the human body in many ways. It has many parts, each with a specific function. Some parts are stronger, more honorable or visible than others, but the body needs every one of them to function properly.[28-35] If one part suffers, all suffer with it.[36] We are all a part of this body.[37]

Live in harmony with each other because this is fitting for followers of Jesus. Do not be proud, but willing to associate with those of low estate.[38,39] You should be a good listener, not anxious to speak and rarely angry.[40] Encourage those who are timid. Take care of those who are weak. Be patient with everyone.[41] Think of ways to motivate each other to acts of love and good works.[42] Encourage each other and build each other up.[43] Teach and counsel each other with God's wisdom.[44] Do not neglect attending the meetings of your congregation. They are meant to encourage and build you up in your faith.[45] Let the peace of Christ rule your heart and your life as a member of the body of Christ.[46]

Do not be deceived; you cannot mock God. You will reap what you sow. You will reap the destruction of your soul if you sow to your own selfish interests, but if you sow to please God, you will reap eternal life.[47,48]

ADULTERY

1   Ex. 20:14
2   Deut. 5:18
3   Matt. 5:27
4   Mark 10:19
5   Luke 18:20
6   Rom. 13:9
7   Lev. 18:20
8   Prov. 6:32
9   Matt. 15:19
10 Mark 7:21
11 James 2:11
12 Matt. 5:28
13 Matt. 5:29
14 Mal. 2:16
15 Mark 10:11
16 Mark 10:12
17 Luke 16:18
18 Matt. 5:32
19 Matt. 19:9
20 1 Cor. 7:15
21 Mal. 2:13
22 Mal. 2:14
23 Mal. 2:15
24 Gen. 2:24
25 Matt. 19:5
26 Mark 10:7
27 Eph. 5:31
28 Jer. 7:9
29 Ezek. 23:37

ADULTERY

Do not commit adultery.[1-6] Do not have sexual relations with anyone else's spouse and defile yourself in this way.[7]

The man or woman who commits adultery lacks judgment and destroys themselves.[8] It shows what is actually in their heart.[9,10] Breaking any one of God's laws makes you guilty of breaking the entire law.[11]

Don't even look at another man or woman with lustful intent. You will already have committed adultery in your heart.[12] Stop any practice and get out of any situation that is causing you to have lust in your heart. Giving up your most cherished temptation is far better than being thrown into hell.[13]

God hates divorce.[14] Anyone who divorces his or her spouse without a legitimate reason and marries another person commits adultery.[15-17] The only exceptions are marital unfaithfulness and abandonment.[18-20]

Honor your marriage and remain faithful to each other.[21] Do not break faith with the spouse of your youth. It causes untold grief.[22,23] Marriage is a covenant partnership created by God for the wellbeing of both you and your children.[24-28]

Abandoning God to worship false gods is spiritual adultery.[29]

ALIEN

1   Ex. 23:9
2   Ex. 22:21
3   Lev. 19:33
4   Ex. 22:21
5   Jer. 7:6
6   Zech. 7:10
7   Deut.10:19
8   Lev. 19:10
9   Lev. 23:22
10 Ex. 12:49
11 Lev. 24:22
12 Num.15:15
13 Jer. 22:3
14 Deut.27:19
15 Ps. 146:9
16 Mal. 3:5
17 Rom. 13:1
18 Num. 9:14
19 Eph. 2:11
20 Eph. 2:12
21 Eph. 2:13
22 Eph. 2:14
23 Eph. 2:18
24 Eph. 2:19
25 Phil. 3:20
26 1 Peter 2:11

ALIEN

Do not oppress or mistreat an alien.[1-5] Do not think evil of them, but show them love.[6-7] Make provision for their basic needs.[8-9]

You must have the same laws for aliens as natural citizens.[10-12] You must guarantee them equal justice because God himself is their defender. Do them no wrong and do not take advantage of them for any reason.[13-16]

Everyone must obey the law.[17] An alien living in your community must celebrate your customs and regulations and be subject to all your laws.[18]

Gentiles were once excluded from citizenship in the kingdom of heaven. However, Christ broke down the barrier walls between Jew and Gentile by his sacrificial death and thus created a common pathway to citizenship in heaven for both by faith in Jesus Christ. You are no longer a foreigner or an alien, but a fellow citizen with all God's people and a member of God's household.[19-24]

As a follower of Jesus, you are now a citizen of heaven.[25] You should think of yourself as an alien and stranger in this world and abstain from sinful desires and practices that war against your soul.[26]

ANGER

1   Ps. 37:8
2   Ps. 4:4
3   Prov. 15:1
4   Prov. 27:4
5   James 1:20
6   Prov. 29:11
7   Eph. 4:26
8   Eph. 4:27
9   Eccl. 7:9
10 Prov. 22:24
11 Prov. 22:25
12 Prov. 29:22
13 1 Tim. 2:8
14 James 1:19
15 Eph. 4:31
16 Col. 3:8
17 Matt. 5:22
18 Ps. 86:15
19 Ps. 103:8
20 Ps. 145:8
21 Ps. 103:8
22 Jonah 4:2
23 Nah. 1:3
24 Ps. 30:5

ANGER

Do not allow yourself to get angry and do not lose your temper.[1] Letting anger control you always leads to a bad outcome and is a sin. Bite your tongue and think about your issues overnight.[2] A gentle answer calms anger, but harsh words make tempers flare.[3] Anger is cruel and overwhelming, and jealousy is even worse.[4]

Your anger does not accomplish the righteous life that God desires for you.[5] Be wise and maintain self-control. Only a fool gives full vent to his or her anger.[6]

Do not let anger control you—it is a sin. Do not let the sun go down while you are still angry.[7] Anger gives the devil a foothold.[8]

Do not be easily provoked to anger—it is foolish.[9]

Do not make friends with a hot-tempered person or associate with anyone who is easily angered, or you may become just like them.[10,11] An angry person stirs up controversy and division, and a hot-tempered person commits many sins.[12]

Keep your place of worship free from anger and controversy.[13]

You should be slow to become angry and slow to speak, but quick to listen.[14] You must get rid of all anger, bitterness, rage, slander, and every form of malice as well as filthy language.[15,16]

Do not be angry with a member of your community because you will face judgment for it. Do not call anyone a hateful or derogatory name or curse them. If you do this, you put yourself in danger of the fires of hell.[17]

The Lord is slow to anger. He is gracious and compassionate and rich in love.[18-22] He is great in power and will not leave the guilty unpunished.[23]

The Lord's anger lasts only a moment for those who repent, but his favor lasts for a lifetime. Weeping may last through the night, but joy comes in the morning.[24]

ANXIETY

1	Ps. 42:11	35	Gal. 6:2
2	Ps. 55:22	36	Matt. 6:34
3	Ps. 139:23	37	1 Peter 5:7
4	Ps. 139:24		
5	Ps. 139:1		
6	Ps. 139:2		
7	Ps. 139:3		
8	Ps. 139:4		
9	Ps. 139:5		
10	Ps. 139:6		
11	Ps. 139:7		
12	Ps. 94:19		
13	Isa. 41:10		
14	Isa. 30:15		
15	Ps. 37:7		
16	Prov. 24:19		
17	Prov. 24:20		
18	Matt. 6:31		
19	Matt. 6:25		
20	Luke 12:29		
21	Luke 12:23		
22	Matt. 6:32		
23	Luke 12:30		
24	Matt. 6:33		
25	Luke 21:34		
26	Matt. 6:27		
27	Matt. 6:26		
28	Matt. 6:28		
29	Matt. 6:29		
30	Matt. 6:30		
31	Phil. 4:6		
32	Phil. 4:7		
33	Eccl. 11:10		
34	Prov. 12:25		

ANXIETY

Do not be anxious or depressed.[1] Cast your anxieties on the Lord, and he will sustain you. Put your hope in God, the one who saves you, and offer praise to him. He will never let the righteous fall.[2]

Tell God about your anxious thoughts. He knows you better than you know yourself. He knows your inner thoughts and your words even before you speak them. He knows when you sit down or stand up, and he surrounds you at all times.[3-11] His presence will calm your anxiety.[12]

Do not be anxious or afraid, because God is with you to strengthen and help you. He will uphold you with his righteous hand.[13] His strength will come to you in times of quietness and trust, in repentance and rest.[14]

Be still in the presence of the Lord, and wait patiently for him to act. Do not be anxious when evil people succeed in their ways and carry out their wicked schemes.[3] Do not be envious of the wicked, because they have no future.[15-17]

Do not be anxious or preoccupied with the details of your everyday life, like whether you will have enough food and drink or enough clothes to wear.[18-20] Life is more important than food and the body more important than clothing.[21] These things dominate the thoughts of unbelievers, but God already knows about all of your needs.[22-23] So set your priority on the kingdom of God and living a righteous life. God will supply everything else that you need.[24]

Be careful that the anxieties of this life do not weigh you down so much that the return of Christ overtakes you unexpectedly.[25] Anxiety and worry cannot add anything to your life, not even a single second.[26] Think about the birds in the air (not one falls without him knowing) and the flowers in the field (which are here today and thrown into the fire tomorrow). Since God cares for them so wonderfully well, he will certainly care for you. Let these examples encourage and strengthen your faith.[28-30]

Do not be anxious about anything. Instead pray about everything. Tell God what you need, even though he already knows, and thank him for all he has done. Then you will experience his peace, which far exceeds anything anyone else can understand. God's peace will protect your heart and mind against anxiety as you live your life of faith in Jesus.[31,32]

Refuse to worry, and keep your body healthy.[33] Find someone who will offer a kind word to cheer you up.[34] Find someone to share your burden. In this way they will be doing God's will.[35]

Do not be anxious about what may or may not happen tomorrow.[36] Give your attention to today's challenges and God will help you deal with the rest when the time comes.[36]

Tell God about your anxiety because he cares about you.[37]

APOLOGETICS

1   1 Peter 3:15
2   2 Tim. 2:15
3   Prov. 23:12
4   2 Peter 3:18
5   2 Peter 1:8
6   1 Cor. 8:1
7   2 Peter 1:5
8   2 Peter 1:6
9   Col. 4:5
10 Col. 4:6
11 1 Tim. 6:20
12 2 Tim. 2:25
13 2 Tim. 3:16
14 2 Tim. 3:15
15 John 20:31
16 1 John 5:13
17 1 John 5:20
18 Acts 4:12
19 Prov. 1:7
20 Prov. 9:10
21 Prov. 2:5
22 Rom. 11:33
23 Jer. 33:3
24 Prov. 2:6
25 James 1:5
26 Col. 1:9
27 Col. 1:10
28 Prov. 19:2

APOLOGETICS

Always be ready to give an answer to anyone who asks you to explain your faith as a believer in Jesus and the hope that you have for eternal life. Do this with gentleness and respect.[1]

Study hard and learn how to interpret and apply the truth of the Bible. This is pleasing to God.[2] Apply yourself to learning.[3] Grow in your knowledge and understanding of Jesus.[4]

Knowledge alone will not make you effective or productive as a follower of Jesus.[5] Knowledge can make you feel smart and important, but it takes love to build up others.[6] Make every effort to temper your knowledge with faith, goodness, self-control, perseverance and godliness.[7,8]

Make the most of every opportunity to interact with non-believers.[9] Be graceful and respectful in your conversation with others, but always willing to challenge their assumptions and answer their questions.[10] Redirect the conversation from godless chatter and human worldviews to the one true source of knowledge, the Word of God.[11] Use gentle persuasion in the hope that God will grant them repentance leading them to a knowledge of the truth.[12]

Scripture is our primary source of ultimate truth. It is a revelation from God that teaches us what is true and right.[13] It gives instruction for salvation through faith in Jesus.[14] It is written so that you can know that Jesus is the Son of God and be assured that you have eternal life by believing in him.[15-17] He is the only true source of salvation.[18]

The fear of the Lord is the beginning of knowledge and wisdom.[19-21] The depth and richness of God's wisdom and knowledge are way beyond our human ability to comprehend.[22] Ask him to show you things you do not know or understand.[23,24] He willingly and generously shares these things with those who ask.[25]

Ask God to fill you with the knowledge of his will so that you can live a productive life, pleasing to him in every way.[26,27]

It is not good to have zeal without knowledge.[28]

ATTITUDE

1	Phil. 2:5	34	Phil. 3:10
2	John 6:38	35	Phil. 3:11
3	Phil. 2:6	36	Eph. 5:20
4	Phil. 2:7	37	1 Thess. 5:18
5	Phil. 2:8	38	Ps. 95:2
6	James 4:7	39	Ps. 100:4
7	James 4:10	40	Ps. 118:1
8	Mic. 6:8	41	2 Cor. 9:15
9	Phil. 2:3	42	Col. 1:12
10	Prov. 8:13	43	Heb. 13:5
11	1 Peter 5:5	44	1 Tim. 6:6
12	Matt. 7:21	45	Col. 3:15
13	Matt. 19:17	46	John 14:27
14	Luke 6:46	47	Phil. 4:6
15	1 John 5:3	48	Phil. 4:7
16	Gal. 5:22	49	Isa. 26:3
17	Gal. 5:23	50	Luke 6:36
18	2 Peter 1:5	51	Col. 3:12
19	2 Peter 1:6	52	Col. 3:13
20	2 Peter 1:7	53	Phil. 4:5
21	2 Peter 1:8	54	Eph. 4:2
22	Eph. 4:23	55	Rom. 15:7
23	Eph. 4:24	56	Eph. 4:32
24	Rom. 12:2	57	1 Peter 3:8
25	1 Thess. 5:16	58	Phil. 2:14
26	Phil. 4:4	59	Matt. 7:1
27	Phil. 3:1	60	1 Peter 2:17
28	Rom. 5:2	61	Titus 1:8
29	Luke 10:20	62	Eph. 5:21
30	James 1:2	63	Eph. 5:1
31	James 1:3		
32	Rom. 5:3		
33	1 Peter 4:13		

ATTITUDE

Have the same attitudes that Jesus demonstrated.[1] He came down from heaven to do the will of God.[2] Although he was God, he humbled himself to serve others, and was obedient to his mission, even to the extent of an unjust and cruel death.[3-5]

You too must be humble in the sight of God.[6-8] Don't be conceited, but think of others as better than yourself.[9] God hates pride and arrogance.[10,11]

You must also be obedient to God's commandments. Only the person who knows and does the will of God can enter the kingdom of heaven.[12-14] Obedience to God's laws is the way you demonstrate your love for him.[15]

Let your attitudes be evidence of your growing faith in God. Love, joy, peace, patience, kindness, goodness, faithfulness, gentleness and self-control demonstrate to others that he is working in your life.[16-20] These qualities will make you productive and effective in your Christian life.[21] Don't adopt the attitudes of your culture, but let your attitudes be transformed and made new by God who wants you to be like him.[22-24]

Be full of the joy of the Lord at all times. It is a safeguard for your soul.[25-27] Rejoice in your hope of heaven and that your name is written there.[28-29] Rejoice when you face trials of any kind because these experiences produce perseverance in your faith.[30-32] Rejoice even in suffering because it is a way to identify with Christ and experience the joy and hope of his resurrection.[33-35]

Be grateful for all things and in all circumstances.[36,37] Come before the Lord with praise and thanksgiving.[38,39] Give thanks to the Lord for he is good, and his love endures forever.[40] Thank him for the indescribable gift of his Son and the promised inheritance of eternal life.[41,42]

Be content with what you have and keep your life free from the love of money.[43] Godliness with contentment is true wealth.[44]

Let the peace of Christ rule in your heart.[45] This will keep you from anxiety as you commit your circumstances to God and thank him for what he has done.[46-48] He will give you perfect peace as you confidently put your trust in him.[49]

You must be compassionate because God is compassionate.[50] Be kind, humble, gentle, patient, accepting, sympathetic and forgiving.[51-57]

Don't be a complainer.[58] Don't be judgmental.[59] Be respectful of everyone.[60] Be hospitable.[61] Be submissive to others out of respect for Christ.[62]

Imitate God's attitudes like a small child imitates an adoring parent.[63]

AUTHORITY

1	Ex.20:3	28	Matt. 28:18	55	Mic. 1:1	82	Rom. 13:1
2	Gen.1:1	29	Matt. 28:19	56	Zeph. 1:1	83	Rom. 13:2
3	Ex. 20:5	30	Matt. 28:20	57	Hag. 1:1	84	1 Peter 2:13
4	Ex. 20:6	31	Mark 16:15	58	Zech. 1:1	85	1 Peter 2:14
5	Jude 25	32	John 14:15	59	Mal. 1:1	86	Titus 3:1
6	Ex. 20:7	33	John 16:13	60	2 Sam. 22:31	87	1 Peter 2:17
7	Ex. 20:8	34	John 16:7	61	Ps. 18:30	88	1 Tim. 2:1
8	James 4:7	35	John 16:8	62	Ps. 33:4	89	1 Tim. 2:2
9	Deut. 6:5	36	John 16:9	63	1 Peter 1:25	90	Acts 5:29
10	Matt. 22:37	37	John 16:10	64	John 20:31	91	Luke 20:25
11	Mark 12:30	38	John 16:11	65	Rev. 22:18	92	1 Cor. 11:
12	Luke 10:27	39	1 Thess. 5:19	66	Rev. 22:19	93	Eph. 5:23
13	John 1:1	40	Eph. 5:18	67	1 Cor. 4:6	94	Eph. 6:1
14	Col. 2:9	41	2 Tim. 3:16	68	2 Tim. 2:15	95	Ex. 20:12
15	Col. 2:10	42	2 Petet 1:21	69	2 Tim. 3:17	96	Eph. 6:2
16	Matt. 9:6	43	2 Peter 1:20	70	James 1:22	97	Eph. 6:5
17	Mark 2:10	44	1 Thess. 2:13	71	Luke 11:28	98	Eph. 6:6
18	Luke 5:24	45	Num. 3:16	72	Matt. 16:16	99	Eph. 6:7
19	Eph. 1:19	46	2 Sam.24:11	73	Matt. 16:17	100	Eph. 6:8
20	Eph. 1:20	47	1 Kings 6:11	74	Matt. 16:18	101	1 Peter 2:18
21	Eph. 1:21	48	2 Kings 20:4	75	Eph. 1:22	102	Eph. 6:9
22	Eph. 1:22	49	Jer. 1:2	76	1 Tim. 3:15	103	Gen. 1:26
23	John 14:6	50	Ezek. 1:3	77	Matt. 20:25	104	Gen. 1:27
24	Acts 4:12	51	Hos. 1:1	78	Matt. 20:26	105	Gen. 1:28
25	John 5:27	52	Joel 1:1	79	Matt. 20:27	106	Rev. 2:26
26	Phil. 2:10	53	Amos 7:16	80	Matt. 20:28		
27	Phil. 2:11	54	Jonah 1:1	81	Heb. 13:17		

AUTHORITY

God is the Supreme Authority in the universe.[1] He created all things in the very beginning.[2] You must not worship any other god.[3,4] Majesty, glory, power and authority belong only to God.[5] You must not misuse his name or forget his holy day.[6,7] Submit to his authority and love him with all your heart, soul, mind and strength.[8-12]

Jesus Christ, also known as "The Word," is God and was present and active in creation.[13] He was sent to earth as a human being, but also as a full representation of God with all the same power and authority.[14,15] He proved his authority to forgive sins by his miracles.[16-18] God's mighty power raised him from the dead and placed him above every other authority in the universe.[19-22] He is the only way back to God.[23,24] He is the final judge.[25] Everyone will be forced to recognize him someday.[26,27] You must respond to his authority by going out into your world to make disciples for him.[28-32]

The Holy Spirit was sent into the world by Jesus and speaks God's truth with his authority about sin, righteousness and judgment.[33-38] Live your life under the authority of the Holy Spirit.[39,40]

All Scripture is authoritative because it is inspired by God.[41] It did not originate with any human idea or interpretation.[42-44] It is the written record of God speaking directly to men who wrote it down.[45-59] It is faithful, flawless, right and true, and will stand forever.[60-63] Do not add or take away anything that is written in the Scripture[64-67] Study the Scripture in order to understand and correctly apply it and then do what it says.[68-71]

The Church is founded on Jesus Christ who is its supreme authority.[72-75] It is the household of God, the pillar and foundation of the truth.[76] Church leaders must not assume a burdensome hierarchy, but engage in servant leadership.[77-80] You must submit to their authority.[81]

You must submit to authority of the government because there is none that exists except that which has been established by God. Consequently, anyone who rebels against this authority is rebelling against God's institution.[82-87] Pray for those in authority so that you may live your life in peaceful religious freedom.[88,89] However, you must obey God's authority rather than that of your government in cases where there is conflict.[90,91]

A husband is subject to the authority of Christ and his wife is subject to his authority in the same way that the Church is subject to the authority of Christ.[92,93] Children are subject to the authority of their parents and must obey and honor them.[94-96] Employees must obey the authority of their employers.[97-101] Employers must recognize a higher authority in heaven who shows no favoritism.[102]

You are created in God's image and given authority to rule over all the earth.[103-105]

Hold on to your faith and do God's will and he will give you authority over the nations.[106]

BAPTISM

1   Acts 2:38

2   Matt. 28:18

3   Matt. 28:19

4   Acts 16:31

5   Rom. 10:9

6   Rom. 10:10

7   Rom. 6:23

8   Eph. 2:8

9   Eph. 2:9

10 Gal. 2:16

11 Acts 19:5

12 Acts 10:47

13 Acts 22:16

14 1 Peter 3:21

15 Rom. 6:3

16 Rom. 6:4

17 Col. 2:12

18 Eph. 4:5

19 1 Cor. 12:13

20 Gal. 3:27

21 2 Cor. 5:17

BAPTISM

You must repent of your sins and turn to God for his forgiveness. You must be baptized in the name of the Father and of the Son and of the Holy Spirit.[1-3]

Believe in the Lord Jesus Christ and you will be saved.[4] Believe in your heart that God raised him from the dead. Only true, heart-felt belief makes you right with God. Confess with your mouth that Jesus is Lord—this proclaims your salvation.[5-6] It is God's gracious gift to you, not based on any merit of your own.[7-9] In fact, there is nothing else you can do to be justified before God.[10]

Water baptism is a visible symbol of the washing away of your sins and your good-faith pledge of faith in the resurrection of Jesus Christ. It should take place soon after belief.[11-14]

In baptism, your old self symbolically died and was buried with Christ. Like Christ, you were raised to new life because you trusted the mighty power of God who raised Christ from the dead.[15-17]

There is only one Lord, one true faith, and one true baptism.[18] Baptism publicly identifies you with Christ and his Church.[19-20]

You are a new creation: the old is gone and the new has come.[21]

BLASPHEMY

1	Ex. 20:7		32	1 Tim. 1:13
2	Deut. 5:11		33	1 Tim. 1:14
3	Ex. 20:3		34	1 Tim. 1:15
4	Ex. 20:4		35	1 Tim. 1:16
5	Ex. 20:5		36	Ezek. 33:11
6	Lev. 19:12		37	1 Tim. 1:13
7	Lev. 22:32		38	1 Tim. 1:14
8	Lev. 24:15		39	1 Tim. 1:15
9	Lev. 24:16		40	Heb. 10:29
10	Titus 1:16		41	Eph 4:30
11	Num. 15:30		42	Matt. 12:24
12	Rom. 2:24		43	Matt. 12:25
13	Heb. 10:29		44	Matt. 12:26
14	Rom. 15:3		45	Matt. 12:27
15	Ps. 69:9		46	Matt. 12:28
16	Mark 15:29		47	Matt. 12:29
17	Mark 15:30		48	Matt. 12:30
18	Luke 5:21		49	Acts 7:51
19	Luke 5:22		50	1 Thess. 5:19
20	Luke 5:23		51	Gen. 6:3
21	Luke 5:24			
22	Heb. 1:3			
23	Matt. 12:30			
24	Matt. 12:31			
25	Matt. 12:32			
26	Luke 12:10			
27	Mark 3:28			
28	Mark 3:29			
29	Mark 3:30			
30	Luke 12:10			
31	1 John 1:9			

BLASPHEMY

You must not misuse the name of the Lord your God in any way. He will hold you accountable for doing so.[1,2]

You must not worship any other god.[3] You must not make an idol representing anything in the sky, or on the earth, or in the sea. You must not bow down and worship any created thing because God will not tolerate affection or worship of any other god. It is a grievous sin. He will severely punish those who worship a false god but will lavish unfailing love "for a thousand generations" on those who love him and obey his commandments.[4,5]

Do not profane the holy name of God by using it to swear dishonestly.[6,7] Do not blaspheme in this way or curse God.[8] Anyone who deliberately blasphemes God and thus brazenly violates the Lord's will must be cut off from your congregation.[9]

Do not claim to know God but actually deny him by your actions.[10] Purposefully ignoring or transgressing the Lord's will is a form of blasphemy.[11] Such actions may cause others to blaspheme the name of the Lord in the same way.[12]

Do not blaspheme the name of Jesus, whose unjust death on a cross makes you holy before God. He endured many insults including that of blasphemy for claiming that he had authority to forgive sins. He actually proved that he does have this authority by performing miracles, something only God can do.[14-21] Jesus is the exact representation of God in a human body, bringing forgiveness of sins to everyone who now believes in him.[22] You are either with him or against him; you either attract others to him or you turn them away from him.[23]

Do not blaspheme the Holy Spirit, because it is the unpardonable sin.[24-30] Every other sin will be forgiven by God if we confesss it to him.[31] He will forgive even the worst of us and will overwhelm you with his grace and love.[32-39] Do not grieve, disdain, or insult the Holy Spirit by the way you live. He brings God's mercy to you and is your guarantee of salvation.[40-41]

Do not ascribe the works of God to the Devil. Do not contrive complex, contradictory explanations of God's work that cannot even stand on their own logic.[42-48] Do not be stubborn and continually resist the Holy Spririt.[49]

Do not continually squelch the work of the Holy Spirit.[50] He will eventually withdraw from your life without you even realizing it until it is too late.[51]

BLESSING

1 Ps. 103:1
2 Ps. 103:2
3 Ps. 103:22
4 Ps. 104:1
5 Ps. 104:35
6 Rom 12:14
7 Matt. 5:44
8 Luke 6:28
9 1 Peter 3:9

William Bunnell

BLESSING

Bless the Lord with all that is within your being. Bless his holy name.[1] Praise him and do not forget all he has done for you.[2] Bless him for all his wonderful works in all places.[3] Bless him for his greatness, honor and majesty.[4] Bless him because the wicked will be no more.[5]

Bless those who persecute you. Bless those who curse you. Bless those who hate you. Bless those who abuse or misuse you. Do not curse them. Love your enemies and do good to them. Pray for them. [5-8]

Do not repay evil with evil or retaliate with insults when you are insulted. Instead, repay with a blessing. This is what God has called you to do, and he will bless you for doing so.[9]

BODY

1	1 Cor. 6:19	35	Prov. 14:30	69	Rom. 7:22
2	1 Cor. 6:20	36	Prov. 4:22	70	Rom. 7:23
3	1 Peter 1:18	37	Matt. 6:22	71	Rom. 7:24
4	1 Peter 1:19	38	Matt. 6:23	72	Rom. 7:25
5	1 Cor. 3:16	39	Luke 11:34	73	Matt. 10:28
6	1 Cor. 6:19	40	Luke 11:36	74	Luke 12:5
7	1 Cor. 3:17	41	James 3:2	75	Rom. 8:11
8	Rom. 12:1	42	James 3:5	76	Rom. 8:23
9	Phil. 1:20	43	James 3:6	77	1 Cor. 15:53
10	Ps. 139:14	44	Col. 2:20	78	1 Cor. 15:42
11	Ps. 139:13	45	Col. 2:21	79	Phil. 3:21
12	Job 31:15	46	Col. 2:22	80	2 Cor. 5:9
13	Isa. 44:2	47	Col. 2:23	81	2 Cor. 5:10
14	Isa. 44:24	48	Mark 7:19		
15	Isa. 49:5	49	Matt. 15:17		
16	Jer. 1:5	50	Matt. 15:18		
17	Ps. 139:15	51	Matt. 15:19		
18	Ps. 139:16	52	Matt. 15:20		
19	1 Peter 2:24	53	Luke 12:22		
20	Isa. 53:5	54	Luke 12:23		
21	Isa. 53:6	55	Matt. 6:31		
22	1 Peter 3:18	56	Matt. 6:32		
23	Col. 1:22	57	Matt. 6:33		
24	Col. 1:23	58	1 Thess. 4:3		
25	Heb. 10:10	59	1 Cor. 6:18		
26	Luke 22:19	60	Rom. 6:12		
27	Matt. 26:26	61	Rom. 6:13		
28	Mark 14:22	62	Rom. 6:19		
29	1 Cor. 11:24	63	Rom. 8:13		
30	Prov. 4:23	64	1 Thess. 4:4		
31	Col. 3:1	65	1 Thess. 5:23		
32	Col. 3:2	66	2 Cor. 7:1		
33	Col. 3:3	67	Matt. 26:41		
34	Col. 3:15	68	Rom. 7:21		

BODY

Honor God with your body. You were bought at a very high price, the precious blood of Christ. You are no longer your own.[1-4] Your body is now a living temple of God because God's Spirit lives in you.[5,6] Don't do anything that harms this human temple, because it is sacred.[7] Offer your body to God as a living sacrifice. This is a spiritual act of worship that is pleasing to God.[8,9]

Your body is mysteriously and wonderfully made.[10] God actually knew you before you were born and knit all the parts of your unformed body together in your mother's womb.[11-18]

Christ bore your sins in his body when he was nailed to the cross. His wounds purchased your forgiveness.[19-21] The death of his physical body, a righteous man for all the unrighteous, brings you to God if you have faith in him.[22-24] You have been made holy through the sacrifice of the body of Jesus Christ once and for all.[25] Eat the bread of communion to remind yourself of the one who sacrificed his body for you.[26-29]

Guard your heart. It is the wellspring of your life.[30] Set your heart and mind on heavenly matters and let them be ruled by the peace of Christ.[31-35] Wisdom is the key to a good life and health for your whole body.[36] Keep your eyes open; otherwise your whole body is full of darkness.[37-40] Watch your tongue, a world of evil among the parts of your body. It can corrupt your whole person and set the course of your life on fire.[41-43]

Don't be bound by harsh man-made rules like "don't touch, taste or handle," which seem wise but lack spiritual value.[44-47] Eat whatever you like. Your body is not corrupted in God's sight by what goes into your mouth, only what comes out of it.[48-52] Don't be preoccupied with your body, food, or clothing. Life is more than this. Seek the kingdom of God above all else.[53-57]

It is God's will for you to be holy and to stay away from all sexual sin.[58] It is a sin against your own body.[59] Do not let sin and evil desires rule over your mortal body.[60-62] Put to death the misdeeds of the body with the help of God's Holy Spirit.[63] Learn to control your body in a way that is holy and honorable.[64] Ask God to make you holy in every way: body, soul, and spirit.[65,66]

Watch and pray so that you will not fall into temptation. Your spirit may be resisting, but your body is weak.[67] This tension often makes you do what you do not want to do and not do what you do want to do.[68-70] Thank God; he will deliver you from this terrible inner conflict.[71,72]

Do not be afraid of those who can kill the body but cannot kill the soul.[73,74] If the Spirit of him who raised Jesus from the dead is living in you, he will give new life and immortality to your body after death.[75-77] What was perishable will be raised from the grave imperishable.[78] He will transform your lowly body so that it will be like the glorious body of Jesus.[79]

Make it your goal to please God with your body because you must appear before the judgment seat of Christ to receive what is due for the things you have done while in the body, whether good or bad.[80,81]

CHARACTER

1	Gal. 5:22	35	Mark 11:22	69	1 Peter 1:15
2	Gal. 5:23	36	John 14:1	70	1 Peter 2:12
3	Gal. 5:19	37	Col. 2:7	71	Titus 2:7
4	Gal. 5:20	38	Philem. 6	72	James 1:26
5	Gal. 5:21	39	1 Peter 1:9	73	James 1:19
6	1 Cor. 13:13	40	Eph. 4:32	74	Col. 4:6
7	Col. 3:14	41	Col. 3:13	75	Eph. 4:29
8	1 Cor. 13:4	42	Luke 11:4	76	Eph. 5:21
9	1 Cor. 13:5	43	Mark 11:25		
10	1 Cor. 13:6	44	Matt. 6:14		
11	1 Cor. 13:7	45	Matt. 6:15		
12	1 Cor. 13:1	46	2 Cor. 2:10		
13	1 Cor. 13:2	47	2 Cor. 2:11		
14	1 Cor. 13:3	48	1 Peter 5:6		
15	1 Thess. 5:16	49	James 4:10		
16	Phil. 4:4	50	Rom. 12:3		
17	Neh. 8:10	51	Rom. 12:16		
18	Rom. 12:12	52	Gal. 5:26		
19	Hab. 3:17	53	Phil. 2:3		
20	Hab. 3:18	54	1 Cor. 10:24		
21	Hab. 3:19	55	Col. 3:12		
22	James 1:2	56	Mark 10:43		
23	James 1:3	57	Matt. 23:11		
24	James 1:4	58	1 Tim. 6:6		
25	1 Thess. 5:18	59	1 Tim. 6:10		
26	Eph. 5:20	60	1 Tim. 6:10		
27	Ps. 50:23	61	Luke 12:15		
28	Ps. 107:1	62	Col. 3:5		
29	2 Cor. 9:15	63	1 John 2:15		
30	Heb. 11:6	64	Matt. 6:19		
31	Heb. 11:1	65	Matt. 6:20		
32	James 2:17	66	Matt. 6:21		
33	James 2:18	67	Phil. 1:11		
34	2 Peter 1:5	68	1 Thess. 4:3		

CHARACTER

Your character as a follower of Jesus should demonstrate the following traits: love, joy, peace, patience, kindness, goodness, faithfulness, gentleness, and self-control.[1,2] This is a dramatic difference from those who follow their own natural inclinations.[3-5]

Love is the greatest and most desirable character trait.[6] It binds all other virtues together into a perfect unity.[7] It is patient, kind, polite, cooperative, forgiving, persistent, hopeful, and enduring. Your character is totally defective without love.[8-14]

Express joy at all times.[15,16] Be joyful even in difficult times. The joy of the Lord is your source of strength.[17-21] Be joyful even when you face trials of many kinds because they develop perseverance and lead to spiritual maturity.[22-24]

Show gratitude in all circumstances because this is God's will for you.[25,26] Thanksgiving is a sacrifice that pleases God and opens your heart to his salvation.[27] Give thanks for his faithful love, which endures forever.[28] Thank him for Jesus, his gift that is too wonderful for words![29]

Faith is essential in pleasing God.[30,31] Genuine faith will be demonstrated by good works.[32,33] Add goodness and knowledge to your faith.[34] Put your faith in God and in his Son, Jesus Christ.[35,36] Be rooted in him and let your life show it.[37] Be active in sharing your faith.[38] The goal of your faith is the salvation of your soul.[39]

Be forgiving of others. It is a requirement for your own forgiveness.[40-45] Holding grudges gives Satan a foothold in your life.[46,47]

Be humble before God, and he will reward you in due time.[48,49] Don't think too highly of yourself, but be willing to associate with people of low position.[50,51] Don't be conceited, selfish or jealous, but think of others as better than yourself.[52-54] Combine humility with compassion, kindness, gentleness and patience.[55] If you want to be a leader, you must become a servant.[56,57]

Be content with what you have. Godly contentment itself is a great treasure.[58] Keep your life free from the love of money, which leads many away from true faith, and greed, which is the same as the sin of idolatry.[59-62] Don't envy what the world has to offer or hoard treasure on earth, but bank it in heaven where it will be safe from loss.[63-65] Your heart will surely be where your treasure is on deposit.[66]

Righteous character is produced in your life by Jesus Christ.[67] It is God's will that you be holy in everything you do.[68,69] Live carefully among your unbelieving neighbors and be an example to them by doing good works of every kind.[70,71] You must control your tongue and be quick to listen, but slow to speak and slow to get angry.[72,73] Be gracious and don't use foul or abusive language. Instead, be helpful and encouraging.[74,75] Be submissive to one another out of reverence for Christ.[76]

CHARITY

1	1 Cor. 13:5		35	1 Cor. 16:2
2	1 Cor. 13:4		36	2 Cor. 8:12
3	1 Cor. 13:6		37	2 Cor. 9:7
4	1 Cor. 13:7		38	2 Cor. 9:6
5	1 Cor.13:13		39	2 Cor. 9:11
6	Col. 3:14		40	2 Cor. 9:12
7	Matt. 2:37		41	2 Cor. 9:13
8	Matt. 22:38		42	2 Cor. 9:15
9	Matt. 22:39		43	Matt. 6:1
10	Gal. 6:2		44	Matt. 6:2
11	1 Tim. 1:5		45	Matt. 6:3
12	1 Cor.16:14		46	Matt. 6:4
13	1 Tim. 5:8		47	Matt. 25:31
14	Gal. 6:10		48	Matt. 25:32
15	1 Peter 4:8		49	Matt. 25:33
16	Luke 14:12		50	Matt. 25:34
17	Luke 14:13		51	Matt. 25:35
18	Luke 14:14		52	Matt. 25:36
19	Lev. 25:37		53	Matt. 25:37
20	Deut. 15:7		54	Matt. 25:38
21	Deut. 15:8		55	Matt. 25:39
22	Deut.15:10		56	Matt. 25:40
23	Heb. 13:16		57	Matt. 5:41
24	Acts 20:35		58	Matt. 25:42
25	1 Tim. 4:12		59	Matt. 25:43
26	1 Tim 6:17		60	Matt. 25:44
27	1 Tim. 6:18		61	Matt. 25:45
28	1 John 3:17		62	Matt. 25:46
29	Luke 12:33		63	Matt. 10:42
30	1 Tim. 6:19		64	1 Cor. 13:1
31	Luke 12:34		65	1 Cor. 13:2
32	Rom. 12:8		66	1 Cor. 13:3
33	2 Cor. 8:7			
34	Matt. 10:8			

CHARITY

Charity means that you always put the welfare of others ahead of your own.[1] It does not keep score, is not rude, or proud. It is patient and kind. It trusts, protects and perseveres. It is the greatest of all virtues.[2-6] It fulfills one of God's greatest commandments.[7-10] It springs from a pure heart, a good conscience and a genuine faith in God.[11]

Practice charity in everything you do.[12] Provide for your relatives. Not to do so is to deny your own faith and would make you worse than an unbeliever.[13] Extend charity to everyone, especially to members of your faith family.[14,15] Extend it to those who could never repay you.[16,18] Do not lend such a person money expecting payment of interest or sell them food for a profit.[19] Do not be hardhearted or tightfisted, but openhanded and generous.[20-22] Sharing with others is a sacrifice that pleases God.[23] It is more blessed to give than to receive.[24] Be an example of charity to others.[25]

Do not put your hope in material wealth, but be rich in good deeds, generous and willing to share.[26,27] The love of God cannot be in you if you have enough money to live well, but do not have compassion for a brother or sister in need.[28] Sell your excess possessions and give to the poor. In this way, you create a bank account in heaven where your wealth is secure.[29,30] Your main focus in this life will surely be in the same place where you deposit your treasure.[31]

Be generous in your giving.[32,33] Freely you have received; freely give.[34] Set aside a sum of money each week in keeping with your income and bring it to your church for collection.[35] Your willingness to give is far more important than the amount, which is determined by what you have and not what you don't have.[36] You should give willingly, not reluctantly or under compulsion because God loves a cheerful giver.[37] If you sow sparingly, you will reap sparingly, but if you sow generously, you will reap generously.[38] Your charity and generosity in giving to others will result in thanksgiving to God by those who receive it.[39-41] Thanks be to God for his indescribably generous gift![42]

Don't do your charity in public to be admired by others because you will lose the promised reward from your Father in heaven.[43,44] Don't let your left hand know what your right hand is doing when you give to someone in need.[45] Do your charity in private and God, who sees what you do in secret, will reward you publicly.[46]

Anything you do for one of the least of society, you do for Jesus and will receive his reward.[47-63]

Your whole life is devoid of meaning if you do not have charity.[64-66]

CHILDREN

1	Luke 18:16		35	Luke 18:17
2	Matt. 19:13		36	Matt. 18:4
3	Matt. 19:14		37	John 1:12
4	Mark 10:14		38	John 1:13
5	Matt. 18:5		39	1 John 5:1
6	Mark 9:37		40	1 John 3:1
7	Matt. 18:14		41	1 John 3:2
8	Matt. 18:6		42	Rom. 8:16
9	Lev. 18:21		43	1 John 3:10
10	Lev. 20:3		44	Heb. 12:7
11	Deut. 12:31		45	Rom. 8:17
12	Deut. 18:10		46	Heb. 12:8
13	Ps.106:37		47	Eph. 5:8
14	Ps.106:38		48	Phil. 2:15
15	Matt.11:25			
16	Prov. 20:11			
17	Ps. 8:2			
18	Matt. 21:16			
19	Matt. 18:3			
20	Eph. 6:1			
21	Col. 3:20			
22	Ex. 20:12			
23	Eph. 6:2			
24	Eph. 6:3			
25	Eph. 6:4			
26	Col. 3:21			
27	Prov. 22:6			
28	Prov. 23:13			
29	Prov. 22:15			
30	Prov. 19:18			
31	Prov. 23:14			
32	Prov. 29:15			
33	Eph. 5:1			
34	Mark 10:15			

CHILDREN

Bring little children to Jesus and do not hinder them, because the kingdom of God belongs to them.[1-4] Welcoming a little child in Jesus's name is the same as welcoming him, and whoever welcomes him welcomes God.[5,6]

God's will is that not a single little child would be lost.[7] Do not cause one of them to sin; it would be better if a millstone were tied around your neck and you were drowned in the depths of the sea.[8]

Child sacrifice is an abomination to God.[9-14]

God has given little children an understanding of certain things that are no longer obvious to even the wise and learned.[15] Even children show by their actions that they know the difference between right and wrong.[16] God loves to hear praise from the lips of infants and children.[17-19]

Children must obey their parents in everything, because this is pleasing to God.[20,21] Honor your father and mother so that things may go well with you and that you may enjoy a long life on the earth.[22-24]

Parents must not frustrate or exasperate their children or they will become discouraged and embittered.[25,26] Instead, train them in the way they should go, the ways that please God, and when they are old, they will not turn away from it.[27] Do not withhold discipline from a child.[28] There is a lot of foolishness in a child's heart, but appropriate discipline drives it away.[29] Do not withhold physical punishment; it will not permanently harm them and may even save their soul from death.[30,31] An undisciplined child is an embarrassment and disgrace to their parents.[32]

Imitate God like a little child imitates his or her parents.[33] You must humble yourself to receive the kingdom of God with the simple faith of a child or you will never enter it.[34-36]

You become a child of God by believing in his Son, Jesus. This comes about by means of a supernatural, not a physical birth.[37,38] You are a child of God if you believe that Jesus is the Christ.[39] How wonderful that because you are a child of God, good things beyond your comprehension lie in store for you![40-41]

You know that you are a child of God because he has put the Holy Spirit in you.[42] Loving God and doing his will are evidences of his presence in your life.[43] God's discipline in your life is also proof that he is treating you as one of his own children.[44] And since you are his child, you are also a co-heir with his Son, Jesus, of all things to come.[45,46]

Live as blameless and pure children of the light in a dark and depraved society.[47,48]

CHOICES

1   Josh. 24:15
2   1 Kings 18:21
3   Deut. 30:19
4   Deut. 30:20
5   Josh. 24:14
6   1 Chron. 28:9
7   Matt. 6:24
8   Luke 16:13
9   James 4:4
10   James 1:8
11   Luke 13:24
12   Matt. 7:14
13   Matt. 7:13
14   Matt. 22:14
15   Prov. 4:14
16   Prov. 4:15
17   Prov. 4:16
18   Ps. 119:30
19   Prov. 3:31
20   Prov. 8:10
21   Prov. 16:16
22   James 2:5
23   1 Cor. 1:28
24   Isa. 44:2
25   James 1:18
26   John 15:16
27   1 Peter 2:9
28   Col. 3:12
29   1 John 2:15
30   James 4:4
31   1 John 2:16
32   1 John 2:17

CHOICES

You must make a choice in life concerning whom you are going to worship and serve: the Lord God Almighty of heaven, or the false gods of your society. The former leads to life and blessing; the latter leads to curses and death.[1-2]

Choose the way of life.[3] Hold fast to the Lord; love and serve him faithfully with wholehearted devotion and a willing mind.[4] Get rid of false gods because the one true God knows every heart and understands every motive.[5,6]

You cannot serve two masters. You will love one and hate the other or be devoted to one and despise the other. You cannot serve both God and money.[7,8] You cannot be a friend of the world and a friend of God at the same time.[9] You must choose and commit to one or the other. Otherwise, you will be conflicted and uncertain in everything you do.[10]

Choose to take the narrow pathway that leads to eternal life. It is a difficult course.[11,12] But the wide pathway that is broad and easy leads to destruction, and most people choose it without much thought.[13] Everyone has to make this choice, but few make the right decision.[14]

Do not even set foot on the path of the wicked.[15] Choose to turn away from it and go another way because those on this path cannot think of anything else but evil.[16,17]

Choose the way of truth and set your heart on God's ways.[18] Do not envy a violent person or choose any of their ways.[19]

Choose God's instruction and knowledge instead of wealth.[20] Choose to pursue wisdom and understanding, which are much better than gold and silver.[21]

God has chosen those who are poor in the eyes of the world to be rich in faith and the humble things of this world to confound the proud.[22,23] He created and formed you in the womb, and now choses to offer you a spiritual rebirth so that you will be the crown jewel of all creation.[24,25] He has chosen you to reproduce this story in others.[26]

You are now part of a chosen people belonging to God.[27] Show it by your compassion, kindness, humility, gentleness, and patience.[28]

Do not choose to be a friend of the world. Friendship with the world is incompatible with love for God.[29] The world and all it values will come to an end, but the person who chooses to do the will of God will live forever.[30-32]

CHRISTIAN COMMUNITY

1	Phil. 1:27		35	Rom. 15:2
2	1 Peter 3:8		36	Acts 14:22
3	1 Cor. 12:25		37	1 Peter 4:1
4	1 Cor. 12:26		38	Jude 22
5	Matt. 20:26		39	Gal. 6:2
6	Mark 10:43		40	James 5:16
7	Matt. 20:27		41	1 Cor. 8:9
8	Mark 9:35		42	James 1:19
9	Matt. 23:11		43	James 1:22
10	Titus 2:7		44	Titus 3:14
11	2 Tim. 2:24		45	Phil. 2:3
12	Titus 1:6		46	1 Tim. 5:21
13	Titus 1:7		47	James 2:1
14	Titus 1:8		48	James 2:9
15	Titus 1:9			
16	Titus 3:2			
17	John 13:34			
18	John 15:12			
19	John 13:35			
20	1 Peter 1:22			
21	1 Peter 3:8			
22	1 John 4:21			
23	1 Peter 3:8			
24	Titus 3:2			
25	Col. 3:12			
26	1 Peter 3:8			
27	Luke 6:36			
28	Rom. 15:7			
29	Col. 3:13			
30	1 Thess. 5:11			
31	Jude 20			
32	Heb. 3:13			
33	Heb. 3:13			
34	Heb. 10:25			

CHRISTIAN COMMUNITY

Live as a citizen of heaven. Conduct yourself in a manner worthy of the Good News about Christ. Be united in purpose and of a single mind—to stand for and defend the gospel.[1,2] There should be no divisions, but each part of your community should have equal concern for each other.[3] If one part suffers, every part suffers; if one part is honored, every part rejoices with it.[4]

Leaders must serve those they lead.[5-7] Whoever wants to be first must take last place and be the servant of everyone else.[8,9] Leaders must be examples by doing good works and reflecting the integrity and seriousness of their beliefs.[10] They must not be quarrelsome, but kind to everyone and patient with difficult people.[11] They must live a blameless life and be faithful to their spouse.[12] They must not be arrogant or quick-tempered, not a heavy drinker, violent or dishonest with money.[13] They must love what is good, live wisely and be just. They must live a devout and disciplined life.[14] They must be able to encourage others with wholesome teaching and show those who oppose the gospel where they are wrong.[15] They must not slander anyone, but be gentle and show true humility to everyone.[16]

Love one another. It is a demonstration of your faith in Christ who gave this commandment.[17,19] You must show sincere love from deep within your heart for each other as brothers and sisters.[20,21] This also shows that you love God.[22]

Be humble and sympathetic with each other.[23] Be gentle and avoid quarrels.[24] Develop a reputation for tenderhearted mercy, kindness, humility, gentleness, and patience.[25,26] You must be compassionate toward others as a reflection of God's compassion on you.[27] Accept one another just as Christ accepted you.[28] Make allowance for each other's faults and forgive anyone who offends you, just as the Lord forgave you.[29]

Encourage one another and build each other up in the faith.[30,31] Do this on a daily basis so that no one will be deceived by sin and hardened against God.[32] Do not neglect meeting together as this is an important source of encouragement.[33,34] This helps others do what is right.[35] Remind each other that we must suffer many hardships to enter the kingdom of God.[36] Suffering for Christ has a way of making us abandon sin.[37] Show mercy to those whose faith is wavering.[38]

Carry each other's burdens and in this way you will fulfill the law of Christ.[39] Confess your sins to each other and pray for each other.[40] Do not allow your freedom in Christ to cause those with a weaker conscience to stumble.[41] Be quick to listen, but slow to speak and slow to get angry.[42]

Don't just listen to God's word. You must do what it says. Otherwise, you are just fooling yourself.[43] Learn to do good by meeting the urgent needs of others and then your faith will be productive.[44] But do so with humility, considering others better than yourself, and don't do anything out of selfish ambition or vain conceit.[45] You must not show favoritism—it is a sin.[46-48]

CHURCH

1	Col. 1:18	30	1 Thess. 5:13
2	Eph. 5:23	31	1 Tim. 5:17
3	Col. 1:15	32	Heb. 10:25
4	Col. 1:19	33	1 Cor. 14:26
5	Matt. 28:18	34	1 Cor. 5:11
6	Eph. 1:22	35	2 Thess. 3:14
7	Matt. 16:18	36	Titus 3:9
8	1 Tim. 3:15	37	1 Cor. 6:4
9	Eph. 3:10	38	Titus 3:10
10	Eph. 4:11	39	1 Tim. 5:3
11	Eph. 4:12	40	1 John 3:11
12	Eph. 4:13		
13	Eph. 4:15		
14	Eph. 4:14		
15	1 Cor. 12:12		
16	1 Cor. 12:27		
17	Eph. 4:16		
18	1 Cor. 12:7		
19	1 Cor. 12:4		
20	1 Cor. 12:5		
21	Rom. 12:6		
22	Rom. 12:7		
23	Rom. 12:8		
24	1 Cor. 12:8		
25	1 Cor. 12:9		
26	1 Cor.12:10		
27	1 Cor.14:26		
28	Heb. 13:17		
29	Thess. 5:12		

CHURCH

The Church is the visible body of Christ in the world.[1] Jesus is the foundation and head of the Church and preeminent in everything.[2] He is the visible image and full expression of the invisible God.[3,4] All authority in heaven and on earth has been given to him by God who has appointed him to be head over everything including the Church.[5,6] The gates of hell itself will not prevail against this Church.[7] It is the foundation and pillar of the truth of the living God.[8] God uses the Church to display his amazing wisdom to unseen rulers and authorities in heavenly places.[9]

Christ has given many different gifts to the Church: apostles, prophets, evangelists, pastors, and teachers. Their responsibility is to equip God's people to do his work and build up the Church, the body of Christ.[10,11] Their goal is to develop maturity in your faith and knowledge in the Lord and help you grow in every way into becoming more like Christ.[12-14]

You are part of the body of Christ if you have put your faith in Jesus. Every part needs to work together in order for this body to function properly.[15-17] So the Holy Spirit has given you a spiritual gift that is to be used to serve the Lord, build up the Church and help each other.[18-20]

If your gift is serving, serve; if it is teaching, teach; if it is encouraging, encourage; if it is contributing money, give generously; if it is leadership, govern diligently; if showing mercy, show it cheerfully.[21-23] You may have the ability to give wise advice, contribute special knowledge, demonstrate great faith, or exercise discernment in spiritual matters.[24-26] All these gifts and abilities are to be used for the strengthening of the Church.[27]

Obey your church leaders and submit to their authority so that their work will be a joy, not a burden. They are accountable to God.[28] Respect them and hold them in the highest regard, especially those whose work is preaching and teaching.[29-31] Be consistent in meeting together. Encourage each other.[32] Bring something to offer: a hymn, word of instruction, new understanding, or anything that helps to the strengthen your congregation.[33]

You must not associate with anyone who calls himself or herself a Christ-follower but is sexually immoral or greedy, an idolater or a slanderer, a drunkard or a swindler. Perhaps this will shame them into changing their ways.[34,35]

Avoid discussions of foolish controversies, spiritual pedigrees, and arguments about the law because these are unprofitable and useless.[36] Appoint judges from within your congregation to rule in cases of interpersonal dispute and immoral behavior.[37] Warn a divisive person twice and after that have nothing to do with them.[38]

Give proper attention those who are really in need.[39]

Love one another.[40]

COMMUNION

1   Matt. 26:26
2   Matt. 26:27
3   Matt. 26:28
4   Mark 14:22
5   Mark 14:23
6   Mark 14:24
7   Luke 22:19
8   1 Cor 11:25
9   1 Cor. 11:26
10   1 Cor. 11:27
11   1 Cor. 11:29
12   1 Cor. 11:28
13   1 Cor. 10:16
14   Rom. 10:9
15   Rom. 10:10
16   1 Cor. 11:31

COMMUNION

Jesus was eating Passover supper with his disciples on the same night that he was betrayed by Judas. He took a loaf of bread, gave thanks to God, broke it, and said, "This is my body, which is broken for you. Eat it in memory of me." [1-5] In the same way after they had eaten, he took a cup of wine, gave thanks, and said, "This cup represents a new covenant between God and his people, an agreement confirmed with my blood, which is to be poured out as a sacrifice for the forgiveness of your sins. Drink it in memory of me." [1-8]

You must solemnly remember that every time you eat this bread and drink this cup, you reenact this memorial of the Lord's death in words and actions. Continue to do so until he returns. [9] If you do this without believing the reality in your heart, you are guilty of mocking the body and blood of the Lord. You eat and drink future judgment on yourself. [10,11]

Examine your heart before you participate in this sacrament. [12] By eating the bread and drinking the wine, you identify yourself with Christ in his death for your sins. [13] Do not participate in this sacrament in an unworthy, careless, or hypocritical manner. True confession and genuine faith are basic requirements. [14,15] Judge yourself, and you will not be judged. [16]

COMPASSION

1   Zech. 7:9
2   Col. 3:12
3   Eph. 4:32
4   Ps.103:13
5   Ps. 103:4
6   Ps. 116:5
7   Ps.119:156
8   Isa. 30:18
9   Isa. 49:13
10   Ias. 54:10
11   Lam. 3:22
12   Lam. 3:23
13   Lam. 3:32
14   Ps. 51:1
15   Ps. 119:77
16   Isa. 63:7
17   2 Cor. 1:3
18   James 5:11
19   Phil. 2:1
20   Phil. 2:2

COMPASSION

Show compassion and mercy to one another.[1] Maintain a wardrobe of virtue and dress yourself with compassion, kindness, humility, gentleness, and patience.[2] Be kind and compassionate to one another, forgiving each other just as God forgave you because of Christ.[3]

The Lord has compassion on those who fear him.[4] He will redeem their life from hell and crown them with love and compassion.[5] He is full of compassion, grace, and righteousness.[6] His compassion is great and he longs to be gracious to you.[7,8]

Rejoice because the Lord comforts and shows compassion to those who are afflicted.[9] Even if the mountains are shaken and the hills disappear, the unfailing love of the Lord for you will never be taken away, nor will his compassion for you ever stop.[10]

Because of the Lord's great love, we are not consumed by our afflictions. His compassions for you will never fail. They are new every morning. Great is his faithfulness![11,12] Although he does allow grief, he will show compassion because of his unfailing love for you.[13]

Ask God to extend his mercy to you. Because of his unfailing love and great compassion, he will blot out the record of all your transgressions.[14] His act of compassion will bring you new life.[15]

Tell others about the Lord's compassion and the many kindnesses he has shown to you in order that others may praise him along with you.[16] He is the source of all compassion and comfort.[17] The Lord is full of compassion and mercy.[18]

Love one another and work together with one mind and purpose since you belong to Christ and have developed his compassion in your own life.[19,20]

CONFESSION

1   1 John 1:9
2   Isa. 43:25
3   Mic. 7:19
4   Ps. 103:12
5   Heb. 8:12
6   Heb. 10:17
7   Acts 3:19
8   Luke 13:3
9   1 John 1:8
10 James 4:9
11 Joel 2:13
12 Joel 2:12
13 Ps. 51:17
14 James 4:8
15 Ezek. 18:31
16 James 4:10
17 Prov. 28:13
18 Num. 32:23
19 Ps. 32:5
20 Num. 5:6
21 Num. 5:7
22 James 5:15
23 James 5:16
24 Rom. 10:9
25 Rom. 10:10
26 Rom. 14:11
27 Phil. 2:11
28 Heb. 3:1
29 Ezra 10:11
30 2 Cor. 9:13
31 1 Tim. 6:12
32 Heb. 13:15
33 2 Tim. 2:19
34 Matt. 3:8

CONFESSION

Confess your sins to God who is both faithful to his own nature and just. He will forgive all of your sins and offer you a full pardon.[1] He will expunge your record; cast it into the depths of the sea; remove it as far away from you as the East is from the West. He promises never to bring them up again![2-6]

Turn to God so that your sins may be wiped out.[7] Unless you do so, you will be permanently separated from God.[8] If you think you have no sin, you are only fooling yourself and are living in total denial of reality.[9]

Let your confession be accompanied by true sorrow and remorse.[10-12] God recognizes the value of a broken and contrite heart.[13] Come close to God, and he will come close to you. Purify your heart and do not let its loyalty be divided between God and the world.[14] Put all your rebellion behind you and develop a new heart and attitude.[15] Humble yourself before God, and he will lift you up in due time.[16]

Do not try to conceal your sin—it will not work.[17] You can be sure that it will catch up with you at some future point.[18] Confess your sin to the Lord, and he will forgive you and wipe away your guilt.[19] If you have harmed another person, you must make full restitution for their loss.[20,21]

Confess your sins to each another and pray for one another for healing when one of you is sick. The earnest prayer of a righteous person has great power and produces wonderful results.[22,23]

Confess with your mouth that "Jesus is Lord" and believe in your heart that God raised him from the dead and you will be saved. Actions by both mind and heart are required.[24,25] Eventually God will require this of everyone.[26,27] If you have confessed Jesus in this way, focus your mind and thoughts on him because you share in a heavenly calling.[28]

Confess your faith in Jesus and then do his will.[29] Obedience must be the natural outcome of your confession because others will see it and offer praise to God for it.[30,31] This is pleasing to God.[32]

Everyone who confesses the name of the Lord must turn away from evil.[33] Prove by the way you live that you have confessed and repented of your sins and turned to God.[34]

CONFIDENCE

1	Heb. 11:1		31	2 Pet 1:5
2	2 Cor. 3:4		32	2 Pet. 1:6
3	Rom. 10:17		33	2 Pet. 1:7
4	1 John 5:13		34	2 Pet. 1:8
5	John 20:31		35	2 Pet. 1:10
6	Heb. 10:35		36	James 1:2
7	Prov. 3:26		37	Rom. 5:3
8	Jer. 17:7		38	James 1:3
9	Isa. 33:6		39	James 1:4
10	Isa. 28:16		40	Rom. 5:4
11	Heb. 4:16		41	Prov. 11:21
12	Eph. 3:12		42	Prov. 16:5
13	Heb. 10:19		43	Eph. 5:5
14	1 John 5:14			
15	Heb. 13:6			
16	1 John 4:17			
17	1 John 4:15			
18	1 John 4:16			
19	1 John 3:21			
20	Phil. 1:6			
21	1 John 2:28			
22	Luke 1:4			
23	Luke 1:1			
24	Luke 1:2			
25	Luke 1:3			
26	2 Tim. 2:15			
27	Rom. 1:16			
28	Rom. 1:17			
29	2 Tim. 3:16			
30	Heb. 6:11			

CONFIDENCE

Faith is confidence that what we hope for will actually happen. It is the conviction that unseen things are absolute realities.[1] Such confidence comes from Jesus Christ and his Word.[2,3] By this, you can know beyond the shadow of a doubt that you have eternal life, a reality and not an illusion.[4,5] Do not throw away this confidence because it will be richly rewarded.[6]

Put your confidence in the Lord. He will protect and bless you.[7,8] He will be a sure foundation for your times; a rich source of salvation and wisdom and knowledge. Those who trust him will never be dismayed. The fear of the Lord is the key to this treasure.[9,10]

Have confidence, because of your faith in Jesus, to come to God for mercy and help, especially when you need it.[11,12] You have this confidence because of his sacrifice on the cross.[13] Your confidence in approaching God is that he will hear anything you ask according to his will.[14] Be confident and unafraid because the Lord is your helper.[15]

Have confidence as you approach the day of judgment because of what Jesus has done.[16] If you acknowledge that he is the Son of God, you can have confidence and rely on God's love for you.[17,18] You can have confidence before God if your conscience is clear.[19]

You can have confidence that God will continue the good work he began in you until it is finished on the day when Jesus returns.[20] Stay in fellowship with him so that you may be confident and unashamed on that day.[21]

Put your confidence in the Gospel. It is a carefully written account of the life and teachings of Jesus and based on eyewitness reports from his first disciples.[22-25] Study it so that you can understand and explain it to others.[26] It reveals God's powerful way of making you righteous in his sight—by faith in Jesus.[27,28] In fact, all Scripture is inspired by God and deserves your full confidence.[29]

Increase your confidence in your hope of eternal life by adding these qualities to your faith: goodness, knowledge, self-control, perseverance, godliness, kindness, and love.[30-33] The more you grow in these, the more confident you will be in your calling and the more productive and useful you will be with your knowledge of Jesus.[34,35]

Be confident in the face of problems and trials of many kinds.[36,37] They help develop perseverance and endurance, maturity, strength of character, and strengthen your confidence in your hope of salvation.[38-40]

Be confident of this: the wicked will not go unpunished, nor will the proud.[41,42] No immoral, impure, or greedy person has any inheritance in the kingdom of Christ.[43]

CONTENTMENT

1 Heb. 13:5
2 1 Tim. 6:10
3 Eccl. 5:10
4 Matt. 6:24
5 1 John 2:15
6 1 John 2:16
7 1 John 2:17
8 Luke 12:15
9 Eph. 5:3
10 Col. 3:5
11 Prov. 23:4
12 Matt. 16:26
13 Mark 8:36
14 Luke 9:25
15 Phil. 4:11
16 Phil. 4:12
17 Phil. 4:13
18 Prov. 19:23
19 1 Tim. 6:6
20 1 Tim. 6:8
21 Luke 12:22
22 Luke 12:23
23 Luke 12:29
24 Luke 12:30
25 John 6:27
26 Matt. 6:33
27 Luke 12:31
28 Col. 3:15
29 Rom. 8:6
30 Isa. 26:3
31 Phil. 4:6
32 Phil. 4:7

CONTENTMENT

Be content with what you have and keep your life free from the love of money, because God will never leave you or forsake you.[1] The love of money is the root of all kinds of evil and causes many to wander away from true faith, piercing themselves through with many sorrows.[2] Those who love money will never think they have enough. It is foolish to think that wealth brings true happiness.[3] You cannot serve two masters. Either you will hate one and love the other or you will be devoted to one and despise the other. You cannot serve both God and money.[4]

Do not be seduced by the world and all it has to offer. Love for the world displaces love for God.[5] The world offers only preoccupation with sex, money and power. These things will all pass away and are not to be compared with pleasing God in this life and living forever with him in the next.[6,7]

Be on your guard against all kinds of greed. The quality of your life is not determined by the value and number of your possessions.[8] Do not allow even a hint of greed in your life. Get rid of it! Greed is the same as the sin of idolatry.[9,10] Do not wear yourself out to get rich, but show some restraint.[11] After all, what would you benefit if you gained the whole world, but lost your own soul?[12-14]

Learn the secret of being content in any circumstance, rich or poor, healthy or sick, honored or despised.[15,16] Christ will give you strength to endure and do all things.[17]

The fear of the Lord leads to a contented life.[18] Godliness with contentment is true wealth.[19]

Be content with what you have.[20] Do not be overly concerned about your daily needs, food, clothing and shelter.[21-25] Make the kingdom of God your top priority and these other things will fall into their proper place.[26,27]

Let the peace of Christ rule your heart and the Spirit control your mind; and be thankful.[28,29] Then you will experience true contentment.[30-32]

DEVIL

1   1 Peter 5:8
2   James 4:7
3   1 Peter 5:9
4   Eph. 6:11
5   Eph. 6:12
6   Eph. 6:13
7   Eph. 6:14
8   Eph. 6:15
9   Eph. 6:16
10   Eph. 6:17
11   Eph. 6:18
12   Eph 4.26
13   Eph. 4:26
14   2 Cor. 2:10
15   2 Cor. 2:11
16   2 Cor. 11:14
17   Eph. 2:2
18   2 Cor. 11:15
19   2 Tim. 2:26
20   2 Cor. 4:4
21   Heb. 2:14
22   Jude 9
23   Zech. 3:2

DEVIL

Be sober and vigilant at all times. Your enemy, the Devil, prowls like a roaring lion looking for someone to devour.[1]

Submit yourself to God. Resist the Devil and he will flee from you.[2] Resist him, standing firm in the faith. Others around the world are undergoing the same kind of suffering.[3]

Put on the full armor of God so that you can take your stand against the schemes and strategies of the Devil.[4] Your battles are not against flesh and blood enemies, but against unseen mighty powers in this dark world and against evil spirits in the heavenly places.[5] You will need every piece of God's armor to resist your enemy, the Devil, and still be standing after your battle is finished.[6] Since this battle is spiritual, you will need spiritual defenses: truth, righteousness, peace, faith, salvation, Scripture, and prayer.[7-11]

Do not let anger stay long in your heart. It will cause you to sin.[12] It gives the Devil a hammerlock on you. Do not allow this to happen.[13]

Forgive anyone who has something against you for the sake of Christ and in order that Satan might not outsmart you. Be aware of his schemes.[14,15]

Satan himself masquerades as an angel of light.[16] He is the commander of the powers in the unseen world and the spirit at work in the hearts of those who refuse to obey God.[17] Don't be surprised that those who serve him also disguise themselves as servants of righteousness.[18] Many have been caught in this trap and are Satan's captives to do his will.[19] He blinds the minds of those who do not believe the gospel so that they cannot see the glorious light of the Good News or understand the message about Christ, who is the exact likeness of God.[20]

Satan holds the power of death for now. However, he will ultimately be destroyed by Christ who died a human death in order to free you from the fear of death.[21]

It is not up to you to rebuke Satan.[22,23]

DEVOTION

1   Deut. 6:5
2   Matt. 2:37
3   Mark 12:30
4   Deut. 6:6
5   Deut. 6:7
6   Deut. 6:8
7   Deut. 6:9
8   1 Chron. 22:19
9   1 Chron. 28:9
10   1 Sam. 2:24
11   Job 11:13
12   Job 11:14
13   Job 11:15
14   Josh. 22:5
15   Ezek. 33:31
16   Ps. 86:2
17   2 Cor. 11:3
18   1 Kings11:4
19   Matt. 6:24
20   Matt. 22:39
21   Rom. 12:10
22   Titus 3:14
23   1 Tim. 1:4
24   Col. 4:2

DEVOTION

Love the Lord your God with all your heart and with all your soul and with all your mind and with all your strength. This is the greatest commandment of all.[1-3] Keep all his commandments in your heart and impress them on your children. Talk about them as you go about your day. Place physical reminders of them in obvious places in your life routines.[4-7]

Devote your heart and soul to seeking the Lord your God.[8] Acknowledge God and serve him with wholehearted devotion and a willing mind, because he searches your heart and understands every motive behind even your thoughts. Seek him and you will find him.[9] Serve him faithfully with all your heart. Think about what great things he has done for you.[10]

Devote your heart to the Lord and reach out to him in prayer. Have nothing to do with sin and evil and you will not be ashamed before him.[11-13]

Love the Lord your God, walk in all his ways, obey his commandments, hold fast onto him, and serve him with all your heart and all your soul.[14] Do not express your devotion with words only, but put it into practice.[15]

Trust God to guard your life because you are devoted to him.[16] Beware that you are not led astray from your sincere and pure devotion to Christ.[17] Even a wise person does foolish things when their heart is not fully devoted to the Lord.[18]

Do not attempt to serve two masters. You will either be devoted to one and despise the other or vice versa. You cannot serve both God and money.[19]

Love your neighbor as yourself. This is the second greatest commandment.[20] Be devoted to one another in brotherly love.[21] Devote yourself to doing what is good in order to live a productive life.[22]

Do not devote yourself to myths and endless genealogies. These promote controversies rather than accomplishing God's work—which is by faith.[23]

Devote yourselves to prayer, being watchful and thankful.[24]

DISABLED PERSONS

1	Lev. 19:14		35	Luke 10:21
2	Deut. 27:18		36	1 Cor. 1:25
3	Heb. 12:13		37	1 Cor. 1:26
4	Rom. 15:1		38	1 Cor. 1:27
5	Ps. 82:3		39	1 Cor. 1:28
6	1 Thess. 5:14		40	1 Cor. 1:29
7	Ps. 82:4		41	2 Cor. 4:4
8	Luke 14:13		42	2 Peter 1:5
9	Acts 20:35		43	2 Peter 1:6
10	Ps. 41:1		44	2 Peter 1:7
11	Isa. 63:9		45	2 Peter 1:8
12	Ps. 12:5		46	2 Peter 1:9
13	Isa. 40:29		47	1 John 2:11
14	Ps. 72:4		48	Rev. 3:17
15	Ps. 72:13		49	2 Cor. 4:18
16	1 Cor. 1:27		50	2 Cor. 4:17
17	Luke 4:18			
18	Isa. 42:7			
19	Matt. 11:5			
20	Matt. 15:31			
21	Matt. 21:14			
22	Mark 8:23			
23	Luke 7:21			
24	Luke 7:22			
25	Mark 7:37			
26	John 9:2			
27	John 9:3			
28	Ps.119:67			
29	2 Cor. 12:7			
30	2 Cor. 12:9			
31	Job 1:7			
32	Job 1:8			
33	Job 1:9			
34	Job 1:10			

DISABLED PERSONS

Do not do anything to make life more difficult for a person with a disability. Do not take advantage of, ridicule, or bully them.[1,2] Rather, do things that make life easier for you and disabled persons alike.[3]

Be patient with anyone who has a disability and bear with their shortcomings and failures, even when it is an inconvenience to you.[4] Help them in areas where they are unable to help themselves.[5,6] Rescue them when they are in trouble.[7] Do something fun for them, knowing they can never repay you.[8] It is more blessed to give than receive.[9] Blessed is the person who has regard for persons with disabilitiy.[10]

God is distressed when he sees one of his children distressed.[11] He knows about violence done to the helpless and disabled. He hears their prayers for relief.[12] He will give relief to the afflicted, strength to the elderly and power to the weak.[13-15] He has chosen the weak to shame those who are strong. He has chosen simple things to confound the wise.[16]

Jesus's mission on earth included healing those who were physically disabled.[17-18] The crippled were given strength to walk, the blind granted vision, the deaf could hear, and the mute speak. Those oppressed with many afflictions including mental illness and disability were cured. He preached the gospel to the poor and marginalized. Much praise to God resulted from all of this.[19-25]

Disability is often not the result of anyone's sin but always a part of God's plan to display good works through his people.[26,27] Disability tends to keep us from being proud or wandering away from God.[28,29] God's power is most evident in the areas of our lives that are weak.[30] Disability can be a result of the battle between God and Satan for your soul.[31-34]

God has made the gospel known even to those with mental disability, while at the same time hidden this knowledge from those who think themselves wise and clever.[35] This "foolish" plan of God is far wiser than any human plan.[36,37] He chooses people the world considers nothing and uses them to bring to nothing the things the world considers important.[38,39] As a result, no one has bragging rights.[40]

Spiritual disability is caused by Satan, who blinds the minds of unbelievers so that they cannot see the light of the gospel of Christ.[41] Make every effort to avoid spiritual disability in your own life by developing the virtues of a mature character: faith, goodness, knowledge, self-control, perseverance, godliness, kindness, and love.[42-48]

Do not fixate on your disability if you have one. Although big to you now, it is small in the big picture and will come to a glorious end.[49] Focus instead on things you cannot see now, things that vastly outweigh your present troubles and that will last forever![50]

DISCIPLESHIP

1	Matt. 28:18
2	Matt. 28:19
3	Matt. 28:20
4	John 12:26
5	John 15:5
6	John 15:6
7	John 15:4
8	John 15:10
9	John 15:8
10	John 12:26
11	John 14:15
12	Matt. 20:26
13	Luke 14:27
14	2 Tim. 2:15
15	Jude 20
16	2 Tim. 2:2
17	Luke 9:23
18	Luke 14:33
19	Matt. 10:38
20	Matt. 10:37
21	Luke 14:26
22	Mark 10:21
23	Matt. 19:29
24	Matt. 19:30
25	Mark 8:35
26	Luke 17:33
27	Luke 9:24
28	John 12:25
29	Matt. 16:26
30	Mark 8:36
31	Luke 9:25
32	John 8:31
33	John 15:8
34	John 13:35

DISCIPLESHIP

Go and make disciples in all nations. Baptize them in the name of the Father and the Son and the Holy Spirit. Do this on the basis of Jesus's authority and command.[1,2] Teach these new disciples to obey all of Jesus's commands.[3]

Spend time with Jesus if you want to be his disciple.[4] He is like a vine and you are like a branch. A branch cannot bear fruit by itself unless it remains attached to its vine. You cannot be fruitful in the kingdom of God unless you remain attached to Jesus.[5-7] Obey Jesus's commands and you will always be attached to him.[8] Bearing fruit pleases God and shows that you are Jesus's disciple.[9]

You must follow Jesus and stay with him if you want to be his disciple.[10] You must show your devotion to him by keeping his commandments.[11] You must be a servant of Jesus and others if you want to be great in the kingdom of heaven.[12] You must be willing to bear your own cross even as he carried his own.[13]

Concentrate on doing your best work for God, especially learning to accurately understand and explain the Scriptures. This pleases God.[14] Build yourself up in your faith and pray in the power of the Holy Spirit.[15] Find a receptive person and teach them about the things you have learned.[16]

You must be willing to renounce your own interests and face the same obstacles that Jesus faced if you want to be his true disciple.[17] You must be willing to bear a cross of your own.[18] Nothing including persons and property must be even close to standing between you and him.[19,21] Give away everything that hinders your devotion or service to him. In this way, you will be depositing a treasure in heaven where it will be held safely for you.[22,23] Many who think of themselves first will find themselves last.[24]

Don't try to hang on to life as you know it or you will lose it. Give up your life for the sake of Jesus and the gospel and you will save it.[25-28] Even if you could keep it for yourself, would it be worth losing your own soul in exchange?[29-31]

You prove yourself a true disciple of Jesus by following his teaching and bearing fruit.[32,33] You prove it to others by loving his disciples.[34]

DISCIPLINE

1   Prov. 22:6
2   Prov. 29:17
3   Prov. 23:13
4   Prov. 23:14
5   Prov. 19:18
6   Prov. 13:24
7   Prov. 22:15
8   Eph. 6:4
9   Prov. 3:11
10   Prov. 3:12
11   Heb. 12:6
12   Heb. 12:10
13   Ps. 119:67
14   Rev. 3:19
15   Heb. 12:7
16   1 Tim. 4:7
17   Titus 1:8
18   2 Tim. 2:15
19   Col. 2:6
20   Col. 2:7
21   Ps. 96:9
22   Ps. 29:2
23   Ps. 46:10
24   Ps. 37:7
25   1 Thess. 5:17
26   Col. 4:2
27   Phil. 4:8
28   Phil. 4:6
29   1 Peter 2:11

DISCIPLINE

Train a child in the way they should go and they will not depart from it when they are old.[1] Discipline your children and they will give you peace and be a delight to your soul.[2] Do not withhold discipline from your child; it will not kill them.[3] There is hope that appropriate punishment will save your child's soul from death.[4,5]

Be committed to discipline your children because it demonstrates that you love them.[6] A child's heart is full of foolishness, but physical discipline will drive it away.[7] Do not exasperate your children by being unreasonable, but bring them up with the discipline and instruction that comes from the Lord.[8]

Do not despise or resent the Lord when he disciplines you.[9] He does this for everyone he loves.[10,11] In the same way that earthly fathers discipline their children, God disciplines us for our own good, and this guides us into a right relationship with him.[12] Affliction tends to bring us back when we stray away from him.[13] Be sincere and repent when God rebukes and disciplines you.[14] Endure any hardship as a form of discipline imposed on you by a loving heavenly Father.[15]

Discipline yourself to be godly, self-controlled, upright, holy, and good.[16,17]

Study the Scriptures and learn to explain them correctly.[18] Continue to follow Jesus and let your life be built on him. Then your faith will grow strong and your life will overflow with gratitude.[19,20]

Worship the Lord in the beauty and splendor of his holiness.[21] Give him the glory and honor due his name.[22]

Be silent and still before the Lord. Learn to know him as your God. Wait patiently for him to act in your life and do not fret when others gain success.[23,24]

Pray at all times.[25] Devote yourself to prayer with an alert mind and a thankful heart.[26]

Set your mind on things that are true and honorable, right and pure, lovely and admirable, and excellent and worthy of praise.[27]

Do not allow yourself to be anxious about anything. Instead, present your requests to God with honest and sincere prayer and thanksgiving for all he has already done for you.[28]

Keep away from worldly desires that wage war against your soul.[29]

DIVORCE

1   Mal. 2:16
2   Mark 10:6
3   Mark 10:7
4   Mark 10:8
5   Mark 10:9
6   1 Cor. 7:39
7   Ex. 20:14
8   Matt. 5:32
9   Matt. 19:9
10   1 Cor. 7:15
11   Luke 16:18
12   Mark 10:11
13   Mark 10:12
14   Matt. 19:8
15   1 Cor. 7:12
16   1 Cor. 7:13
17   1 Cor. 7:16
18   1 Cor. 7:14
19   Mark 10:5
20   Mal. 2:13
21   Mal. 2:14
22   Mal. 2:15

DIVORCE

God hates divorce.[1]

God created human beings as male and female in the very beginning.[2] He planned that both should leave their parents and be united to each other so as to no longer be two, but one.[3,4] Do not separate what God has joined together.[5]

You are bound to your spouse until death. After that, the surviving spouse is free to remarry.[6]

Do not commit adultery.[7]

Divorce is permissible in the case of marital unfaithfulness.[8,9]

Divorce is permissible in the case of abandonment.[10]

Divorce for any other reason is prohibited. Divorcing your spouse without just cause is morally equivalent to adultery.[11-13] From the beginning, divorce was never God's intention.[14]

An unbelieving spouse does not justify divorce.[15,16] As a believer, you bring holiness and influence into your marriage and may even bring salvation to your spouse.[17] You also influence your children who would otherwise not learn about the spiritual purposes of God.[18]

Hard hearts bring on divorce and separation from both God and your spouse.[19] Divorce causes untold grief.[20]

Do not break faith with the spouse of your youth. Marriage is a covenant partnership created by God for the wellbeing of you both and your children.[21,22]

DOUBT

1   John 14:1

2   James 4:8

3   Luke 24:38

4   Luke 24:39

5   Matt. 14:31

6   Rom. 10:17

7   Heb. 4:12

8   Luke 1:4

9   1 John 5:13

10   John 20:27

11   Heb. 11:1

12   Matt. 17:20

13   Matt. 1:21

14   Mark 11:23

15   James 1:5

16   James 1:6

17   James 1:7

18   James 1:8

19   Ps. 73:1

20   Phil. 1:6

21   James 1:2

22   James 1:3

23   Rom. 5:3

24   James 1:4

25   Rom. 5:4

26   Rom.14:23

27   Jude 22

DOUBT

Do not let your heart be controlled by doubt. Trust in God; trust also in his Son, Jesus Christ.[1] Come near to God, and he will come near to you. Wash your hands and purify your heart of its double-minded, unstable, and indecisive ways.[2]

Do not allow questions of doubt to take over your life of faith. Look at the reality of Jesus's life and death and what he has done for you.[3,4]

Why do you doubt? It is because you lack faith.[5] How do you gain faith? Faith comes from hearing the gospel of Christ delivered to you through the Word of Christ, that is the Scriptures.[6] They are sharper than a surgeon's scalpel, cutting through everything including doubt and defense.[7] They are reliable and written so that you can know beyond the shadow of a doubt that you have eternal life.[8,9]

Stop doubting evidence that you can see.[10] Have confidence even in things you cannot see—by faith.[11] Even the very smallest amount of faith without doubt can move the mountains in your life.[12-14]

If you have doubts, ask God for his help. He gives wisdom generously to all without finding fault.[15] But you must believe and not doubt or you cannot expect to receive anything from the Lord.[16] Otherwise, you are like a wave of the sea, blown about by the wind; double-minded and unstable in everything you do.[17-18]

There is no doubt about it: God is good.[19] There should be no doubt in your mind that God has started a good work in your heart and will continue this good work until he finishes it on the very day Jesus returns.[20]

You should be happy when you face difficulties in life because they develop perseverance and endurance.[21,23] These two virtues develop strength of character and help remove doubt about your salvation.[24,25]

If you have doubts about any lifestyle issues, you should abstain. Otherwise, you are not following your convictions, and this would be a sin against God.[26]

Be merciful to those who doubt.[27]

DRUNKENNESS

1   Prov. 23:20

2   Prov. 23:2

3   Isa. 5:11

4   Isa. 5:22

5   1 Cor. 5:11

6   1 Cor. 6:10

7   Luke 12:29

8   Rom. 14:17

9   Luke 12:19

10   Luke 12:20

11   1 Cor. 10:24

12   1 Cor. 10:23

13   Rom. 14:21

14   1 Cor. 10:31

15   1 Cor. 10:32

16   Eph. 5:18

DRUNKENNESS

Do not join those who drink too much wine or gorge themselves on too much meat and good food. Drunkards and gluttons come to poverty and laziness clothes them in rags.[1,2] Woe to those who rise up early in the morning to run after their drinks and stay up late at night until they are inflamed with alcohol.[3] Woe to those who are heroes at drinking wine and champions at mixing drinks![4]

You must not associate with anyone who claims to be a Christ-follower and is a drunkard.[5] Such a person will not inherit the kingdom of God.[6]

Do not set your heart on what you will eat or drink. Do not worry about that.[7] The kingdom of God is not about eating or drinking, but about righteousness, peace, and joy in the Holy Spirit.[8]

On the other hand, beware the easy, carefree, and foolish life of "eat, drink, be merry" when you think you have it made. Death may come suddenly and you find out you are not really prepared![9,10]

Don't be preoccupied with your own self-interest, but with the good of others.[11] Everything is permissible, but not everything is beneficial or constructive.[12] It is better not to eat meat or drink wine if that is an issue that offends the conscience of another Christian.[13] Whether you eat or drink or whatever you do, do it all for God's glory.[14] Do not cause anyone to stumble in their faith because of what you do.[15]

Do not get drunk on wine because that will ruin your life. Instead, be filled with and controlled by the Holy Spirit.[16]

EMPLOYEES

1   1 Peter 2:18
2   Eph. 6:5
3   Eph. 6:6
4   Col. 3:22
5   Col. 3:23
6   Eph. 6:7
7   Col. 3:24
8   Eph. 6:8
9   1 Tim. 6:1
10 Titus 2:9
11 Titus 2:10
12 Col. 3:25
13 Eph. 6:9
14 Col. 4:1
15 Phil. 2:14
16 Phil. 2:15
17 1 Cor. 10:31

EMPLOYEES

Submit to the authority of your employers and bosses with all due respect, not only to those who are good and considerate, but also to those who are harsh.[1] Do what they ask, not only when they are watching, or just to win their favor, but with a sincere heart and out of reverence for the Lord. Follow their instructions just as you would follow his. This is an example of doing the will of God from your heart.[2-4]

Work willingly at whatever you do. Do your job wholeheartedly as if you were doing it for the Lord and not for men.[5,6] Remember that the boss you are really working for is Christ, and that he will compensate you for whatever good you have done with an eternal inheritance.[7,8]

Treat your employer with full respect so that the name of God will not be slandered.[9] Try to please him or her and do not talk back to them.[10] Do not steal from them, but show that you can be fully trusted, so that in every way you will make the teaching about God our Savior attractive.[11] If you do what is wrong, you will pay a price.[12]

Employers must treat their employees in the same way. Do not threaten them because you know that you both have the same Master in heaven, and there is no favoritism with him.[13,14]

Do everything without arguing or complaining so that no one can criticize you.[15,16]

Whatever you do, do it all for the glory of God.[17]

ENEMIES

1   Matt. 5:44

2   Luke 6:27

3   Luke 6:35

4   Prov. 25:21

5   Prov. 25:22

6   Rom. 12:20

7   Luke 6:28

8   Luke 6:29

9   Luke 6:35

10   Rom. 12:21

11   Prov. 24:17

12   James 4:4

13   1 John 2:15

14   1 John 2:16

15   Col. 1:21

16   Rom. 5:10

17   Heb. 10:26

18   Heb. 10:27

19   1 John 2:17

20   1 Peter 5:8

21   1 Peter 5:9

22   James 4:7

23   1 Cor. 15:26

24   Rom. 6:23

25   John 11:25

ENEMIES

Love your enemies. Pray for those who persecute you.[1] Do good to those who hate you.[2] Do good things for them and lend to them without expecting to get anything back.[3] If an enemy is hungry, give them food to eat; if thirsty give them something to drink. By acting in this way, you heap burning coals of fire on their head.[4-6]

Bless those who curse you. Pray for those who hurt you.[7] If someone slaps you on the cheek, don't strike back. Just turn the other cheek. If someone demands your coat, offer them your shirt too.[8] This kind of behavior pleases God because he is kind even to the ungrateful and the wicked. He will give you a great reward someday.[9]

Do not be overcome by evil, but overcome evil with good.[10] Do not gloat over the misfortune of your enemy.[11]

Do not be a friend to the world. It makes you an enemy of God and shows that you have rejected him.[12-14] At one time you were his enemy, at least in your mind if not your behavior, and separated from him by your evil thoughts and actions.[15] But even though you were his enemy, he reconciled you to himself through the death of his Son.[16]

Do not continue to deliberately commit sin now that you know the truth of the gospel. You can only live in fear of the horrible judgment reserved for the enemies of God if you do.[17,18] But the person who does what pleases God will live forever.[19]

Be self-controlled and alert. Your personal enemy, the Devil, prowls around like a hungry lion, looking for someone to devour.[20] Resist him and stand firm in your faith. You can be sure that you are not alone.[21,22]

Death is the last enemy to be destroyed.[23] It is the result of sin.[24] The person who believes in Jesus will live, even after they die.[25]

ENVY

1	Ex. 20:17	28	James 3:17
2	Deut. 5:21	29	James 3:13
3	Prov.2 3:17	30	Luke 12:15
4	Prov. 3:31	31	Matt.16:26
5	Prov. 24:19	32	Col. 3:5
6	Ps. 73:2	33	1 John 2:15
7	Ps. 73:3	34	1 John 2:16
8	Ps. 73:4	35	1 John 2:17
9	Ps. 73:5	36	Heb. 13:5
10	Ps. 73:6	37	1 Tim. 6:6
11	Ps. 73:7	38	1 Tim. 6:10
12	Ps. 73:8	39	1 Tim. 6:9
13	Ps. 73:9	40	Rom. 13:9
14	Prov. 24:1	41	1 Cor. 13:4
15	Prov. 23:6		
16	1 Tim. 6:6		
17	Prov.14:30		
18	Gal. 5:26		
19	Rom. 1:29		
20	Mark 7:22		
21	Mark 7:23		
22	Gal. 5:19		
23	Gal. 5:20		
24	Gal. 5:21		
25	1 Peter 2:1		
26	James 3:15		
27	James 3:16		

ENVY

Do not be envious.[1] Do not covet your neighbor's spouse or be envious of their house or anything that belongs to your neighbor.[2]

Do not let your heart envy ungodly or violent persons or choose any of their ways.[3,4] Do not envy the wicked or be jealous when you see their prosperity. They have no struggles or burdens like the rest of us, but they have become conceited, callous, scoffers, hateful, arrogant, and oppressive. They demand power and control over both heaven and earth.[5-13] Don't even envy their company and fine delicacies.[14,15] A contented heart leads to a healthy body; envy is like a cancer in your bones.[16,17]

Do not let yourself become envious of anyone else.[18] Envy is part of your old sinful nature and comes from your heart.[19-21] Following its desires leads to many evils including hostility, jealousy, anger, selfish ambition and an immoral life. You cannot live this way and expect to inherit the kingdom of God.[22-24]

Get rid of all envy, jealousy, malice, deceit, hypocrisy, and slander of every kind.[25] Envy and selfish ambition are earthly, unspiritual and demonic and lead to disorder and evil of every kind.[26,27] Envy is not part of God's wisdom, which is pure, peace loving, gentle, sincere, full of mercy and good deeds, and willing to yield to others.[28] Prove that you understand this by living an honorable life, doing good works with humility.[29]

Beware of greed! The quality of your life cannot be measured by adding up the value of your assets.[30] Even if you acquire unimaginable wealth in life, but lose your own soul, you will be bankrupt when you die.[31] Greed is the moral equivalent to the sin of idolatry, worshipping anything or anyone other than God.[32] Do not envy the world or anything it has to offer. It will pass away one day, but you will live forever if you do the will of God.[33-35]

Do not envy wealth, but be content with what you have.[36] Contentment and godliness preclude envy and constitute great wealth by themselves.[37] On the other hand, the love of money causes all kinds of evil and has led many away from their faith and into ruin and destruction.[38,39]

Love your neighbor as yourself. This is the way to fulfill the requirements of the law.[40]

Love is patient and kind. It does not envy.[41]

EVIL

1	Ps. 97:10		28	Eph. 2:5
2	Amos 5:15		29	2 Cor. 5:17
3	Rom. 12:9		30	1 Peter 4:2
4	Job 28:28		31	1 Peter 5:8
5	Prov. 14:16		32	Jer. 17:9
6	Prov. 3:7		33	2 Cor. 11:14
7	Prov. 16:6		34	1 Peter 5:9
8	1 Thess. 5:22		35	James 4:7
9	Eph. 5:11		36	Eph. 4:27
10	Ps. 141:4		37	Eph. 6:13
11	Prov. 4:14		38	Eph. 6:16
12	Prov. 4:27		39	1 Cor. 14:20
13	2 Chron. 12:14		40	Heb. 5:14
14	3 John 11		41	Rom. 12:2
15	Ps. 34:14		42	Ps. 34:13
16	Ps. 37:27		43	1 Peter 3:10
17	1 Peter. 3:11		44	Matt. 5:37
18	Amos 5:14		45	James 3:8
19	Isa. 55:7		46	James 3:6
20	Rom. 6:12		47	Matt. 5:39
21	1 Peter 1:14		48	Rom. 12:17
22	Col. 3:5		49	1 Peter 3:9
23	2 Tim. 2:22		50	Rom. 12:21
24	James 1:21		51	Rom. 14:16
25	Col. 1:21		52	Eph. 5:16
26	Eph. 2:2		53	Eph. 5:11
27	Eph. 2:4		54	2 Peter 3:3

EVIL

All those who love the Lord must hate evil and love good.[1-3] Fear the Lord and shun evil.[4-7] Have nothing to do with any kind of evil.[8,9] Do not let your heart be drawn to it or keep company with evil persons.[10-12] You risk falling into this trap if your heart is not set on seeking the Lord.[13]

Do not imitate what is evil, but only what is good.[14] Turn to the Lord and forsake your wicked ways and evil thoughts.[15-19] Do not let the evil desires of your former life—sexual immorality, impurity, lust, and greed, which is the same as idolatry—control you.[20,22] Get rid of all filth and evil in your life, pursue righteousness, faith, love and peace, and humbly accept the word of God, which has the power to save your soul.[23,24]

You were once an enemy of God because of your evil thinking and behavior, obeying the Devil who is the commander of powers in the unseen world.[25,26] But God is rich in mercy and loves you so much that he gave you life when he raised Christ from the dead.[27,28] Faith in Christ makes you a new person. The old self is gone and is replaced by a new self.[29] So don't live the rest of your life for earthly or human desires, but rather for the will of God.[30]

Be sober and vigilant at all times.[31] Your heart is more deceitful than you realize, and desperately wicked. No one can fully understand it.[32] Your enemy is the Devil, and he prowls like a roaring lion looking for someone to devour. He even masquerades as an angel of light.[33]

Submit yourself to God. Resist the Devil, stand firm in your faith, and he will flee from you.[34,35] Do not even give him a foothold.[36] Protect yourself with the full armor of God so that you can stand your ground in the face of evil.[37,38]

Be as innocent as a baby when it comes to evil.[39] Train yourself to distinguish good from evil.[40] Let God transform you into a new person and your mind into a new way of thinking, and then you will learn to know God's good, pleasing and perfect will for yourself.[41]

Watch your tongue. Keep it from evil and deceitful speech.[42,43] Let your "yes" be "yes" and your "no" be "no."[44] No one can tame the tongue. It is a restless evil, full of deadly poison.[45] It is also a fire, a world of evil among the parts of the body. It can corrupt your whole person and set the whole course of your life on fire![46]

Do not resist an evil person. If someone slaps you on the cheek, turn the other one also.[47] Do not repay anyone evil for evil or insult for insult, but with a blessing because this is your calling so that you may inherit a future blessing.[48,49]

Do not be overcome by evil, but overcome evil with good.[50] Do not allow what you consider to be good to be spoken of as evil.[51] Make the most of every opportunity because the times are evil.[52] Expose the evil deeds of darkness, but otherwise have nothing to do with them.[53]

Understand that in the last days, scoffers will gain control, expressing their own evil desires.[54]

FAITH, Part 1

1   Heb. 11:6
2   Heb. 11:1
3   James 2:17
4   James 2:18
5   James 2:19
6   James 2:22
7   James 2:24
8   James 2:26
9   Mark 11:22
10 John 14:1
11 John 6:40
12 John 14:6
13 Acts 4:12
14 John 8:24
15 Acts 20:21
16 Rom. 1:17
17 Rom. 3:22
18 2 Cor. 5:7
19 Gal. 3:11
20 1 Peter 1:9
21 Rom. 5:1
22 Eph. 2:8
23 Heb. 12:2
24 1 Pet.er1:8
25 2 Tim. 3:15
26 2 Tim. 3:16
27 1 Cor. 2:5

FAITH, Part 1

Without faith, it is impossible to please God. You can only approach him if you believe that he exists and that he responds to and rewards those who sincerely and earnestly seek him.[1] Faith is the confidence that what we hope for will actually happen. It gives us assurance about things we cannot see.[2]

True faith must be accompanied by action—otherwise it is not real.[3,4] Even the devils believe that there is one God—and tremble![5] Genuine faith expresses itself and is demonstrated by good works.[6] Belief alone that is not demonstrated by good works is not genuine and does not bring justification before God.[7] Faith without works is dead.[8]

Put your faith in God.[9] Trust also in Jesus Christ.[10] It is God's will that everyone who believes in his Son will be resurrected after death to have eternal life.[11] Jesus is the Way, the Truth, and the Life. No one can come to God except through him.[12] God's salvation cannot be found anywhere else. He has given no other name under heaven by which we can be saved.[13] You will die in your sins if you do not put your faith in Jesus for salvation.[14]

You must turn to God and repent of your sins and place your faith in the Lord Jesus.[15] The gospel reveals how we are made righteous before God.[16] It comes through faith in Jesus Christ.[17] So the righteous must live by faith, not by sight.[18,19]

The goal of your faith is the salvation of your soul.[20] Once you are justified before God by faith, you will have a good relationship with him through the Lord Jesus Christ.[21] For it is by his grace you have been saved, through faith—nothing you have done yourself. It is a gift from God.[22]

Fix your eyes on Jesus, the source and object of your faith and the one who brings it to full maturity.[23] Love him, and believe in him, even though you do not see him now, and you will be filled with an inexpressible and glorious joy.[24]

Learn the holy Scriptures, which tell how to accept the salvation that comes through faith in Jesus Christ.[25] All Scripture is inspired by God and is useful for training in a life of faith and righteousness.[26] They show that your faith and its expression are based on God's power and not the wisdom of man.[27]

FAITH, Part 2

1   Matt. 17:20
2   Rom. 12:3
3   1 Cor. 13:2
4   Heb. 10:22
5   Jude 20
6   Col. 2:7
7   2 Tim. 2:22
8   1 Tim. 6:11
9   2 Peter 1:5
10   1 Tim. 6:12
11   Eph. 6:16
12   1 Peter 5:9
13   1 Cor. 16:13
14   1 Tim. 1:19
15   James 1:3
16   1 Peter 1:7
17   Philem. 6
18   Rom. 14:1
19   Prov. 3:5
20   Prov. 3:6
21   Prov. 3:7
22   Isa. 2:22

FAITH, Part 2

You can do amazing things even if your faith is as small as a tiny seed.[1] However, do not think of yourself more highly than you ought, but with sober judgment in accordance with the amount of faith God has given you.[2] Even if you have a faith that can move mountains, you are nothing if you do not also have love.[3]

Draw near to God with a sincere heart and with full confidence in your faith.[4] Build yourself up in your most holy faith by being deeply rooted in Christ.[5,6] Pursue faith, righteousness, love, gentleness, and peace with a pure heart.[7,8] Make every effort to add goodness to your faith and knowledge to your goodness.[9]

Fight the good fight of faith.[10] Faith is a shield in your spiritual battle against the Devil with which you can extinguish all his flaming arrows.[11] Resist him, standing firm in the faith, courageous and strong.[12,13] Hold on to faith and a good conscience.[14]

Be joyful in trials because the testing of your faith develops perseverance.[15] Trials come so that your faith, which is much more valuable than gold, can be proven genuine and honoring to Christ.[16]

Be active in sharing your faith so that you will have a full understanding of every good thing you have in Christ.[17]

Accept a person whose faith is weak without passing judgment on disputable matters.[18]

Trust in the Lord with all your heart and do not lean on your own understanding. Acknowledge him in all your ways, and he will give you direction. Do not be wise in your own eyes.[19-21] Do not put your faith in mankind who has but a breath in his nostrils and is not trustworthy.[22]

FAITHFULNESS

1	Gal. 5:22	30	Lam. 3:23
2	Prov. 3:3	31	Deut. 32:4
3	Deut. 6:10	32	Ps. 25:10
4	Deut. 6:11	33	Ps. 33:4
5	Deut. 6:12	34	Ps. 111:7
6	2 Chron. 19:9	35	Ps. 92:1
7	Deut. 6:17	36	Ps. 92:2
8	Deut. 6:18	37	Ps. 89:2
9	Matt. 25:21	38	Josh. 24:14
10	Rom. 12:12		
11	Heb. 10:23		
12	Rev. 2:10		
13	Rev. 14:12		
14	2 Thess. 3:3		
15	Jude 20		
16	Jude 21		
17	2 Tim. 2:13		
18	1 Cor. 10:13		
19	1 John 1:9		
20	Ps. 146:6		
21	Ps. 117:2		
22	Ps. 119:90		
23	Ps. 100:5		
24	Ex. 34:6		
25	Ps. 86:15		
26	Ps. 57:10		
27	Ps. 108:4		
28	Ps. 36:5		
29	Lam. 3:22		

FAITHFULNESS

Faithfulness must be a quality of your character. It is an evidence that the Holy Spirit is shaping your life.[1] Never let love and faithfulness leave you. Bind these virtues around your neck, and write them on the tablet of your heart.[2]

Be careful to remain faithful to the Lord in times of prosperity. There is a great tendency to forget all he has done for you and take the credit yourself when everything is good.[3-5]

Serve the Lord faithfully and with your whole heart because you fear the Lord.[6] Keep his commandments, and do what is right and good in his sight so that things will go well for you.[6-8]

You should want to hear his "well done" at the end of your days.[9]

Be faithful in your prayer life, patient in affliction, joyful in hope.[10] Hold on tightly to the hope you profess because the one who gives you this hope is faithful to fulfill his promises.[11]

Be faithful during suffering and persecution, even to the point of death, and you will receive a reward in heaven.[12] This requires patient endurance on the part of those who do God's will and remain faithful to Jesus.[13] The Lord is faithful and will strengthen and protect you from Satan during these trying times.[14]

Be faithful to each other, and build each other up in your faith, and pray in the power of the Holy Spirit as you await the return of Jesus who will bring eternal life. By doing this, you will keep yourself safe in God's love.[15,16]

God is faithful even if you are not. He cannot deny himself.[17] He is faithful to you in your temptations and will protect you by providing a way to escape them.[18] If you fail and sin, he is faithful to his own nature and will not only forgive your sin but purify you from all unrighteousness.[19]

The Lord, the maker of heaven and earth, will remain faithful forever.[20-23] He is compassionate and full of grace, slow to anger, and abounding in love.[24,25] His faithfulness reaches every corner of the universe.[26-28] His mercies never cease—they are new every morning. Great is his faithfulness![29,30]

The Lord is a rock. All his ways are perfect and just, loving and faithful, and totally trustworthy. He does nothing wrong. He is faithful and upright in all he does.[31-34]

Praise the Lord, and proclaim his love and faithfulness both morning and night.[35-37]

Fear the Lord, and serve him faithfully.[38]

FAMILY

1	Gen. 1:27	30	2 Tim. 3:16
2	Mark 10:6	31	Eph. 5:33
3	Gen. 2:24	32	Col. 3:18
4	Matt. 19:5	33	Eph. 5:22
5	Mark 10:7	34	Eph. 5:23
6	Mark 10:8	35	Eph. 5:24
7	Eph. 5:31	36	Eph. 5:21
8	Mark 10:9	37	Prov. 31:10
9	Matt. 19:9	38	Prov. 12:
10	Ex. 20:14	39	Prov. 19:14
11	Eph. 5:25	40	Col. 3:20
12	Eph. 5:28	41	Eph. 6:1
13	Eph. 5:33	42	Ex. 20:12
14	1 Peter 3:7	43	Deut. 5:16
15	Col. 3:19	44	Lev. 19:3
16	1 Cor. 13:4	45	Matt. 19:19
17	1 Cor. 13:5	46	Eph. 6:2
18	1 Cor. 13:6	47	Mark 10:19
19	1 Cor. 13:7	48	Prov. 1:8
20	1 Cor. 13:8	49	Prov. 6:20
21	1 Cor. 13:13	50	Prov. 23:22
22	Eph. 6:4	51	Prov. 4:1
23	Col. 3:21	52	1 Tim. 5:4
24	James 1:19	53	1 Tim. 5:8
25	Prov. 22:6	54	Eph. 2:19
26	Deut. 6:5		
27	Deut. 6:6		
28	Deut. 6:7		
29	1 Tim. 3:4		

FAMILY

At the time of creation, God created human beings in his own image, both male and female.[1,2] For this reason, a young person should leave their parents and be united to a spouse. They will become one flesh.[3-7] Because this union is God's design, no one should split it apart.[8] Anyone who does so by divorcing their spouse, except for marital unfaithfulness, commits adultery.[9] Do not commit adultery.[10]

Husbands must love their wives just as Christ loved the church. He gave up his life for her.[11] Husbands must also love their wives as much as they love their own bodies.[12,13] Be considerate of your wife and treat her with honor and respect as you live together. She is your equal partner in God's gift of new life. Treat her as you should so that your prayers will not be hindered.[14] Love your wife and do not be harsh with her.[15] Love is patient, kind, polite, never jealous or proud, not self-centered, not easily angered, and does not keep score. Love values truth and righteousness. It protects, trusts, hopes, and perseveres. It is unfailing. It is the greatest and most enduring human virtue.[16-21]

Fathers must bring their children up with training and instructions from the Lord.[22] Do not exasperate or embitter them.[23] Be quick to listen, slow to speak, and slow to become angry.[24] Train your children in the way they should go and they will not turn away from it when they are old.[25] Impress the commandments of the Lord upon the hearts of your children. Talk about them as you go about your daily activities. Teach them to love the Lord with all their heart and soul.[26-28] See that they treat their parents with proper respect.[29] Use Scripture in training your children in the right way to live. It is God's word and his way.[30]

Wives must respect their husbands.[31] Wives must submit to their husbands.[32-33] The husband is the head of the wife in the same way that Christ is the head of the church, and just as the church submits to Christ, the wife is to submit to the husband.[34,35] Each must courteously respect the other out of reverence for Christ.[36] A wife of noble character is worth more than rubies. She is her husband's crown. She is a gift from the Lord.[37-39]

Children must obey their parents because this pleases the Lord and is the right thing to do.[40,41] Honor and respect your parents because this gives you promise for a long life.[42-47] Pay attention to the instruction and wisdom they give to you.[48-51]

Put your religion into practice by caring for your own family members in need. In this way, you not only repay your parents and grandparents, but please God.[52] If anyone does not provide for their relatives, especially immediate family, they deny the faith and are worse than an unbeliever.[53]

Faith in Jesus Christ makes you part of the family of God.[54]

FASTING

1   Joel 2:12

2   Ps. 51:16

3   Ps. 51:17

4   Zech. 7:5

5   Zech. 7

6   Isa. 58:2

7   Isa. 58:3

8   Isa. 58:5

9   Isa. 58:6

10   Ias. 58:7

11   Zech. 7:9

12   Zech. 7:10

13   Matt. 6:16

14   Matt. 6:17

15   Matt. 6:18

FASTING

Return to the Lord with all your heart, with fasting and weeping and mourning.[1] Your broken and contrite heart is acceptable and pleasing to God.[2,3]

You must focus on the Lord and not yourself when you fast.[4,5] You must be sincere in seeking the Lord, to know his ways, his will, and his presence.[6] You must set aside your own interests during this time.[7] It must be more than just going through the motions.[8]

This is the kind of fasting that pleases God: Loosen the chains of injustice and set the oppressed free (widows, orphans, aliens and the poor). Break every yoke of bondage. Share your food with the hungry. Provide the poor wanderer with shelter. Cloth the naked. Do not abandon your own family. Do not think evil of each other.[9-12]

Do not do anything to make a show of your fasting so that other people will notice. That is a hypocritical show only for others.[13] Look and act normally so that it will not be obvious to others that you are fasting. Your heavenly Father will see what you do in secret and reward you openly.[14,15]

FEAR

1 Ps. 56:3

2 Isa. 12:2

3 Ps. 27:1

4 Ps. 34:4

5 Isa. 43:1

6 Josh. 1:9

7 Deut. 31:6

8 Isa. 41:10

9 Isa. 41.13

10 Ps. 46:1

11 Zeph. 3:17

12 Isa. 51:12

13 Deut. 3:22

14 Rev. 1:17

15 Mark 4:39-40

16 2 Tim. 1:7

17 John 14:27

18 Ps. 23:4

19 Heb. 2:14

20 Heb. 2:15

21 1 Peter 5:7

22 Ps. 55:22

23 1 Peter 3:14

24 Phil 4.6,7

25 Matt. 6:34

26 Luke 12:22-26

27 1 John 4:18

28 Rom. 8:38-39

FEAR

Put your trust in God when you are afraid.[1,2] He is your light and salvation; the stronghold of your life. Do not be afraid of anyone.[3] Pray to God, and he will answer and free you from all your fear.[4] He has redeemed you and called you by name. You are his.[5]

Be strong and courageous. Do not be discouraged or terrified by any situation you face because the Lord your God is with you. He will never leave you nor forsake you.[6,7] Do not be afraid, because he will strengthen and help you. He will hold you by your right hand.[8,9]

Let God be your refuge and strength. He will always be present to help in times of trouble.[10] He is mighty to save. He takes great delight in you; you bring him joy. He will quiet your fears with his love.[11] So do not be afraid of mere humans who wither like the summer grass and disappear.[12,13]

Do not be afraid. God is sovereign, the Alpha and Omega, the first and the last.[14] Fear shows a lack of faith.[15] Fear does not come from God; only courage, love and self-discipline.[16] Do not be worried or afraid. Jesus promised you his special kind of peace of mind and spirit.[17]

Do not fear death because God will be with you even then.[18] Jesus died a human death so that he might destroy the one who holds the power of death—that is the devil—and free those who are held in slavery by their fear of death.[19,20]

Give all your worries and cares to God because he cares for you.[21] He will sustain you and never let you fall.[22] Don't be afraid even if you suffer for doing what is right because God will reward you for it.[23]

Do not worry or be anxious about anything—not tomorrow or even life itself. Instead, pray to God. Tell him your anxieties and requests and at the same time be thankful to him for what you have and what you are. He will grant you a peace of mind and spirit that transcends human understanding and guard your heart against anxiety.[24-26]

There is no fear in perfect love.[27] Nothing can separate you from God's love, including your fears for today and your worries about tomorrow.[28]

FEAR GOD

1	Ecc. 12:13		28	Prov. 1:7
2	Deut. 10:20		29	Isa. 33:6
3	Ps. 33:8		30	Deut. 5:29
4	1 Peter 1:17		31	Ps. 147:11
5	1 Sam. 12:24		32	Ps. 103:11
6	Prov. 23:17, 18		33	Ps. 103:17
7	Ps. 33:8-9		34	1 Peter 1:17
8	Gen. 1:1		35	Acts 10.34
9	Ps. 33:6		36	Acts 10:35
10	Jer. 5:22-24		37	Prov. 14:27
11	Ps. 89:7		38	Ex. 20:20
12	Ps. 96:4-5		39	Ps. 85:9
13	Ps. 33:5		40	Ps. 111:10
14	Ps. 130:3-4		41	Ps. 112:1
15	Luke 1:50		42	Prov. 15:16
16	Ps. 103:13			
17	Ps. 145:19-20			
18	Deut 10:12-13			
19	1 Sam. 12:24			
20	Prov. 8:13			
21	Prov 3:7-8			
22	Prov. 3:7			
23	Ps. 19:9			
24	Ex. 20:7			
25	Ps. 86:11			
26	Ps. 111:10			
27	Prov. 9:10			

FEAR GOD

Fear God and keep his commandments. This is the whole duty of mankind.[1] Fear him, worship him, cling to him.[2] Stand in awe and reverent fear of him, because he judges each person impartially[3,4] Serve him faithfully and think of all the wonderful things he has done for you.[5] Do not let your heart be jealous of sinners, but always be zealous for the fear of the Lord. This is a sure future hope for you.[6]

Revere the Lord; show awe and respect for him. He spoke and the heavens and the earth and everything seen and unseen came into being.[7-10] He is more awesome than all who surround him.[11] All other gods are but powerless idols; the Lord made the heavens.[12] He loves righteousness and justice. The earth is full of his unfailing love.[13]

Honor and respect God, because he does not keep a record of sins.[14] He offers forgiveness and shows mercy and compassion to those who fear him.[15,16] He fulfills the desires of those who fear him.[17]

Fear the Lord your God. Walk in all his ways. Love him and serve him faithfully with all your heart and soul. Observe all his commands and decrees. Consider all the great things he has done for you.[18,19]

To fear God is to hate evil. He hates pride, arrogance, evil behavior, and perverse speech.[20] Shun evil.[21,22] The fear of the Lord is pure, enduring forever. His commandments are righteous and fair.[23]

Do not misuse the name of the Lord your God, as in curses or silly banter.[24] Fear God's name, and learn his ways. Walk in light of his truth with an undivided heart.[25]

The fear of the Lord is the beginning of wisdom and knowledge.[26-28] He will be a sure foundation for your times; a rich store of salvation, wisdom, and knowledge. The fear of the Lord is the key to this treasure.[29]

Incline your heart to fear God and keep all his commandments.[30] He delights in those who fear him and put their hope in his unfailing love.[31] His love for those who fear him is as high as the heavens are above the earth.[32] His love is from everlasting to everlasting to those who fear him.[33]

Live your life in reverent fear of God, who does not show favoritism but accepts everyone who fears him and does what is right.[34-36]

The fear of the Lord is a fountain of life.[37] It will keep you from sinning.[38] It will bring you to salvation.[39] It is the source of wisdom and understanding.[40] It will bring you true happiness.[41]

Better is a little with the fear of the Lord than great wealth with turmoil.[42]

FORGIVENESS

1	Ex. 34:5		30	2 Chon. 7:14
2	Ex. 34:6		31	Eph. 4:32
3	Ex. 34:7		32	Col. 3:13
4	Num. 14:18		33	Luke 17:4
5	Ps. 86:5		34	2 Cor. 2:10
6	Ps. 130:4		35	2 Cor. 2:11
7	Ps. 103:3		36	Luke 11:4
8	Mic. 7:18		37	Mark 11:25
9	1 John 1:9		38	Matt. 6:14
10	Mic. 7:19		39	Matt. 6:15
11	Ps. 103:12		40	Matt. 18:35
12	Isa. 43:25		41	Mark 3:28
13	Heb. 8:12		42	Matt. 12:31
14	Heb. 10:17		43	Matt. 12:32
15	Ps. 32:5		44	Mark 3:29
16	Acts 3:19		45	Luke 12:10
17	Acts 16:31			
18	Luke 1:77			
19	Matt. 9:6			
20	Luke 5:24			
21	Acts 4:12			
22	Matt. 26:28			
23	Eph. 1:7			
24	Col. 1:14			
25	Acts 13:38			
26	Acts 10:43			
27	1 John 2:12			
28	Matt. 6:12			
29	1 John 1:9			

FORGIVENESS

God is the ultimate source of forgiveness. He is compassionate and gracious, patient, and generously extends love and faithfulness to all those who call on his name. He forgives all kinds of wickedness, rebellion and sin. He does not stay angry forever but delights in showing mercy.[1-8]

Confess your sins to God, and change your ways. He is just and faithful to his own nature and will forgive them all.[9] He actually wipes them out, sending them to the bottom of the sea or hurling them away from us as far as the east is from the west.[10-11] On top of that, he promises to never bring them up again.[12-14] His forgiveness will lift your burden of guilt and bring a new sense of freedom to your soul.[15,16]

Believe in Jesus for the forgiveness of your sins.[17,18] He is the only one who has the authority to forgive your sins and provide salvation for your soul.[19-21] He shed his blood and died so that he could bring about the forgiveness of your sins.[22] The forgiveness of your sins and the redemption of your soul come through him.[23-25] Everyone who sincerely believes in him receives forgiveness of sins through his name.[26,27]

Pray to God for the forgiveness of your sins.[28] You must admit and confess them in order for God to forgive.[29] Be humble, seek to know God, and turn away from any sin in your life, and he will hear your prayer and forgive you.[30]

Forgive whatever grievances you may have against one another. Bear with each other; be kind and compassionate, forgiving each other just as the Lord forgave you.[31,32] If someone sins against you multiple times, you must forgive them multiple times.[33] An unforgiving heart gives Satan a chokehold on your life.[34,35]

You must be willing to forgive everyone who has ever sinned against you if you expect God to forgive you. He will not forgive you if you do not sincerely forgive from your heart any other person.[36-40]

Every sin except persistent rejection of God and his Holy Spirit can be forgiven.[41-45]

FREEDOM

1	Gal. 4:5		30	Rom. 8:1
2	Luke 4:18		31	Rom. 8:2
3	Isa. 42:7		32	Rom. 8:3
4	John 14:1		33	Rom. 8:4
5	John 14:6		34	Gal. 5:1
6	2 Cor. 3:15		35	Gal. 5:13
7	2 Cor. 3:16		36	1 Peter 2:16
8	2 Cor. 3:17		37	Rom. 6:15
9	John 8:32		38	Rom. 6:1
10	John 8:36		39	Gal. 5:13
11	Rom. 8:1		40	1 Cor. 8:9
12	Rom. 8:2		41	Rom. 14:13
13	Heb. 9:15		42	1 Cor. 10:29
14	Col. 1:22		43	1 Cor. 8:12
15	Rom. 6:22		44	Rom. 14:20
16	Rom. 8:2		45	Rom. 14:1
17	Rom. 8:8		46	1 Cor. 10:23
18	Heb. 2:15		47	1 Cor. 10:24
19	Rom. 6:14		48	1 Cor. 10:31
20	Gal. 5:1		49	Rom. 14:18
21	Rom. 8:3		50	Rom. 14:12
22	Gal. 3:19			
23	Gal. 3:22			
24	Gal. 3:23			
25	Gal. 3:24			
26	Gal. 3:25			
27	Gal. 2:16			
28	Gal. 5:4			
29	Gal. 5:6			

FREEDOM

Jesus Christ was sent by God to earth to bring freedom to those imprisoned by the Law of Moses and to release those oppressed by spiritual blindness and darkness.[1-3] Put your trust in this Jesus because he is the Way, the Truth, and the Life. He is the only way to find God and true freedom.[4,5] When God's Holy Spirit is present, there is freedom from spiritual blindnes.[6-8] When Jesus and his truth sets you free, you are truly free.[9-10]

Jesus Christ sets you free from the penalty of sin and death when you put your trust in him[11-14] He has set you free from the power of sin in your life.[15,16] He has set you free from your sinful human nature so that you can please God.[17] He has set you free from the fear of death.[18]

Christ has set you free from the obligations of the Law of Moses.[19,20] That law could only point out your sins; it could never save you from them.[21,22] Now that Jesus has come, faith in him—not keeping the Law—is the only way to please God.[23-33] So don't let yourself be burdened by the yoke of the Law.[34]

Do not use your freedom as an excuse for evil.[35,36] You are not free to live as you like just because you are free from the Law of Moses. You cannot deliberately continue to live in sin just because you have the false hope that God will forgive you anyway.[37,38] Use your freedom to serve others in love.[39]

Do not allow the exercise of your freedom to become a stumbling-block to someone else who is weak in faith.[40,41] Eating or drinking might not be a matter of conscience to you, but your freedom of practice might encourage others to do something that they really think is wrong. This is a sin against the other believer and thus a sin against Christ.[42-44]

Accept a weaker believer without passing judgment on disputable matters.[45] Not everything that is permissible is beneficial or constructive.[46] Don't be concerned just for your own good. You want to live well, but your foremost efforts should be to help others live well also.[47] So let your lifestyle glorify God in everything you do.[48] If you serve Christ with this attitude you will please God and serve as an example to others.[49]

You will have to give a personal account to God for your actions.[50]

GENEROSITY

1	Deut. 15:10		30	Col. 3:5
2	Deut. 15:11		31	Matt. 6:24
3	Prov. 3:27		32	Luke 12:33
4	Prov. 14:31		33	Matt. 19:21
5	Prov. 19:17		34	Mark 10:21
6	Prov. 22:9		35	Luke 18:22
7	Psa. 37:21		36	Matt. 6:21
8	1 Tim. 6:18		37	Matt. 23:23
9	Heb. 13:16		38	Ps. 112:5
10	1 Peter 4:10		39	Matt. 10:8
11	Rom. 12:8		40	Acts 20:35
12	2 Cor. 9:11		41	2 Cor. 9:15
13	2 Cor. 9:12			
14	2 Cor. 9:13			
15	Matt. 6:1			
16	Matt. 6:2			
17	Matt. 6:3			
18	Matt. 6:4			
19	Matt. 5:16			
20	Mal. 3:10			
21	1 Cor. 16:2			
22	2 Cor. 9:7			
23	2 Cor. 9:6			
24	1 Tim. 6:17			
25	1 Tim. 6:18			
26	1 Tim. 6:19			
27	Matt. 6:19			
28	Matt. 6:20			
29	Luke 12:15			

GENEROSITY

Give generously to the needy and do so without a grudging heart.[1] There will always be poor people; share freely with them.[2] Do not withhold good from those who deserve it when it is in your power to act.[3] Anyone who oppresses the poor shows contempt for their Maker, but whoever is kind to the needy honors God.[4] When you are kind to the poor, you lend to the Lord, and he will reward you for your generosity.[5] Righteous people are generous.[6,7]

Be generous in good deeds and willing to share with those in need.[8,9] Use your gifts to serve others, spreading God's grace in many different ways.[10] If your gift is contributing to the needs of others, give generously.[11] This not only meets their need, but also causes them to give praise to God.[12,13] Your generosity proves that you are obedient to the Good News of the gospel of Christ.[14]

Don't be motivated to do your good deeds publicly just to be seen by others. The attention you get in this way will be your only reward. Don't let your right hand know what your left hand is doing. Give your gifts privately and God will reward you publicly.[15-18] Somehow, at the same time, you must let others see your good works and praise God in heaven.[19]

Set aside a sum of money on a regular basis in proportion to your income and assets and bring it to your church.[20] You must decide in your own heart how much you will give. Don't do this reluctantly or under pressure because God loves a cheerful giver.[21,22] Remember to give generously so that you may receive generously.[23]

Don't trust in your money. Use it to do good along with your good works.[24-26] Don't hoard treasure here on earth, but store it up in heaven where it will never run out or be vulnerable to theft, inflation or market fluctuations.[27,28] Beware greed—it is part of your earthly nature. The quality of your life cannot be measured by the number of your possessions.[29,30]

You cannot serve God and be enslaved to money.[31] Sell off some of your possessions and give to the poor and you will make a deposit in heaven.[32-35] Your heart will surely follow the money.[36]

Generosity is not a matter of law. It is a matter of justice, mercy and faithfulness.[37,38]

Freely you have received; freely give.[39] It is more blessed to give than to receive.[40]

Thank you, God, for the incredibly generous gift of your Son![41]

GENTLENESS

1   Phil. 4:5
2   Gal. 5:22
3   Gal. 5:23
4   Col. 3:12
5   1 Tim. 6:11
6   1 Tim. 3:2
7   1 Tim. 3:3
8   2 Tim. 2:24
9   1 Peter 3:3
10   1 Peter 3:4
11   Matt. 5:3
12   Matt. 5:4
13   Matt. 5:5
14   Matt. 5:6
15   Matt. 5:7
16   Matt. 5:8
17   Matt. 5:9
18   Prov. 15:1
19   Prov. 25:15
20   1 Cor. 4:21
21   Eph. 4:15
22   1 Peter 3:15
23   James 3:17
24   Eph. 4:2
25   Eph. 4:32
26   2 Tim. 2:25
27   Gal. 6:1
28   1 Kings 19:12
29   Matt. 11:29

GENTLENESS

Let gentleness be an obvious part of your reputation.[1] The virtues of your Christian character should include gentleness, love, joy, peace, patience, kindness, goodness, and faithfulness along with humility.[2-4]

Pursue gentleness, righteousness, godliness, faith, love and endurance.[5] Church leaders must be gentle, above reproach, temperate, self-controlled, respectable, hospitable, not a lover of wine or money, and not quarrelsome or resentful, but kind and able to teach.[6-8]

Let your personal attractiveness come from a gentle and quiet inner self. This is of great value in God's sight.[9,10] He blesses both your seen and unseen virtues.[11-17]

A gentle answer breaks down indifference and rigid defenses, but harsh words stir up anger. A gentle tongue can break a bone![18,19]

A gentle and loving spirit is better than a whip.[20] So speak the truth, but always with love, gentleness and respect. And always be prepared to give an answer to anyone who asks about the hope you have as a result of following Jesus. Do this with gentleness and respect.[21,22]

Wisdom that comes from God is gentle, pure, considerate, merciful, impartial, and sincere.[23]

Be gentle, patient and humble, and tolerate differences in one another with love.[24] Be kind and compassionate, forgiving others just as God has forgiven you because of Christ.[25] Gently debate those who oppose you in the hope they will come to understand the truth.[26]

Gently restore anyone who is caught in a sin, but repents, thinking of yourself as if you were to be in a similar situation.[27]

God often speaks in a gentle whisper, not in dramatic ways.[28]

Learn from Jesus who is gentle and humble. Live in his way and you will have peace and quiet in your soul.[29]

GOD HATES...

1	Mal. 3:5	30	Deut. 27:23	59	Zech. 8:17
2	Deut. 5:18	31	Ezek. 22:11	60	Deut. 27:16
3	Prov. 16:5	32	Deut. 27:19	61	Ezek. 18:13
4	Prov. 8:13	33	Prov. 17:15	62	Ezek. 22:12
5	Ps. 101:5	34	Mal. 3:5	63	Ps. 11:5
6	Deut. 27:21	35	Zech. 8:17	64	Ps. 5:6
7	Deut. 27:25	36	Prov. 6:19	65	Mal. 2:16
8	Deut. 18:9	37	Prov. 6:17	66	Zech. 8:17
9	Deut. 18:10	38	Ps. 5:6	67	Ps. 5:6
10	Deut. 22:5	39	Deut. 27:24	68	Prov. 6:17
11	Deut. 27:18	40	Prov. 6:17	69	Ezek. 22:2
12	Prov. 20:23	41	Ezek. 18:12	70	Deut. 27:24
13	Prov. 11:1	42	Ezek. 22:7	71	Prov. 15:9
14	Prov. 20:10	43	Mal. 3:5	72	Psa. 101:3
15	Prov. 20:23	44	Deut. 27:16	73	Psa. 101:4
16	Lev. 19:35	45	Prov. 11:20	74	Prov. 6:18
17	Deut. 25:15	46	Prov. 15:9	75	Ps. 5:5
18	Deut. 25:16	47	Prov. 15:26	76	Prov. 15:26
19	Deut. 27:17	48	Prov. 6:18	77	Prov. 6:18
20	Mal. 2:16	49	Psa. 101:4	78	Deut. 18:9
21	Titus 1:16	50	Prov. 11:20	79	Deut. 18:10
22	Prov. 15:8	51	Prov. 8:13	80	Deut. 18:11
23	Ezek. 18:12	52	Prov. 15:8	81	Deut. 18:12
24	Mal. 1:14	53	Isa. 1:13	82	Mal. 3:5
25	Deut. 27:15	54	Ps. 101:5	83	Luke 16:15
26	1 Peter 4:3	55	Isa. 61:8		
27	Jer. 17.5	56	Ezek. 18:12		
28	Deut. 27:20	57	Ps. 101:3		
29	Deut. 27:22	58	Ps. 5:6		

GOD HATES...

ADULTERY[1,2]

ARROGANCE[3-5]

BESTIALITY[6]

BRIBERY[7]

CHILD SACRIFICE[8,9]

CROSS DRESSING[10]

MISTREATMENT OF DISABLED[11]

DISHONEST BUSINESS PRACTICES[12-19]

DIVORCE[20]

FALSE WORSHIP[21-24]

IDOL WORSHIP[25-27]

INCEST[28-31]

INJUSTICE[32-36]

LYING[37,38]

MURDER[39-]

OPRESSION OF THE POOR[41-43]

DISHONORING PARENTS[44]

PERVERSE HEART[45-50]

PERVERSE SPEECH[51]

SACRIFICE OF THE WICKED[52,53]

SLANDER[54]

STEALING[55,56]

TREACHERY[57-59]

USURY[60-62]

VIOLENCE[63-70]

WICKED WAYS[71-77]

WITCHCRAFT; SORCERY; DIVINATION[78-82]

WORLDLY STANDARDS[83]

GOD LOVES...

1	Deut. 30:10	30	Ps. 33:5	59	Ps. 87:2
2	Zeph. 3:17	31	Ps. 37:28	60	Rom. 5:8
3	1 John 4:16	32	Ps. 146:8	61	Eph. 2:4
4	John 16:27	33	Deut. 7:9	62	Heb. 2:9
5	1 John 4:10	34	Prov. 15:9	63	1 John 4:9
6	Rom. 5:8	35	Ps. 103:11	64	John 15:10
7	Jer. 31:3	36	Matt. 5:4	65	John 10:17
8	John 15:9	37	Matt. 5:6	66	John 15:9
9	1 John 4:10	38	Matt. 5:8		
10	John 16:27	39	Matt. 5:9		
11	Rom. 5:8	40	Matt. 5:10		
12	Eph. 2:4	41	Matt. 5:11		
13	1 John 4:9	42	Mic. 7:18		
14	Mark 10:21	43	Mic. 6:8		
15	John 11:36	44	Matt. 5:7		
16	John 17:26	45	Mic. 7:18		
17	John 3:16	46	Deut. 30:10		
18	Jer. 9:24	47	John 14:21		
19	Jer. 9:24	48	John 14:15		
20	Ps. 33:5	49	John 15:10		
21	Ps. 99:4	50	2 Cor. 9:7		
22	Mic. 6:8	51	Mic. 6:8		
23	Psa. 11:7	52	Matt. 5:3		
24	Isa. 61:8	53	Matt. 5:5		
25	Ps. 37:28	54	Zeph. 3:17		
26	Ps. 11:7	55	Isa. 63:9		
27	Jer. 9:24	56	Jer. 31:3		
28	Ps. 33:5	57	2 Chron. 2:11		
29	Prov. 15:9	58	Deut. 7:9		

GOD LOVES...

YOU[1-13]

PEOPLE[14-16]

THE WORLD[17]

KINDNESS[18]

JUSTICE[19-26]

RIGHTEOUSNESS[27-30]

RIGHTEOUS PEOPLE[31-41]

MERCY[42-44]

FORGIVENESS[45]

OBEDIENCE[46-49]

CHEERFUL GIVER[50]

HUMILITY[51-53]

ISRAEL[54-58]

JERUSALEM[59]

SINNERS[60-63]

JESUS[64-66]

GOLDEN RULE

1   Matt. 7:12
2   Luke 6:31
3   Lev. 19:18
4   Matt. 19:19
5   Matt. 22:39
6   Mark 12:33
7   Luke 10:27
8   Gal. 5:14
9   Rom. 13:9
10   James 2:8
11   Rom. 13:10
12   Mark 12:31
13   Mark 12:30

GOLDEN RULE

Do for others the kinds of things you would like them to do for you. This is the essence of all that is taught in the law and the prophets.[1,2]

Love your neighbor in the same way you love yourself.[3-7] The entire law of Moses is summed up in this single commandment.[8-11] Only one commandment is greater than this: Love the Lord your God with all your heart and all your soul and all your mind and all your strength.[12,13]

GOSPEL

1	Matt. 28:19
2	Matt. 28:20
3	Mark 16:15
4	Mark 16:16
5	Mark 1:15
6	John 3:16
7	Luke 19:10
8	Luke 4:18
9	Isa. 61:1
10	Isa. 61:2
11	1 Cor. 15:2
12	1 Cor. 15:3
13	1 Cor. 15:4
14	1 Cor. 15:5
15	1 Cor. 15:6
16	1 Cor. 15:7
17	1 Cor. 15:8
18	Acts 1:3
19	2 Tim. 2:8
20	Rom. 1:16
21	Gal. 1:11
22	Rom. 16:26
23	1 Cor. 2:10
24	Col. 1:26
25	Rom. 1:17
26	Rom. 16:25
27	Col. 1:27
28	Col. 1:22
29	2 Cor. 5:18
30	2 Cor. 5:19
31	Eph. 3:6
32	Eph. 1:13
33	2 Cor. 5:20
34	Phil. 1:27

35	2 Tim. 1:8
36	Eph. 6:15
37	Mark 8:35

GOSPEL

Go into all the world and preach the gospel to every human being.[1] Make disciples in every nation, baptizing them in the name of the Father and of the Son and of the Holy Spirit. Teach them to obey all of Jesus's commands.[2,3] Whoever believes and is baptized will be saved, but whoever does not believe will be condemned.[4]

Repent and believe the gospel for the kingdom of God has come.[5] God loved the world so much that he gave his one and only Son so that everyone who believes in him will no longer face eternal death but will have eternal life.[6] Jesus came to seek and save those who are lost.[7] He came to preach the gospel to the poor, heal the brokenhearted, preach deliverance to captives, recovering sight to the blind, and set at liberty those who are imprisoned.[8-10]

You must believe this gospel if you are to be saved: 1) Christ died for your sins. 2) He was buried but was raised to life again on the third day. 3) He appeared after this to Peter and James, the rest of the apostles, a crowd of over five hundred, and lastly to the apostle Paul.[11-19]

Do not be ashamed of the gospel of Christ. It is the power of God bringing salvation to everyone who believes, regardless of race or ethnicity.[20] This gospel is not based on human reasoning nor was it made up by "enlightened" men.[21] This Good News is a direct revelation from God given to holy men who recorded it in their prophetic writings.[22] It remained a "mystery," hidden for ages, but is now further revealed by the Holy Spirit to those who have faith.[23-26] This mystery is Christ in you, your hope of heaven.[27]

The good news of the gospel is that Christ, through his death, has reconciled you to God, holy and free from all guilt.[28-30] This includes Gentiles as well as Jews.[31] You have been given the Holy Spirit as his seal of approval.[32] Now he wants you to be his representative on earth, pleading with others on Christ's behalf, "Be reconciled to God."[33]

Live your life in a manner worthy of the gospel of Christ.[34] Don't be afraid to speak up for the Lord, and be willing to suffer for the gospel if you are called to do so.[35] Prepare for your spiritual battles with a thorough knowledge of the gospel of peace.[36]

Don't try to hang on to the life you planned to live for yourself or you will actually lose it. Give it up for Jesus and the sake of the gospel and you will find true fulfillment.[37]

GOSSIP

1   Lev. 19:16
2   Ex. 23:1
3   Prov. 17:4
4   Rom. 1:18
5   Prov. 12:22
6   Ps. 101:5
7   Prov. 6:17
8   Prov. 6:19
9   James 5:9
10   1 Peter 2:1
11   Eph. 4:31
12   Col. 3:8
13   Rom. 1:29
14   Rom. 1:28
15   Rom. 1:29
16   Prov. 20:19
17   Prov. 11:13
18   Prov. 16:28
19   Prov. 25:23
20   1 Tim. 5:13
21   Prov. 18:8
22   Prov. 26:20

GOSSIP

You must not spread false rumors or repeat malicious gossip to others.[1,2] Gossip and suppressing the truth are wicked behaviors and infuriate God.[3,4] He will not tolerate slander and detests gossip, which stirs up trouble among family and friends.[5-8]

Don't gossip about others or you will incur the judgment of God.[9] Have nothing to do with slander and its accompanying vices: anger, rage, bitterness, malice, envy, hypocrisy, and filthy language.[10-12]

Gossip is the product of a depraved mind.[13-15]

Avoid a person who talks too much. A gossip betrays confidence, stirs up trouble, and alienates close friends.[16-18] A gossiping tongue causes anger as surely as a north wind brings rain.[19]

Idleness often produces gossips and busybodies who repeat things that should not be said.[20] The words of a gossip are like choice morsels that are easily swallowed.[21]

A quarrel dies down without gossip like a fire goes out without wood.[22]

GOVERNMENT

1   Matt. 22:21

2   Luke 20:25

3   Rom. 13:1

4   Rom. 13:2

5   Rom. 13:4

6   Rom. 13:5

7   Titus 3:1

8   Rom. 13:6

9   Rom. 13:7

10   1 Peter 2:17

11   Ex. 22:28

12   1 Tim. 2:1

13   1 Tim. 2:2

14   1 Tim. 2:3

15   Luke 12:11

16   Luke 12:12

17   Eph. 6:10

18   Eph. 6:12

19   Eph. 6:11

20   Eph. 6:13

21   Col. 3:15

22   Phil. 3:20

GOVERNMENT

Give to the government what is due it and to God what is due him.[1,2]

Submit to the governing authorities because all authority comes from God and those in positions of authority have been placed there by God.[3] Anyone who rebels against authority is rebelling against what God has instituted.[4] They are God's servants for your good.[5] Submit to them not only to avoid punishment, but to keep a clear conscience.[6,7] Pay your taxes and give respect and honor to those who are in authority.[8,9,10] Do not curse the president.[11]

Pray earnestly and thankfully for your government and those in authority that you may live a peaceful and quiet life with complete religious freedom.[12,13] This is good and pleases God.[14]

Do not worry about how you will defend yourself if you are brought before a government agency. The Holy Spirit will give you instructions at that time.[15,16]

Be strong in the Lord.[17] You are engaged in spiritual warfare, not against flesh-and-blood enemies, but against evil rulers and governments of the unseen world, against mighty powers of the dark world and against evil spirits in the heavenly places.[18] So you must use all the spiritual defenses that God has provided to resist and stand firm against all the strategies of the Devil.[19,20]

Let the peace of Christ govern your heart.[21]

Remember that your spiritual citizenship is in heaven.[22]

GREATEST COMMANDMENTS

1	Deut. 6:5	28	1 John 2:3
2	Deut. 10:12	29	1 John 2:4
3	Deut. 11:1	30	1 John 2:5
4	Deut. 11:13		
5	Deut. 11:22		
6	Deut. 19:9		
7	Deut. 30:16		
8	Deut. 30:20		
9	Josh. 22:5		
10	Josh. 23:11		
11	Matt. 22:37		
12	Mark 12:29		
13	Mark 12:30		
14	Luke 10:27		
15	Lev. 19:18		
16	Matt. 5:43		
17	Matt. 19:19		
18	Matt. 22:39		
19	Mark 12:31		
20	Mark 12:33		
21	Luke 10:27		
22	Rom. 13:9		
23	James 2:8		
24	Gal. 5:14		
25	John 13:34		
26	John 13:35		
27	1 John 2:6		

GREATEST COMMANDMENTS

Love the Lord your God with all your heart and all your soul and all your mind and all your strength. This is the most important command ever given to the human race .[1-14]

The second most important commandment is to love your neighbor as yourself.[15-23] In fact, the entire law of Moses can be summed up in this single command.[24]

Love one another just like Jesus loves you. This is a new commandment from him.[25] You will demonstrate to others that you are a true follower of Jesus if you show love to others.[26]

You must obey God's commandments if you claim to follow Jesus.[27] This is proof that you have a right relationship with God.[28-30]

GREED

1   Luke 12:15

2   Prov. 23:4

3   1 John 2:15

4   1 John 2:16

5   1 John 2:17

6   1 Tim. 6:10

7   1 Tim. 6:9

8   Matt. 6:24

9   Col. 3:5

10   Ex. 20:3

11   Eph. 5:3

12   1 Cor. 5:11

13   Luke 11:39

14   Heb. 13:5

15   1 Tim. 6:6

16   Matt. 16:26

17   Mark 8:36

18   Luke 9:25

19   Matt. 6:19

20   Matt. 6:20

21   Luke 12:33

22   Prov. 19:17

23   Matt. 6:21

GREED

Be on your guard—watch out for all kinds of greed. The value of your life is not determined by the abundance of your possessions.[1] Do not wear yourself out to get rich; have the wisdom to show restraint.[2]

Do not crave everything you see. Love for the world and the things it has to offer displaces love for God. The two are incompatible.[3] And this world and everything in it will one day be gone. Only those who do what pleases God will live forever.[4,5]

The love of money is a root of all kinds of evil. People eager to get rich tend to wander away from the faith and open themselves up to all kinds of temptation that often plunges them into ruin and destruction.[6,7] You cannot serve two different masters effectively because you will eventually be devoted to one and despise the other. You cannot serve both God and money.[8]

Crucify greed in your life. It is the same as the sin of idolatry.[9,10] There must not even be a hint of greed in your life.[11] Don't even associate with anyone who claims to follow Christ, but is greedy.[12] Beware hypocrisy, making yourself appear generous to others but actually being greedy in your heart and mind.[13]

Keep your life free from the love of money and be content with what you have.[14] Godliness with contentment is itself great wealth.[15] After all, what would you benefit if you were to acquire the whole world and lose your own soul? Would it really be worth it?[16-18]

Do not hoard your treasure on earth where it is vulnerable to depreciation and theft.[19] Instead, store up for yourself treasure in heaven where it will be secure.[20] Sell some of your possessions and give to the poor. In this way you create treasure in heaven and a sure reward.[21,22]

You can be sure that your heart will always follow the money.[23]

HATE

1   Luke 6:27

2   Luke 6:28

3   Matt. 5:44

4   1 Peter 3:9

5   Lev. 19:17

6   Ex. 23:5

7   Rom. 12:9

8   Prov. 13:5

9   Amos 5:15

10 Heb. 1:9

11 1 John 3:13

12 Luke 21:17

13 John 15:18

14 John 15:23

15 John 3:20

16 John 8:12

17 Matt. 5:14

18 1 John 4:20

19 1 John 2:11

20 Titus 3:3

21 1 John 3:15

22 Matt. 6:24

23 Luke 16:13

HATE

Do good to those who hate you. Love your enemies.[1] Bless those who curse you and pray for those who persecute and mistreat you.[2,3] Do not repay evil with evil or insult with insult, but with a blessing, because this is your calling, and you will inherit a blessing.[4]

Don't secretly hate another person. If you have something against them, get it out in the open.[5] If you see them or their property in distress, be sure to help them.[6]

Hate what is evil.[7,8] Love what is good; maintain justice in your courts.[9] Jesus hates wickedness, but loves righteousness.[10]

Do not be surprised if people in the world hate you because you follow Jesus.[11,12] Keep in mind that they hated him first.[13] The person who hates Jesus also hates his Father, God.[14]

Those who do evil hate the light because it exposes their wicked deeds.[15] Jesus is the light of the world.[16] So are you if you follow him.[17]

You cannot hate another person and at the same time claim to love God. If you cannot love someone you have seen, it is impossible to love God whom you have not seen.[18] You are in darkness and denial if you harbor hatred for another person.[19]

Those who hate others end up being hated themselves.[20] Hatred is the moral equivalent of murder.[21]

Do not try to serve two masters at the same time. It is impossible. You will eventually hate either one or the other. You cannot serve both God and money.[22,23]

HOLINESS

1	Lev. 19:2		30	Ps. 99:9
2	Lev. 20:26		31	Ps. 29:2
3	1 Peter 1:16		32	Heb. 10:10
4	1 Peter 1:15		33	Col. 3:12
5	2 Tim. 1:9		34	Col. 3:13
6	1 Thess. 4:7		35	Col. 3:14
7	Heb. 10:10		36	Col. 3:15
8	Mic. 6:8		37	Col. 3:16
9	Deut. 6:5		38	Jude 20
10	Deut. 26:16		39	2 Cor. 7:1
11	1 Kings 8:61		40	1 Thess. 4:3
12	Josh. 1:8		41	Rom. 12:2
13	Ps. 119:11			
14	Ps. 15:2			
15	Ps. 15:3			
16	Ps. 15:4			
17	Ps. 15:5			
18	Ps. 34:13			
19	Ps. 34:14			
20	Ps. 24:4			
21	Prov. 23:17			
22	1 Peter 1:15			
23	1 Peter 1:16			
24	Isa. 6:3			
25	Matt. 5:48			
26	1 Peter 3:15			
27	Matt. 6:33			
28	Ex. 20:8			
29	Ex. 31:13			

HOLINESS

Be holy because God is holy.[1-3] Be holy in all you do.[4] God has saved you and called you to a holy life—not because of anything you have done, but because of his grace.[5,6] He has made you holy through the sacrifice of his Son, Jesus Christ.[7]

This is what the Lord requires: act justly, love mercy, and walk humbly with your God.[8] Love the Lord your God with all your heart, soul, mind, and strength.[9] You must be fully committed to the Lord and live by his decrees and obey his commandments.[10,11] Do not neglect the Scriptures, but meditate on them day and night so that you can be careful to do everything written in them.[12] Hide them in your heart; they will keep you from sin.[13]

Your walk must be blameless, and you must always do the right thing. Speak the truth from your heart.[14] Do not slander another or do your neighbor harm.[15] Despise an evil person and honor those who fear the Lord. Keep your promises even when it hurts.[16] Lend your money generously and do not accept a bribe.[17] Keep your tongue from evil and your lips from speaking lies.[18] Turn from evil and do good. Seek peace and pursue it.[19] Keep your hands clean and your heart pure.[20] Do not let your heart envy sinners, but always be zealous for the fear of the Lord.[21]

You must be holy in everything you do, because God is holy.[22-25] In your heart, set Christ apart as Lord of your life.[26] Prioritize his kingdom and his righteousness first in your life.[27] Remember the Sabbath Day by keeping it holy.[28] It is a sign of God's promises and a reminder that he is the one who makes you holy.[29] Worship the Lord your God because he is holy.[30,31]

It is God's will to make you holy through the sacrifice of the body of Jesus Christ.[32] So you must clothe yourself with tenderhearted mercy, kindness, humility, gentleness and patience.[33] Make allowance for each other's faults and forgive anyone who offends you. The Lord forgave you, so you must forgive others.[34] Above all, clothe yourself with love, which binds all virtues together in perfect harmony.[35] Let the peace of Christ rule in your heart. Always be thankful.[36] Let the message about Christ, in all its richness, fill your life. Teach and counsel others with all the wisdom he gives. Sing psalms and hymns and spiritual songs to God with a thankful heart.[37]

Build yourself up in your most holy faith and pray with the help of the Holy Spirit.[38] Get rid of everything that contaminates body and spirit. Perfect holiness out of reverence for God.[39]

It is God's will that you be sanctified; that is, engaged in the process of being made holy.[40] So do not copy the customs and behavior of the world, but let God transform you into a new person by changing the way you think.[41]

HOLY SPIRIT

1	Eph. 4:30	30	2 Cor. 5:5
2	Eph. 1:13	31	Rom. 8:16
3	Eph. 4:25	32	Rom. 8:14
4	Eph. 4:28	33	Gal. 5:22
5	Eph. 4:26	34	Gal. 5:23
6	Eph. 4:27	35	Rom. 8:5
7	Eph. 4:31	36	Rom. 8:6
8	Eph. 4:29	37	Rom. 8:13
9	Eph. 5:4	38	Gal. 5:17
10	Eph. 5:3	39	Matt. 12:32
11	1 Thess. 5:19	40	Mark 3:29
12	Eph. 4:17	41	Luke 12:10
13	Eph. 4:18	42	Heb. 10:29
14	1 Cor. 6:19	43	Heb. 3:7
15	1 Cor. 6:20	44	Heb. 3:8
16	1 Cor. 6:18	45	Gen. 6:3
17	Eph. 5:15	46	2 Cor. 6:2
18	Eph. 5:17	47	Eph. 4:30
19	Eph 5:17	48	John 15:26
20	Prov. 20:1	49	Titus 3:6
21	Prov. 23:32	50	Titus 3:5
22	Prov. 23:20	51	Eph. 4:23
23	1 Cor. 5:11	52	Isa. 11:2
24	Rom. 13:13	53	Eph. 4:30
25	Acts 2:38	54	Eph. 6:18
26	Luke 11:13	55	Jude 20
27	Acts 5:32	56	Eph. 4:3
28	Rom. 5:5	57	2 Tim. 1:14
29	Gal. 5:16		

HOLY SPIRIT

Do not grieve God's Holy Spirit by the way you live. Remember that he has identified you as his own and guaranteed your salvation on the last day if you believe the gospel.[1,2] So, stop telling lies, and don't steal from others.[3,4] Don't let anger control you because it gives the devil a foothold.[5,6] Don't harbor bitter feelings or slander anyone.[7] Don't use foul or abusive language, obscenities, or engage in foolish talk or coarse joking.[8,9] There should not even be a hint of sexual immorality or greed in your life.[10]

Do not smother the fire of the Holy Spirit in your life.[11] Do not live as non-believers do because they are hopelessly confused.[12] Their minds are full of darkness and they have wandered far from God because they have closed their minds and hardened their hearts against him.[13]

Honor God with your body because it is a temple of his Holy Spirit who lives in you. You are no longer your own because he has bought you with a very high price.[14,15] Run from sexual immorality. It is the most destructive sin against your own body.[16] Be careful and don't be foolish about this, but be wise and understand God's will this matter.[17,18]

Be filled with and controlled by the Holy Spirit, and not with intoxicating substances, which lead to reckless indiscretion and ultimately destroy you.[19] Drugs and alcohol mock you, and in the end, bite like a poisonous snake.[20,21] Stay away from people who overindulge.[22-24] Repent of your own sins, obey God, and he will fill your heart with his love and give you the gift of the Holy Spirit.[25-28] This Spirit is God's guarantee of your salvation.[29-32] His presence and work in your life is shown by your character: love, joy, peace, patience, kindness, goodness, faithfulness, gentleness and self-control.[33,34] Let your mind be controlled by the Spirit and you will not live according to your sinful desires, which are contrary to what the Holy Spirit desires.[35-38]

Do not blaspheme the Holy Spirit. This sin will not be forgiven, either in this age or in the one to come.[39-41] Think of the punishment in store for those who trash the Son of God who gave his life and blood to make us right with God. They have insulted and disdained the Holy Spirit who brings God's mercy to us.[42]

Do not harden your heart to the voice of the Holy Spirit.[43,44] He will not contend with you forever—certainly not after you die.[45] Today is the day of salvation.[46]

Do not insult the Holy Spirit of God.[47] He was sent by Jesus to be your helper in life and to bring about spiritual rebirth and transformation of your thoughts and attitudes.[48-51] He brings you wisdom and understanding, counsel and power, knowledge, and the fear of the Lord.[52] Do not give him grief.[53]

Pray with the help of the Holy Spirit on all occasions with all kinds of prayers and requests.[54,55] Make every effort to maintain peace and unity through the Spirit.[56] Guard your faith with the help of the Holy Spirit who lives in you.[57]

HONESTY

1	Lev. 19:11	30	Psa.145:18
2	Col. 3:9	31	Psa. 15:1
3	Ex. 20:16	32	Psa. 15:2
4	Deut. 5:20	33	John 8:44
5	Prov. 6:16	34	Eph. 6:14
6	Prov. 6:17	35	John 3:3
7	Prov. 6:19	36	John 14:6
8	Psa. 5:6	37	Acts 4:12
9	Zech. 8:17	38	John 8:32
10	Prov.12:22	39	1 Cor. 13:6
11	Prov. 19:9	40	1 Tim. 1:5
12	Eph. 4:25	41	1 John 3:18
13	Eph. 4:15		
14	Prov.24:26		
15	Prov.26:28		
16	Psa. 34:13		
17	1 John 1:8		
18	1 John 1:6		
19	1 John 1:9		
20	Lev. 19:35		
21	Lev. 19:36		
22	Deut25:15		
23	Prov.23:10		
24	Deut27:17		
25	Deut27:25		
26	Psa. 15:5		
27	Ps119:163		
28	Psa. 51:6		
29	Heb. 11:6		

HONESTY

Do not tell a lie.[1,2] Do not give false testimony against your neighbor.[3,4] The Lord hates a lying tongue and a false witness.[5-10] Those who tell lies will perish.[11]

Be honest with each other because you are part of the kingdom of God.[12] Speak the truth in love.[13] An honest answer is like a kiss on the lips.[14] A lying tongue expresses hate to those it hurts.[15] Keep your tongue from evil and your lips from speaking lies.[16]

If you think you are not guilty of sin, you are not being honest with yourself and in denial.[17] If you claim to follow Christ, but do not do what he says, you are a total hypocrite, and you will perish.[18] If you confess your sin, he will forgive you and purge your record of all wrongdoing.[19]

Do not use false standards or measurements in your business dealings.[20-22] Do not secretly move an ancient boundary stone or encroach on someone else's property.[23,24] Do not accept a bribe.[25,26] God hates and abhors falsehood of any kind.[27] He wants you to be honest from the first moments of your life.[28]

Without faith, it is impossible to please God. You must first believe that he exists and that he rewards those who seek him with an honest heart.[29,30] Only those who honestly speak the truth from a sincere heart can expect to be in God's presence.[31,32]

The Devil is a liar and the father of lies.[33] Stand firmly against him, supported and strengthened by truth.[34]

The honest truth is that you cannot hope to be part of the kingdom of God unless you are born again.[35] Faith in Jesus is the only way that can happen and the only way to God.[36,37] This is the truth, and it can set you free.[39]

Honesty is an important component of love.[39] True love comes from a pure heart, a good conscience and a sincere faith.[39]

Be honest in your actions toward others as a way to demonstrate the truth of the gospel.[40,41]

HOPE

1	Ps. 42:11	28	Lam. 3:25	55	Rom. 5:3
2	Ps. 42:5	29	Col. 1:5	56	Rom. 5:4
3	Ps. 42:11	30	Heb. 11:1	57	Heb. 6:19
4	Ps. 43:5	31	Col. 1:27	58	1 Cor. 13:13
5	Ps. 130:7	32	Titus 1:2		
6	Ps. 55:22	33	Titus 2:13		
7	Rom. 12:12	34	Rom. 8:23		
8	Ps. 131:3	35	Rom. 5:5		
9	Job 13:15	52	1 Peter 1:13		
10	Lam. 3:18	37	Titus 2:13		
11	Lam. 3:19	38	Col. 1:23		
12	Lam. 3:20	39	1 Peter 1:3		
13	Lam. 3:21	40	1 Peter 1:21		
14	Lam. 3:22	41	2 Thess. 2:16		
15	Lam. 3:23	42	Titus 3:7		
16	Ps. 52:9	43	Titus 1:2		
17	1 Tim. 4:10	44	Gal. 5:5		
18	Ps. 147:11	45	Rom. 8:23		
19	Ps. 33:18	46	1 John 3:2		
20	Isa. 40:31	47	2 Cor. 1:22		
21	Ps. 31:24	48	2 Cor. 5:5		
22	Jer. 29:11	49	2 Cor. 4:18		
23	Rom. 15:4	50	1 Thess. 5:8		
24	Ps. 130:5	51	1 Peter 3:15		
25	Ps. 27:14	52	Heb. 10:23		
26	Ps. 62:5	53	1 John 3:3		
27	Lam. 3:26	54	1 Tim. 6:17		

HOPE

Put your hope in God. Do not be depressed or anxious.[1-5] Put your hope in the Lord because his love for you is unfailing, and he offers full redemption for your soul.[5] Cast your cares on the Lord, and he will sustain you.[6] Be joyful in your hope, patient in affliction, and faithful in prayer.[7]

Put your hope in the Lord now and in the future.[8] Even though your life seems marked by uncertainty, loss, disappointment, affliction, wandering, bitterness, or depression, remember this, that the Lord has great love for you. His compassions for you will never fail—they are new every morning. How great is his faithfulness![9-15]

Put your hope in the good name of the living God, the Savior of all who trust him.[16,17] He delights in those who put their hope in his unfailing love.[18,19] Those who put their hope in the Lord have a constant source of renewed strength. They will soar on wings like eagles; they will run and not grow weary, they will walk and not faint.[20] Be strong and take heart because of your hope in the Lord.[21] He has plans to give you hope and a future.[22]

Put your hope in the Scriptures and what is written there.[23,24] Wait patiently in your hope of God's salvation.[25-27] He is good to those whose hope is in him.[28]

Hope is the foundation of faith and love.[29] Faith is the confidence that what we hope for will actually happen.[30] Hope resides in a mystery: Christ in you.[31] Faith and knowledge rest on the hope of eternal life, promised by God from the beginning of time.[32] Your most blessed hope is the glorious appearing of your great God and Savior, Jesus Christ.[33] Your hope also includes the Holy Spirit in you, a preview of a glorious future when your body will finally be released from the effects of sin and suffering.[34] This hope will not disappoint you.[35]

Set your hope fully on that wonderful day when Jesus will return.[36,37] This hope is presented in the gospel of Jesus Christ.[38] Through his resurrection from the dead, you were born again into a new and living hope.[39,40] This hope is that of eternal life in a new body characterized by freedom from sin and suffering.[41-45] We know that we will become like Jesus and see him face to face.[46] We have the Holy Spirit as a guarantee of this hope in what is to come.[47,48]

In view of your hope, focus your attentions on things that are unseen, but of eternal value.[49] Your character should be that of hope, self-control, faith, and love.[50] Make Christ pre-eminent in your heart and always be prepared to explain to others the hope that is yours.[51] Hold unswervingly to the hope you profess and let it be a motivation to purity.[52,53] Do not put your hope in wealth because it is uncertain.[54] Rejoice when you run into trials and problems because they help you develop endurance, strong character and the confident hope of salvation.[55,56] This hope is a strong and trustworthy anchor for your soul.[57]

Hope, faith, and love are the three greatest character traits.[58]

HUMILITY

1	Rom. 12:3		30	Prov. 27:1
2	1 Peter 5:6		31	Matt. 6:1
3	James 4:10		32	Phil. 2:3
4	Matt. 18:4		33	Rom. 12:10
5	Luke 14:11		34	Prov. 27:2
6	Matt. 20:16		35	Phil. 2:4
7	Matt. 19:30		36	Col. 3:12
8	Matt. 20:26		37	Titus 3:2
9	Luke 22:26		38	Eph. 4:2
10	Matt. 23:8		39	Col. 3:13
11	Matt. 23:9		40	Titus 3:2
12	Matt. 23:10		41	Rom. 12:16
13	Matt. 23:12		42	James 1:9
14	Matt. 20:28		43	James 1:10
15	Mark 10:45		44	Col. 2:18
16	John 13:15		45	Col. 2:22
17	Phil. 2:5		46	Col. 2:23
18	Phil. 2:7		47	James 3:13
19	Phil. 2:8		48	James 4:7
20	Mic. 6:8		49	1 Cor. 13:4
21	Prov. 8:13			
22	Prov. 16:5			
23	Prov. 6:16			
24	Prov. 6:17			
25	Ps. 5:5			
26	Ps. 101:5			
27	James 4:6			
28	Prov. 3:34			
29	Matt. 5:5			

HUMILITY

Don't think you are better than you really are. Be honest in your evaluation of yourself. Measure yourself by the amount of faith God has given you.[1]

Humble yourself before the LORD, and he will lift you up in due time.[2,3] Humility on earth is greatness in the kingdom of heaven.[4] Everyone who builds themselves up will be humbled.[5] Those who are last in this world will be first in the next one.[6,7] Those who want to be great must be servant-leaders.[8,9] Even religious leaders should shun titles that set themselves above others.[10-13]

Consider the example of Jesus who came to serve, not to be served.[14,15] You should follow his example.[16] You should have the same attitude as his. He demonstrated the virtue of humility by serving others and enduring crucifixion on a cross.[17-19]

God requires humility, along with mercy and justice.[20] He hates pride and arrogance.[21-26] He opposes the proud, but gives grace to the humble.[27,28] He blesses those who are humble.[29]

Do not boast about what you will accomplish tomorrow. You have no idea what the day holds for you.[30] Don't do your "acts of righteousness" just so others can see them.[31]

Don't do anything out of selfish ambition or just to impress others, but humbly consider others better than yourself.[32,33] Let praise for you come from someone else's lips and not your own.[34] Don't simply look out for your own interests, but also for the interest of others.[35]

Develop a reputation for humility, compassion, kindness, gentleness, and patience.[36,37] Be patient with one another, making allowance for each other's faults, and forgiving whatever grievances you may have against them.[38,39] Show true humility to everyone.[40]

Live in harmony with one another. Do not be proud, but willing to associate with people of low position. Do not be conceited.[41] The person living in humble circumstances should take pride in their high position in Christ, but the rich should take pride in their low position since they and their wealth will pass away like a wildflower in the heat of midsummer.[42,43]

Beware false humility seen in those who insist on following man-made rules. While these appear authentic, they are destined to pass away because they are of human origin.[44-46]

If you are wise and understand God's intentions for you, prove it to others by living an honorable life and doing good works with the humility that comes from wisdom.[47]

Humble yourself before God. Resist the Devil and he will flee from you.[48]

Love is humble. It does not boast nor is it proud.[49]

HYPOCRISY

1   Ps. 26:4

2   Mark 7:6

3   Matt. 15:8

4   Luke 12:1

5   Luke 20:46

6   Luke 20:47

7   Matt. 23:23

8   Luke 11:42

9   Matt. 23:3

10 Matt. 23:13

11 Matt. 23:15

12 Matt. 23:25

13 Matt. 23:27

14 Matt. 23:29

15 Matt. 6:2

16 Matt. 6:4

17 Matt. 6:5

18 Matt. 6:6

19 Matt. 6:16

20 Matt. 6:18

21 Luke 6:42

22 Matt. 7:5

23 1 Cor. 5:11

24 Luke 13:15

25 Luke 6:46

26 Matt. 7:21

27 James 1:22

HYPOCRISY

Beware hypocrites and do not allow them to be a part of your life.[1] They make a big show of saying and doing the right things, but their hearts are actually far away from God.[2,3]

Beware hypocrisy in some religious leaders.[4] They are pretentious and love public recognition. They offer lengthy prayers for show, but are secretly deceitful. They will be severely punished by God.[5,6] They emphasize tithing, but neglect justice, mercy, faithfulness, and love of God.[7,8] Do not do what they do because they do not practice what they preach.[9]

Beware hypocrisy in the self-righteous. They make it difficult for anyone to enter the kingdom of heaven.[10] They go to great lengths to win a single convert and then teach them to be equally self-righteous.[11] They appear clean on the outside, but inside they are full of greed and self-indulgence.[12,13] They memorialize their ancestors, but deny their faults.[14]

Do not give to the needy as the hypocrites do, with great fanfare so that they will be honored publicly.[15] God sees what you do in secret, and he will reward you for it.[16] Do not pray as hypocrites do in such a way so that they will be seen by others.[17] Pray behind closed doors and God will reward you for it.[18] Do not be obvious to others when you are fasting, as hypocrites do, but be obvious only to God who sees what you do in secret and rewards you accordingly.[19,20]

Do not be hypocritical when you see minor imperfections in others. Consider your own shortcomings and correct those first.[21] Take the plank out of your own eye and then you will see more clearly to remove the speck in someone else's eye.[22]

Avoid anyone who calls themselves "Christian," but is openly immoral in any way because they are hypocrites.[23]

Do not be hypocritical in your observance of the Sabbath.[24]

Do not be a hypocrite by calling Jesus "Lord" and then not doing what he says.[25] Only those who do the will of God can enter the kingdom of heaven.[26,27]

IDOLS

1	Ex. 20:3	28	Jer. 25:6	55	1 Cor. 6:9
2	Deut. 5:7	29	Jer. 25:7	56	Rev. 21:27
3	Lev. 19:4	30	Isa. 65:3	57	Rev. 21:8
4	Ex. 20:4	31	Deut. 7:25	58	Rev. 22:15
5	Deut. 5:8	32	Ezek. 5:9	59	Ps. 24:4
6	Deut. 4:23	33	Ezek. 11:18		
7	Deut. 4:25	34	Ezek. 16:36		
8	Deut. 4:16	35	Ezek. 11:21		
9	Ex. 20:23	36	Deut. 29:17		
10	Isa. 44:10	37	Jer. 32:34		
11	Ps. 115:4	38	Deut. 27:15		
12	Jer. 10:15	39	Deut. 4:24		
13	1 Sam. 12:21	40	Deut. 32:21		
14	Jer. 10:14	41	Ezek. 14:6		
15	Jer. 10:8	42	Jer. 4:1		
16	Hos. 4:12	43	1 Cor. 10:7		
17	Hab. 2:19	44	1 Cor. 10:14		
18	Lev. 26:1	45	1 John 5:21		
19	Ex. 20:5	46	Gal. 5:19		
20	Deut. 5:9	47	Gal. 5:20		
21	Ex. 20:2	48	Rom. 1:21		
22	Ex. 20:6	49	Rom. 1:22		
23	Deut. 5:10	50	Rom. 1:23		
24	Jer. 10:16	51	Rom. 1:25		
25	Isa. 40:19	52	Rom. 1:24		
26	Isa. 48:11	53	1 Cor. 5:11		
27	Isa. 42:8	54	Josh. 24:14		

IDOLS

You must have no other god except the Lord your God.[1-3] Do not make an idol of any kind or an image of anything in the heavens or on the earth or in the sea.[4-6] Do not corrupt yourself by making idols of any kind to rival God;[7] not of any shape including that of a man or a woman; not even of gold or silver.[7-9]

Only a fool would make his own god, an idol that cannot help.[10] Idols are merely things made of silver and gold. They are worthless and are ridiculous lies![12] Do not turn away from God to worship useless idols; they can do you no good.[13] The whole human race is foolish in this regard.[14,15] They ask a piece of wood for advice. They think a stick or a speechless stone can tell them the future.[16] An idol covered over with silver and gold cannot tell you what to do because it has no life inside.[17]

Do not set up carved images or sacred pillars or sculptured stones for the purpose of worship.[18] You must not bow down to them or worship them in any way because God demands your unrivaled worship.[19,20] He alone has rescued you from slavery and lavishes his unfailing love on generations of those who love him and keep his commandments.[21-23]

God is not an idol. He is the Creator of everything that exists.[24] Can he be compared to an idol formed in a mold, overlaid with gold, and decorated with silver chains?[25] He will not let his reputation be tarnished or share his glory with idols.[26,27]

Do not provoke God to anger by worshiping idols made with human hands.[28] He is furious with idol worship.[29] He is insulted by the practice.[30] It is an abomination; a detestable practice in his eyes.[31-38] He is a jealous God, a consuming fire.[39] He wants you to worship him alone, and not anything or anyone else.[40] Therefore, repent and get rid of your idols and return to worshiping the one true God.[41,42]

Do not worship an idol.[43-45] Idolatry will eventually result if you follow your own natural desires.[46,47] Knowing God without worshipping him leads to mental confusion and intellectual darkness.[48] Such people think they are wise, but instead are fools. They exchange the glory of God for images made to look like mortal mankind, birds, animals and reptiles. They exchange the truth of God for a lie, and worship and serve things that are created rather than the Creator himself. So God lets them have their way to do whatever they want. The result is degrading sexual impurity.[49-52] Do not even associate with anyone who claims to follow Jesus and worships an idol.[53]

Fear the Lord and worship him wholeheartedly. Get rid of all of your idols forever.[54] No one who worships an idol can enter the kingdom of heaven.[55-58] Only those whose hands and hearts are pure and who do not worship idols.[59]

JOY

1	1 Thess. 5:16	28	Ps. 100:1	55	1 Peter 1:6
2	Phil. 4:4	29	Ps. 66:1	56	Rom. 12:12
3	Phil. 4:4	30	Ps. 47:1	57	Rom. 5:3
4	Phil. 3:1	31	Ps. 98:4	58	Rom. 5:4
5	Ps. 32:11	32	Ps. 118:24	59	1 Peter 4:13
6	Ps. 64:10	33	Ps. 104:34	60	Phil. 3:10
7	Ps. 68:3	34	Ps. 97:1	61	Gal. 5:22
8	Ps. 119:162	35	Ps. 96:11	62	Gal. 5:23
9	Ps. 119:14	36	Luke 10:20	63	Rom. 14:17
10	Ps. 19:8	37	Luke 15:10	64	Heb. 13:17
11	Prov. 15:13	38	Ps. 13:5	65	Rom. 12:15
12	Ps. 34:8	39	Heb. 12:2		
13	Ps. 126:3	40	1 Peter 1:8		
14	Acts 14:17	41	Rom. 5:2		
15	Ps. 16:11	42	Rom. 5:11		
16	Acts 2:28	43	John 15:10		
17	Ps. 32:11	44	John 15:11		
18	Ps. 97:12	45	John 16:24		
19	Ps. 64:10	46	Acts 2:28		
20	Ps. 32:11	47	Ps. 31:7		
21	Ps. 100:2	48	Ps. 94:19		
22	Ps. 81:1	49	James 1:2		
23	Ps. 149:5	50	James 1:3		
24	Ps. 107:22	51	Luke 6:22		
25	Ps. 95:1	52	Matt. 5:11		
26	Ps. 68:4	53	Luke 6:23		
27	Ps. 33:3	54	Matt. 5:12		

JOY

Be full of joy all of the time.[1,2] Rejoice in the Lord at all times.[3-7] Rejoice in God's commandments and promises like one who has found great treasure or has great riches.[8-9] The commandments of the Lord are right and bring joy to the heart. [10] Joy in your heart puts happiness on your face.[11]

Taste and see that the Lord is good. You will find joy and blessing.[12] He has done great things for you and filled you with joy.[13,14] He will show you the path of life and fill you with joy and eternal pleasures in his presence.[15,16] Rejoice in the Lord with all the righteous people, and praise his Holy name.[17-20]

Worship the Lord with joy.[21] Sing to God for joy. Shout aloud with cries of joy to the Lord, the Rock of your salvation.[22-30] Express your joy with jubilant song and music.[31] Rejoice and be happy in this day that the Lord has made.[32] Meditate and rejoice in the Lord—this is pleasing to him.[33] Let the heavens rejoice and the earth and the sea be filled with joy because the Lord reigns![34,35]

Rejoice that your name is written in heaven.[36] There is great joy in heaven over every single sinner who repents.[37] Trust in God's unfailing love and rejoice in your salvation.[38] Fix your eyes on Jesus and believe in him, even though you do not see him now, and you will be filled with an inexpressible and glorious joy.[39,40] Rejoice in your hope of the glory of God and your reconciliation to him through our Lord Jesus Christ.[41,42] Obey his commandments and you will experience his love and share his joy.[43,44]

Pray to God in Jesus's name and find abundant and complete joy in his answers.[45] He will show you the way for your life and fill you with the joy of his presence.[46] He knows your affliction and the anguish of your soul, and his consolation brings joy to your soul.[47,48]

Consider it pure joy whenever you face trials of many kinds.[49] Trials test your faith and give it a chance to grow.[50] You are blessed when people hate you, exclude you, insult and slander you because of Jesus.[51,52] Rejoice and dance for joy because you will have a great reward in heaven—just like the prophets of old who were treated in the same way.[53,54] So be truly happy because there is wonderful joy ahead, even though you have to endure many trials for some part of your life.[55]

Be joyful in hope, patient in affliction, faithful in prayer.[56] Rejoice in your sufferings because they produce perseverance, character, and hope.[57,58] Rejoice that your suffering identifies you with Christ in his suffering. In this way, you become part of a fellowship of those who share suffering with him and will be overjoyed when he is finally revealed in all his glory .[59,60]

Let the Holy Spirit produce good character in your life: joy, love, peace, patience, kindness, faithfulness gentleness, and self-control.[61,62] The kingdom of God is a matter of joy, peace, and righteousness.[63]

Obey your spiritual leaders so that their task will be a joy and not a burden for them.[63]

Rejoice with those who rejoice and weep with those who weep.[65]

JUDGMENT

1	Heb. 9:27	30	1 Cor. 11:31
2	Mark 1:15	31	John 7:24
3	Acts 26:20	32	Rom. 14:1
4	1 Peter 4:5	33	Rom. 14:13
5	Acts 17:31	34	James 4:12
6	Rom. 2:16	35	Rom. 2:3
7	1 Peter 1:17	36	James 4:11
8	1 Peter 1:17	37	Matt. 5:22
9	Rev. 16:7	38	Matt. 12:36
10	Ps. 7:11	39	1 Cor. 11:27
11	Rom. 11:33	40	1 Cor. 11:28
12	2 Cor. 5:10	41	1 Cor. 11:29
13	Acts 10:42	42	James 3:1
14	John 5:22	43	Heb. 4:12
15	2 Tim. 4:1		
16	Isa. 11:3		
17	Isa. 11:4		
18	Jude 15		
19	1 Peter 1:17		
20	John 7:24		
21	Deut. 1:17		
22	Prov. 31:9		
23	2 Chron. 19:6		
24	Matt. 7:1		
25	Luke 6:37		
26	Rom. 12:3		
27	Rom. 14:10		
28	Matt. 7:2		
29	Rom. 2:1		

JUDGMENT

You are destined to die—and after that to face judgment.[1] Repent of your sins, and believe the gospel.[2] Prove your repentance by doing good works.[3]

You will have to face God who will judge everyone, both the living and the dead.[4] He has set a time when he will do this, and it will expose both your actions and your thoughts. He has no favorites.[5-7] He will judge with equity, truth, and justice.[8,9] He is a righteous judge whose wisdom and knowledge are great and his judgments unquestionable.[10,11]

As a believer, you will have to stand before Christ to be judged for the works you have done on earth.[12] He is the one who has been appointed by God to judge everyone.[13-15] He will not judge by appearances but with righteousness and justice toward the poor and needy. He will convict all the ungodly for what they have done and their rejection of him.[16-18]

Live your life in a way that is different from those around you who follow the world's culture.[19] Stop judging by mere appearances.[20] Do not show partiality in court but hear both small and great alike.[21] Defend the rights of the poor and needy.[22] Remember that you are not just judging for people but for the Lord.[23]

Do not judge and you will not be judged. Do not condemn and you will not be condemned. Forgive and you will be forgiven.[24,25]

Do not look down on others or think more highly of yourself than you should, but use sober judgment for self-evaluation.[26,27] We will all have equal accountability and standing on judgment day.[28] Beware judging others because in so doing you often find yourself guilty of doing the same things.[29] If you first judge yourself, you will not come under judgment.[30]

Don't judge others based on appearance.[31] Accept those whose faith is weak without passing judgment on controversial matters or putting a stumbling block in their way.[32,33] You have no right to judge others. There is only one lawgiver and judge, the one who is able to save and destroy.[34] You will be judged when you judge others while guilty of doing the same things.[35]

Don't speak ill of another Christian.[36] Never call anyone a demeaning name. You will be in danger of the fire of hell.[37] You will be accountable on judgement day for every careless word you have ever spoken.[38]

Examine your heart before partaking of communion. Eating the bread and drinking the cup in an unworthy manner brings judgment on yourself.[39-41]

Not many should be teachers. They will be judged more strictly.[42]

The Scriptures are able to judge the thoughts and attitudes of your heart.[43]

JUSTICE

1	Mic. 6:8	30	Lev. 5:1
2	Ps. 37:28	31	Isa. 10:1
3	Heb. 1:9	32	Matt. 23:23
4	Zech. 7:9	33	Matt. 9:13
5	Isa. 56:1	34	Matt. 12:7
6	2 Chron. 19:7	35	Matt. 5:6
7	Deut. 16:19	36	Acts 17:31
8	Ex. 23:8		
9	Isa. 5:23		
10	Luke 3:14		
11	Prov. 31:9		
12	Prov. 31:8		
13	Jer. 22:3		
14	Deut. 24:17		
15	Zech. 7:10		
16	Deut. 27:19		
17	Deut. 24:17		
18	Ex. 23:6		
19	Mal. 3:5		
20	Isa. 1:17		
21	Ex. 23:2		
22	Lev. 19:15		
23	Deut. 1:17		
24	Ex. 23:6		
25	Ex. 23:3		
26	Isa. 58:5		
27	Isa. 58:6		
28	Isa. 58:7		
29	Deut. 19:15		

JUSTICE

Act justly, love mercy, and walk humbly with your God. These are his basic requirements for your life.[1] He loves justice and hates evil.[2,3]

Maintain true justice by doing what is right and showing mercy and compassion.[4,5] Administer true justice and judge with integrity because the Lord does not tolerate perverted justice, partiality, or the taking of bribes.[6] Never twist justice or show partiality. Never accept a bribe, because it will corrupt wise and righteous decisions. It blinds the eyes of those who see and twists the words even of the righteous.[7-9] Do not extort money or accuse people falsely.[10]

Speak up for those who cannot speak for themselves.[11] Advocate justice for those being crushed by powerful interests. Do not convict an innocent person.[12,13] You must provide true justice to foreigners living legally in your land.[14]

You must protect orphans and widows. You must uphold the rights of the oppressed and the destitute. Do not oppress the widow, the orphan, the alien, or the poor. Do not have prejudice in your heart against them.[15] The person who withholds justice from these vulnerable people is cursed.[16] Do not deprive the alien or the orphan of justice or take the cloak of the widow as a pledge.[17] Do not deny justice to the poor in their lawsuits or defraud laborers of their wages.[18,19] Encourage the oppressed. Defend the cause of the orphan and widow. Defend the rights of the poor and needy.[20]

Do not pervert justice by giving misleading statements when you give testimony in a lawsuit.[21]

Do not twist justice in legal matters by favoring the poor or being partial to the rich and powerful. Always judge fairly.[22] Do not show partiality in judging; hear both small and great alike.[23] Do not deny justice to the poor nor show them favoritism in a lawsuit.[24,25] Free those who are wrongly imprisoned. Let the oppressed go free, and remove the chains that bind them. Share your food with the hungry, and give shelter to the homeless. Give clothes to those who need them, and do not hide from relatives that need your help.[26-28]

A matter must be established by the testimony of two or three witnesses. One is not enough.[29] Speak up if you know or have seen something wrong that is relevant to public interest. It is a sin not to do so.[30]

Woe to those who make unjust laws and issue oppressive decrees.[31] Woe to hypocritical lawmakers who neglect the important matters of law: justice, mercy, and faithfulness.[32-34]

God blesses those who hunger and thirst for justice. They will be satisfied.[35]

God has set a day for judging the world with justice. It is certain that Jesus Christ will be the judge because God has raised him from the dead.[36]

KNOWLEDGE

1	Prov. 1:7	28	2 Pet. 1:7
2	Prov. 9:10	29	2 Pet. 1:8
3	Prov. 2:6	30	John 8:31
4	Prov. 3:5	31	John 8:32
5	Prov. 3:7	32	1 Cor. 2:14
6	Prov. 3:6	33	1 Cor. 2:12
7	Prov. 8:10	34	Col. 1:9
8	Prov. 23:12	35	Col. 1:10
9	Prov. 2:2	36	Col. 3:10
10	Prov. 2:4	37	Titus 1:2
11	Prov. 8:11	38	Eph. 3:19
12	Prov. 10:14	39	Phil. 1:9
13	Prov. 15:14	40	2 Peter 1:3
14	Prov. 18:15	41	Titus 1:1
15	Prov. 2:5	42	1 Tim. 6:20
16	Rom. 11:33	43	Eph. 5:6
17	Ps. 19:1	44	2 Peter 3:17
18	Ps. 19:2	45	Prov. 19:2
19	Rom. 1:20	46	1 Cor. 8:1
20	Isa. 33:6		
21	2 Cor. 4:6		
22	Col. 2:3		
23	1 Tim. 2:4		
24	Luke 1:77		
25	2 Peter 3:18		
26	2 Peter 1:5		
27	2 Peter 1:6		

KNOWLEDGE

The fear of the Lord is the beginning of knowledge.[1] Knowledge, wisdom and understanding come from him.[2,3] Trust in the Lord with all your heart and do not depend on your own understanding.[4] Do not be wise in your own eyes.[5] Acknowledge him in everything you do, and he will guide your path.[6]

Choose knowledge and instruction rather than silver and gold.[7-10] Wisdom is more valuable than rubies.[11] Seek knowledge and store it up because it is the wise and discerning thing to do.[12-14] Through it, you will understand the fear of the Lord and find the knowledge of God.[15]

God's knowledge is rich and deep.[16] All of creation displays it day after day and night after night.[17,18] Creation declares his power and divine nature so that no one has an excuse for not knowing something about God.[19] He will be the sure foundation for your time, a rich store of knowledge, wisdom, and salvation. The fear of the Lord is the key to this treasure.[20]

The same God who created light in the beginning now makes his light shine in your heart so that you can have knowledge of the glory of God and his Son, Jesus Christ.[21] In him are hidden all the treasures of wisdom and knowledge.[22] He wants you to come to a knowledge of the truth of salvation through the forgiveness of your sins.[23,24]

Grow your knowledge of Jesus.[25] Expend every effort to add knowledge to your faith. Also add goodness, self-control, perseverance, godliness, kindness and love. These qualities will make you effective in your knowledge of Jesus.[26-29] Knowing him and doing his will brings you to a knowledge of truth, and this truth will set you free from all your past.[30,31]

Knowing God requires spiritual knowledge that cannot be understood without the help of the Holy Spirit.[32,33] You can be filled with the knowledge of his will through all spiritual wisdom and understanding.[34] This leads to a life worthy of the Lord, pleasing him in every way, doing good works, and growing in the knowledge of God.[35]

You are a new self being renewed in knowledge in the image of your Creator.[36] Your faith and knowledge rest on the hope of eternal life, promised by God who does not lie.[37] You have increasing knowledge and depth of insight into God's love, which actually surpasses knowledge.[38,39] This knowledge gives you everything you need for life and godliness.[40,41]

Beware false knowledge. Turn away from empty chatter and false ideas.[42] Do not be deceived with empty words or intentionally false ideas because the wrath of God will eventually come on those who are disobedient.[43,44]

It is not good to have zeal without knowledge.[45]

Knowledge puffs up, but love builds up.[46]

LIFESTYLE, Part 1

1	Rom. 12:2		30	Gal. 6:2
2	Eph. 4:17		31	Col. 3:14
3	Eph. 4:18		32	Phil. 1:27
4	Eph. 4:19		33	1 Thess. 4:7
5	Col. 2:8		34	Col. 3:5
6	Eph. 5:6		35	Gal. 5:19
7	John 8:12		36	Eph. 5:3
8	John 16:13		37	Eph. 5:5
9	James 1:5		38	Rom. 13:13
10	Eph. 5:8		39	Gal. 5:20
11	Eph. 5:9		40	Col. 3:8
12	Eph. 5:10		41	James 4:11
13	Col. 3:1		42	Eph. 4:31
14	Col. 3:2		43	1 Peter 2:1
15	Phil. 4:8		44	Col. 3:9
16	Heb. 12:2		45	Gal. 5:21
17	Heb. 12:1		46	Eph. 4:28
18	Gal. 5:22		47	Eph. 4:29
19	Gal. 5:23		48	Eph. 5:4
20	Col. 3:15		49	1 Thess. 4:4
21	Col. 3:16			
22	James 1:19			
23	James 1:20			
24	Eph. 4:26			
25	Eph. 4:27			
26	Eph. 5:21			
27	Col. 3:12			
28	Col. 3:13			
29	Gal. 6:1			

LIFESTYLE, Part 1

Do not conform to the lifestyles and worldviews of your unbelieving culture.[1] Do not live as unbelievers who do not know the will of God. Their thinking is futile, and their understanding is darkened because of their persistent rejection of God. They eventually lose all sensitivity to him and give themselves over to sensuality and materialism.[2-4]

Don't be fooled by deceptive philosophical ideas and traditions that originate in human minds rather than in Christ.[5] These empty words will lead you to disobey God's commands and subject you to his wrath.[6] Follow Jesus, the Light of the World, and you will never walk in darkness.[7] His Holy Spirit will guide you into all truth.[8] Ask God if you need wisdom for living; he grants it generously.[9] You should no longer be in the dark about these things but living in the light of the Lord's commands, which produce righteousness, goodness and truth.[10,11] This is pleasing to God.[12]

Set your mind on God's issues, not earthly ones. You have a new life in Christ, so set your sights on the realities of heaven. Be preoccupied with things that are true, noble, right, pure, lovely and admirable.[13-15] Fix your eyes on Jesus, the source and object of your faith, and get rid of everything that hinders your life in him and the sins that so easily trip you up, and run with perseverance the race set out for you.[16,17]

Let the Holy Spirit develop these characteristics in you: love, joy, peace, patience, kindness, goodness, faithfulness, gentleness and self-control.[18,19] Let the peace of Christ rule your heart and be thankful.[20] Let the word of Christ dwell in you richly.[21] Be quick to listen, slow to speak and slow to become angry because anger does not bring about the righteous life that pleases God.[22,23] It leads to sin and gives the Devil a foothold.[24,25]

Submit to one another out of reverence to Christ.[26] Be known for your compassion, kindness, humility, gentleness and patience.[27] Bear with each other and forgive whatever grievances you may have against one another.[28] Gently restore a wayward friend, remembering your own vulnerability to temptation.[29] Carry each other's burdens and in this way fulfill the law of Christ.[30] Above all, exercise love, the greatest of all virtues.[31]

Conduct yourself in a manner worthy of the gospel of Christ.[32] God has called you to live a holy life.[33] Therefore, you must get rid of anything belonging to your unholy human nature: sexual immorality, impurity, lust, evil desires, and greed, which is the same as idolatry.[34-37] Drunkenness, envy, sorcery, hostility, quarreling, jealousy, slander, gossip, anger, rage, malice, selfish ambition, constant objections, lying, and stealing make you unfit for the kingdom of Christ.[38-46] Do not let any unwholesome talk come out of your mouth including obscenity, foolish talk, or coarse joking.[47,48] Learn to control yourself in a way that pleases God.[49]

LIFESTYLE, Part 2

1	1 Thess. 4:11	29	Col. 3:19	57	Rom. 12:20
2	1 Peter 3:16	30	Eph. 5:33	58	Luke 6:35
3	1 Peter 2:12	31	Eph. 5:22	59	Rom. 12:19
4	1 Peter 2:13	32	Col. 3:18	60	Rom. 12:17
5	Rom. 13:1	33	Eph. 5:24		
6	Rom. 13:4	34	Eph. 5:23		
7	1 Tim. 2:2	35	Eph. 6:4		
8	1 Peter 2:14	36	Col. 3:21		
9	1 Tim. 2:1	37	Eph. 6:1		
10	1 Peter 2:17	38	Col. 3:20		
11	1 Peter 2:15	39	Eph. 6:2		
12	1 Peter 2:18	40	Eph. 6:3		
13	Eph. 6:5	41	Heb. 13:5		
14	Col. 3:22	42	1 Tim. 6:6		
15	Eph. 6:6	43	Prov. 23:4		
16	Eph. 6:7	44	1 Tim. 6:10		
17	Col. 3:23	45	Matt. 6:19		
18	Eph. 6:8	46	Matt. 6:20		
19	Col. 3:24	47	1 Tim. 6:17		
20	Eph. 6:9	48	1 Tim. 6:18		
21	Gen. 2:24	49	1 Tim. 6:19		
22	Matt. 19:5	50	Eph. 5:5		
23	Mark 10:7	51	Matt. 6:24		
24	Eph. 5:31	52	Matt. 6:21		
25	Eph. 5:21	53	Rom. 12:21		
26	Eph. 5:25	54	Rom. 12:18		
27	Eph. 5:28	55	Matt. 5:44		
28	Eph. 5:33	56	Luke 6:27		

LIFESTYLE, Part 2

Make it your ambition to lead a quiet life, to mind your own business, and to do meaningful work.[1] Live such a good life that even though unbelievers criticize you, they will have to recognize your good works, which glorify God.[2,3]

Submit yourself for the Lord's sake to all those in governmental authority.[4,5] They are God's means of maintaining social order and allowing you to live a peaceful and quiet life with religious freedom.[6-8] Pray for them, and show proper respect for them.[9,10] It is God's will that you silence the ignorant talk of foolish people by doing so.[11]

Employees must submit to their employers with respect and sincerity of heart, not only to those who are good and considerate, but also to those who are harsh.[12-14] Work not only when they are watching in order to win their favor, but like you are an employee of Christ, wholeheartedly doing the will of God.[15-17] Be assured that you will receive a reward from the Lord—it is really him that you are serving.[18,19] Employers treat your employees in the same way. Do not threaten them since you both have a Master in heaven who does not show favoritism.[20]

A man should leave his father and mother and take a wife, and these two thus become one.[21-24] Husbands and wives must submit to each other out of reverence for Christ.[25] Husbands must love their wives just as they love their own bodies, and even just as Christ loves the church.[26-28] Do not be harsh with them.[29] Wives must respect their husbands.[30] Wives are to submit to the authority of their husbands just as the church submits to the authority of Christ.[31-34] Fathers must not embitter their children, but bring them up in the training and instruction of the Lord.[35,36] Children are to obey their parents because this pleases God.[37,38] Honor your parents so that you may enjoy a long life here on earth.[39,40]

Keep your life free from the love of money.[41] Godliness with contentment is a great investment.[42] Do not wear yourself out to get rich.[43] The love of money is a root of all kinds of evil, causing many to wander from the faith and into many sorrows and much regret.[44] Do not store up for yourself treasures on earth where they can be lost, but store up for yourself treasure in heaven where it is secure.[45,46] Do not put your hope in wealth but in God who richly provides us with everything for our enjoyment.[47] Be generous, willing to share, and rich in good deeds, thus providing a firm foundation for the coming age.[48,49] Do not be greedy—it is a sin equivalent to idolatry.[50] You cannot serve two masters—both God and money.[51] Your heart will surely be where you put your treasure.[52]

Do not be overcome by evil, but overcome evil with good.[53] If possible on your part, live in harmony with everyone.[54] Love your enemies, and pray for those who persecute you. Do good to those who hate you, lend to them without expecting repayment. Feed them and give them drink. You please God in this way because he is kind to the ungrateful, and your reward in heaven will be very great.[55-58] Do not take revenge or repay evil with evil. Leave that up to God.[59,60]

LOVE, Part 1

1	Deut. 6:5	30	Num. 14:18	59	1 John 4:7
2	Matt. 22:37	31	Eph. 3:19	60	1 John 4:8
3	Matt. 22:38	32	Eph. 3:18	61	1 John 4:12
4	Mark 12:29	33	Eph. 2:4	62	Eph. 3:18
5	Mark 12:30	34	Eph. 2:4	63	Eph. 3:19
6	1 John 5:3	35	Rom. 5:5	64	Eph. 3:17
7	1 John 5:3	36	Gal. 5:22	65	1 Cor. 13:13
8	1 John 2:5	37	1 Chr. 16:34	66	Col. 3:14
9	John 14:15	38	1 Kings 8:24	67	1 Cor. 13:4
10	John 14:21	39	Deut. 5:10	68	1 Cor. 13:5
11	John 15:10	40	Ex. 15:13	69	1 Cor. 13:6
12	Mark 12:31	41	Isa. 54:10	70	1 Cor. 13:7
13	Matt. 22:40	42	Lam. 3:22	71	1 Cor. 13:8
14	Gal. 5:14	43	Lam. 3:23	72	1 Cor. 13:1
15	Rom. 13:9	44	Lam. 3:32	73	1 Cor. 13:2
16	1 John 4:21	45	Ps. 100:5	74	1 Cor. 13:3
17	John 13:34	46	Ps. 103:11		
18	1 John 4:21	47	Ps. 147:11		
19	John 13:35	48	Ps. 33:5		
20	1 John 4:20	49	Rom. 8:38		
21	1 John 4:19	50	1 John 4:11		
22	1 John 4:16	51	1 John 4:19		
23	1 John 4:7	52	1 Peter 4:8		
24	1 John 4:10	53	2 John 6		
25	Rom. 5:8	54	John 13:34		
26	1 John 4:9	55	John 15:12		
27	John 3:16	56	Rom. 12:10		
28	1 John 3:1	57	Rom. 12:9		
29	Ex. 34:6	58	Heb. 13:1		

LOVE, Part 1

Love the Lord your God with all your heart, mind, soul and strength. He is the one true God. This is the first and most important commandment.[1-5] You show that you love God by keeping his commandments.[6-8] In the same way, you show that you love Jesus by keeping his commandments.[9-11]

Love your neighbor as yourself. This is the second greatest commandment and is equally important with the first.[12] The entire law of Moses is based on these two commandments.[13-15]

Love your Christian brothers and sisters as an expression of your love for God.[16] This is Christ's command.[17,18] This love will demonstrate to the world that you are a follower of Jesus Christ.[19] No one can honestly say they love God whom they have not seen if they cannot love another Christ-follower whom they have seen.[20] You should love others because God loved you first.[21]

God is love and love comes from him.[22,23] This is true love, not that you loved God, but that he loved you, even when you were still a sinner.[24,25] God has shown his great love for you by sending his one and only Son into the world to pay the penalty for your sins. If you believe in him, you will never perish, but have eternal life.[26,27] His love for you is so great that he calls you his child.[28] He is compassionate and gracious, slow to anger, and overflowing with love and faithfulness to you. He will forgive every kind of sin and rebellion.[29,30] His love surpasses knowledge,[31,32] is rich in mercy,[33,34] and can be reproduced in your life by the Holy Spirit.[35,36] Give thanks to God; he is good, and his love will never fail you.[37-48] Nothing can ever separate you from God's love![49]

Since God loved you first and loved you that much, you surely must love others in the same way.[50-53] Love others just as Jesus loves you.[54,55] Love deeply from your heart with genuine affection.[56,57] Love each other as brothers and sisters.[58] If you do not love one another, you do not know God because God is love.[59,60] Although no one has ever seen God, he lives in you if you love others, and his love is brought to full expression in and through you.[61] Experience the love of Christ and you will be empowered with the fullness of life that comes from God.[62-64]

Love is the greatest virtue, and binds all others into perfect unity.[65,66] Love is patient and kind and never jealous or proud. It is not rude and does not demand its own way. It is not irritable and does not keep score. It rejoices when truth wins out, but not when injustice reigns. It never gives up and never loses faith but is always hopeful and endures through every circumstance.[67-70]

Regardless of your accomplishments, you are nothing without love.[71-74]

LOVE, Part 2

1	Eph. 5:2	28	Luke 6:35
2	1 Cor. 16:14	29	Eph. 5:28
3	1 John 3:18	30	Col. 3:19
4	Rom. 12:9	31	Eph. 5:25
5	Eph. 4:2	32	Eph. 5:33
6	1 Cor. 8:9	33	Titus 2:4
7	Rom. 14:15	34	Heb. 13:5
8	Rom. 13:8	35	Eccl. 5:10
9	1 John 3:17	36	1 Tim. 6:10
10	Eph. 4:15	37	Matt. 6:24
11	Heb. 10:24	38	Luke 16:13
12	1 Tim. 6:11	39	1 John 2:15
13	2 Tim. 2:22	40	1 John 2:16
14	1 Thess. 5:12	41	1 John 2:17
15	1 Thess. 5:13		
16	Rom. 16:16		
17	1 Cor. 16:20		
18	2 Cor. 13:12		
19	1 Thess. 5:26		
20	1 Peter 5:14		
21	Col. 3:14		
22	Rom. 13:10		
23	Matt. 5:44		
24	Luke 6:35		
25	Luke 6:27		
26	Luke 6:28		
27	Luke 6:29		

LOVE, Part 2

Live a life full of love, following the example of Christ.[1,2] Don't just pretend to love others, but show love by your actions.[3,4] Always be humble and gentle, making allowances for each other's faults.[5] Be careful that your lifestyle is not offensive to a weaker believer, causing them to stumble in their Christian walk. This would not be acting in love.[6,7] Owe no one anything except your obligation to love.[8] If a Christian brother or sister has a need that you can meet, show compassion as an expression of your love for God.[9] Speak the truth in love with each other.[10] Think of ways to motivate one another to do acts of love and good works.[11] Run from things that stimulate youthful lusts and pursue righteous living, faith, love, perseverance and gentleness.[12,13] Respect and love your religious leaders.[14,15] Greet one another with Christian love—a holy kiss.[16-20] Above all, let genuine love be your outstanding characteristic. Love fulfills the requirements of God's law.[21,22]

Love your enemies and pray for those who persecute you.[22-26] Turn the other cheek if someone slaps you on the face. If they demand your coat, offer your shirt also.[27] Lend to them without expecting to be repaid and your reward in heaven will be very great because you are truly acting like children of the Most High God who is kind even to those who are unthankful and wicked.[28]

Husbands, you must love your wife as much as you love your own body.[29] Never treat them harshly.[30] Love your wife just like Christ loved the church. He gave up his life for her.[31]

Wives, you must love and respect your husband. You must also love your children.[32,33]

Do not love money; be satisfied with what you have.[34] Otherwise, you will never think you have enough.[35] Love of money is the root of all evil and has caused many to wander away from true faith and pierce themselves with many sorrows.[36] You cannot serve two masters—God and money. You will come to love one and despise the other.[37,38]

Do not love the world or anything in the world. If you love the world, the love of God is not in you.[39] Everything in it—sex, money, power—will pass away.[40] But the person who does the will of God will live forever.[41]

MARGINAL ISSUES

1	Rom. 14:1	30	1 Cor. 8:10
2	Rom. 14:22	31	1 Cor. 8:11
3	Rom. 14:2	32	1 Cor. 8:12
4	Rom. 14:3	33	1 Cor. 8:13
5	Rom. 14:6	34	Rom. 14:21
6	Rom. 14:5	35	1 Cor. 8:12
7	Rom. 14:6	36	Rom. 15:2
8	1 Tim. 3:9	37	Acts 24:16
9	1 Thwaa. 4:3		
10	John 6:4		
11	1 Cor. 6:9		
12	1 Cor. 6:10		
13	1 Tim. 1:19		
14	1 Peter 3:16		
15	1 Cor. 4:4		
16	Rom. 14:23		
17	1 Cor. 10:23		
18	Rom. 14:14		
19	Rom. 14:15		
20	Rom. 14:7		
21	Rom. 14:17		
22	Rom. 14:18		
23	Rom. 14:10		
24	Rom. 14:12		
25	Rom. 14:13		
26	Rom. 14:19		
27	Rom. 14:20		
28	Rom. 15:1		
29	1 Cor. 8:9		

MARGINAL ISSUES

Accept another believer who is new or weak in faith, and don't argue with them about what they think is right or wrong.[1] Keep whatever you believe about disputable matters between yourself and God.[2]

Some believers think that it is acceptable to eat anything while others believe it is only acceptable to eat vegetables.[3] Those who feel free to eat anything must not look down on those who don't. And those who don't eat certain foods must not condemn those who do because God has accepted both.[4] Both want to please God, and both give thanks before eating.[5]

Some believers think one day is more holy than another day and others think every day is alike. Both worship the Lord on a special day to honor him and should be fully convinced that whichever day they choose is acceptable to God.[6,7]

The deep truths of the faith are not marginal, and you must hold on to them.[8] It is God's will that you believe in Jesus and that you be sanctified.[9,10] No one who rejects God's way of life will inherit the kingdom of God.[11,12] Hold on to your faith with a good conscience. Some have rejected its truth and have shipwrecked their faith.[13]

Keep your conscience clear so that you can shame those who speak maliciously against your good behavior.[14] Even a clear conscience does not make you innocent—the Lord is the Judge.[15] If you have doubts about whether or not you should do something, you are sinning if you go ahead and do it because you are not following your convictions.[16]

Many things are permissible but not beneficial or constructive.[17] If you sincerely believe some activity is permissible, but another believer believes it is wrong, then it is wrong for that person.[18] And if they are distressed by your practices, you are not acting in love if you persist in doing them. Do not let this ruin someone for whom Christ died.[19] You don't live just for yourself.[20] The kingdom of God is more than freedom of lifestyle. It is about living a life of goodness, peace, and joy.[21] You serve Christ by denying yourself in these matters, and this pleases God.[22]

Don't condemn other believers or look down on them for their choices.[23] You both will have to give a personal account to God.[24,25] Build each other up and aim for harmony in the church.[26] Don't tear apart the work of God over these issues.[27]

You must be considerate of those who are sensitive about marginal issues or have a greater vulnerability to their attraction.[28,29] You must be careful so that exercising your freedom in Christ does not encourage anyone to violate their own conscience and stumble in their faith walk.[30-33] It is better not to eat meat or drink wine or do anything else that might cause another believer to stumble.[34] This would be a sin against the believer and against Christ.[36]

You should help others to do what is right and build them up in the Lord.[37]

MARRIAGE

1	Gen. 1:26		30	1 Cor. 7:11
2	Gen. 1:27		31	1 Cor. 7:13
3	Gen. 2:18		32	1 Cor. 7:14
4	Gen. 2:25		33	1 Cor. 7:16
5	Gen. 2:8		34	Eph. 5:21
6	Gen. 2:9		35	Eph. 5:28
7	Gen. 1:28		36	Eph. 5:33
8	Gen. 1:28		37	Eph. 5:25
9	Gen. 2:22		38	Eph. 5:23
10	Gen. 2:23		39	1 Peter 3:7
11	Gen. 2:24		40	Eph. 5:22
12	Eph. 5:31		41	Eph. 5:24
13	Matt. 19:4		42	1 Peter 3:1
14	Matt. 19:5		43	Eph. 5:33
15	Eph. 5:31		44	1 Peter 3:2
16	Matt. 19:6		45	1 Peter 3:3
17	Prov. 5:18		46	1 Peter 3:4
18	1 Cor. 7:3		47	Eph. 5:32
19	1 Cor. 7:4		48	2 Cor. 6:14
20	1 Cor. 7:5			
21	Mal. 2:15			
22	Heb. 13:4			
23	Matt. 19:9			
24	Matt. 5:32			
25	Mark 10:11			
26	Mark 10:12			
27	Luke 16:18			
28	Ex. 20:14			
29	1 Cor. 7:10			

MARRIAGE

God created human beings in his own image—a reflection of his own nature.[1] He created them male and female in perfect relationship with each other.[2,4] He put them in a perfect environment and in charge of all of creation.[5,6] He instructed them to have children.[7,8]

God's creation mandate is for a man to leave his father and mother and be united to his wife, and they will become one flesh.[9-15] What God has joined together in this way must not be torn apart by anyone.[16]

Rejoice in the spouse of your youth—let him or her be a source of pleasure and blessing for you.[17] Fulfill your marital duties to each other; your bodies belong to each other.[18,19] Do not deprive each other of sexual satisfaction.[20] The Lord has made you one, so guard your heart and remain loyal to the spouse of your youth.[21] Marriage is to be honored by all and the marriage bed kept pure because God will judge the adulterer.[22]

Anyone who divorces his or her spouse—except for marital unfaithfulness—and marries another, commits adultery.[23-27] You must not commit adultery.[28] You must not divorce an unbelieving spouse unless they are unwilling to live with you.[29-33]

Spouses must submit to each other out of reverence for Christ.[34]

Husbands must love their wives as much as they love themselves and their own bodies.[35-36] Love your wife just like Christ loved the church and gave himself up for her.[37] You are to be her champion just as Christ is the Savior of the church.[38] Be considerate of your wife and treat her with respect so that nothing will hinder your prayers. She is an equal heir of God's gracious gift of life.[39]

Wives must submit to their husbands as to the Lord.[40] This relationship reflects the submission of the church to Christ.[41,42] You must respect your husband.[43] Let him see your purity and reverence.[44] Let your beauty come from your inner self and not makeup or fine clothes and jewelry.[45] The unfading beauty of a gentle and quiet spirit is of great worth in God's sight.[46]

Marriage is a reflection of the profound mystery of the relationship of Christ and his church.[47]

Do not marry an unbeliever. This is an unequal union. Light and darkness cannot coexist nor can righteousness and wickedness.[48]

MATURITY

1	1 Thess. 4:3		30	Phil. 3:9
2	Heb. 6:3		31	Phil. 3:10
3	1 Cor. 14:20		32	Phil. 3:11
4	Heb. 5:13		33	Phil. 3:12
5	Heb. 6:1		34	Phil. 3:13
6	Heb. 6:2		35	Phil. 3:14
7	Heb. 5:12		36	Phil. 3:15
8	1 Peter 2:1		37	Rom. 12:11
9	1 Peter 2:2		38	Phil. 2:12
10	2 Peter 3:18		39	2 Thess. 1:3
11	2 Peter 1:5		40	1 Tim. 4:12
12	2 Peter 1:6		41	James 1:2
13	2 Peter 1:7		42	James 1:3
14	2 Peter 1:8		43	James 1:4
15	Col. 1:10		44	Eph. 4:11
16	Rom. 12:2		45	Eph. 4:12
17	2 Tim. 2:15		46	Eph. 4:13
18	1 Thess. 5:17		47	Eph. 4:14
19	John 13:34		48	Eph. 4:15
20	Mark 16:15			
21	Heb. 5:14			
22	Eph. 3:17			
23	Eph. 3:16			
24	Eph. 3:18			
25	Eph. 3:19			
26	Phil. 1:9			
27	Phil. 1:10			
28	Phil. 1:11			
29	Phil. 3:8			

MATURITY

It is God's will that you become spiritually mature.[1,2] Do not be childish in your understanding of spiritual matters, like an infant who lives on milk and doesn't know how to do what is right.[3,4] Don't dwell on the basic teachings about Christ, like salvation, baptism, etc. going over them again and again.[5,6] Rather move on to solid food like issues of righteousness, which train you to distinguish good from evil.[7] Get rid of all evil behavior, deceit, jealousy, hypocrisy, and unkind speech so that you can grow into a full experience of your salvation.[8,9]

Grow in the grace and knowledge of your Lord and Savior, Jesus Christ.[10] Make every effort to add to your faith: goodness, knowledge, self-control, perseverance, godliness, kindness, and love.[11-13] These qualities are the marks of maturity in your life.[14] They will help you know God and be effective in doing his good work, pleasing him in every way.[15]

Do not conform to the patterns of this world, but let your worldview be transformed by the gospel.[16] Study the Scriptures so that you can correctly understand and apply them to your life.[17] Pray in every situation.[18] Love one another.[19] Share the good news of the gospel with everyone in your world.[20] These disciplines will give you the skill to recognize the difference between right and wrong.[21]

Let Christ dwell in your heart by faith.[22] Let his Spirit strengthen your inner being.[23] Understand and experience the enormous love of Christ, which surpasses knowledge and will lead to spiritual maturity.[24,25] Let your love for him increase in knowledge and insight so that you will be able to discern what is pure and blameless and develop a character that pleases God.[26,28]

Compare everything else in your life to the surpassing greatness of knowing Jesus as your Lord.[29] Through him, you gain a righteousness in God's sight that does not come from anything you can do, but only through faith in Christ.[30] Get to know him and the power of his resurrection along with the fellowship of his suffering.[31] Forget your past efforts and failures and press on to win the prize of your calling, your resurrection from the dead. This is a mature view of your life of faith.[32-36] Be zealous in your spiritual life as you serve the Lord.[37]

Work hard to show the application of your salvation in your life with deep reverence and fear.[38] Let your faith grow and your love for others increase.[39] Be an example in speech, life, love, faith, and purity.[40] Consider problems and trials an opportunity for joy because they challenge your faith and develop perseverance. Perseverance develops maturity making you complete and lacking nothing.[41-43]

Church pastors and teachers have the responsibility to equip God's people to do his work and build up the church. The goal of this is maturity, a unity of faith and knowledge that measures up to the full and complete standard of Christ.[44-46] No longer immature like a child, you should not be influenced by people who try to trick you with clever lies that only sound like the truth.[47]

You should grow in every way to be more and more like Christ.[48]

MEDITATION

1	Isa. 46:9	29	Ps. 77:11	57	Ps. 139:17
2	Isa. 46:10	30	1 Chron. 16:12	58	Ps. 139:18
3	Ps. 37:7	31	Psa. 105:5	59	Ps. 104:34
4	Zech. 2:13	32	Psa. 145:5	60	Ps. 19:14
5	Ps. 46:10	33	Ps. 119:15		
6	1 Kings 19:11	34	Isa. 55:9		
7	1 Kings 19:12	35	2 Tim. 2:8		
8	Ps. 48:9	36	Rom. 13:14		
9	Ps. 25:6	37	John 5:39		
10	Rom. 4:8	38	1 Tim. 4:13		
11	Ps. 139:17	39	Josh. 1:8		
12	Ps. 139:18	40	Ps. 1:2		
13	Ps. 4:4	41	Ps. 119:11		
14	Ps. 139:23	42	James 1:2		
15	Ps. 139:24	43	James 1:3		
16	Ps. 119:78	44	James 1:4		
17	Ps. 119:15	45	Ps. 119:67		
18	Ps. 119:23	46	Ps. 119:71		
19	Ps. 119:48	47	Phil. 4:8		
20	Ps. 119:48	48	Col. 3:1		
21	Ps. 119:97	49	Rom. 12:2		
22	Ps. 119:99	50	Ps. 77:4		
23	Num. 15:39	51	Ps. 77:5		
24	Num. 15:40	52	Ps. 77:6		
25	1 Thess. 2:12	53	Ps. 63:6		
26	Eccl. 12:1	54	Ps. 119:148		
27	Ps. 77:12	55	Ps. 1:2		
28	Ps. 143:5	56	Ps. 119:55		

MEDITATION

Meditate on God. He is supreme; there is no other.[1] His purposes will stand forever; he will do all that pleases him.[2] Be still before the Lord, and wait patiently for him to speak or act. This is the way to get to know God.[3-5] He often does not speak or act in spectacular ways—like tornadoes, earthquakes, or fires—but in a quiet and gentle whisper.[6,7]

Meditate on his unfailing love and mercy.[8-9] Contemplate the forgiveness of your sins and that they will never be counted against you.[10] Thoughts like these are very precious and calming and are so many in number that they outnumber the grains of sand on the beach.[11,12] Search your heart, and listen quietly for God when you cannot sleep.[13] Also let God search your heart to expose your anxious thoughts and anything that does not please him.[14,15]

Meditate on God's precepts, statutes, laws, and decrees, which are specific expressions of his will.[16-20] Meditate on them all day long. They will give you great insight.[21,22] Place reminders of them where you will see them so that you will not forget to obey them.[23,24] Think about living your life worthy of him.[25] Do this while you are young, before the troubles of life make you cynical.[26]

Meditate on the works, miracles, and mighty deeds God has done.[27-29] Think of the judgments he has pronounced.[30,31] They speak of his majesty and splendor.[32] Consider his way of doing things, which is much higher than yours.[33,34]

Meditate on Jesus Christ, whose resurrection is the crux of the gospel.[35] Immerse yourself in his love and goodness, and do not think about how to gratify the desires of your sinful nature.[36]

Meditate on the Scriptures. Focus on reading them. They tell of Jesus Christ and are the key to understanding eternal life.[37,38] Hold them near and dear.[39] Take delight in them day and night.[40] Hide them in your heart. They are your strongest defense against sin against God.[41]

Meditate in your suffering. Trials and tests develop perseverance, which leads to maturity of your faith.[42-44] They also encourage obedience and humility.[45-46]

Meditate on things that are true, noble, reputable, pure, compelling, gracious, lovely, admirable, excellent, or praiseworthy.[47] Fill your mind with the concerns of the kingdom of God.[48] He will use this to transform you into a new person by changing the way you think.[49]

Meditate on all these things during the night when you cannot sleep.[50-54] Think of your faithful God and all his wonderful promises.[55,56] You will fall asleep trying to remember and count them, and when you awaken, he will still be there with you.[57,58]

May your meditation be pleasing to God.[59,60]

MERCY

1   Mic. 6:8

2   Zech. 7:9

3   Matt. 5:7

4   Matt. 23:23

5   Hos. 6:6

6   Matt. 9:13

7   Luke 18:13

8   Titus 3:5

9   Eph. 2:4

10 Ps. 51:1

11 Isa. 55:7

12 Mic. 7:18

13 Rom. 12:1

14 Heb. 4:16

15 Luke 6:36

16 James 2:13

17 Jude 22

18 Jude 23

19 Rom. 12:8

MERCY

Love mercy, act justly, and walk humbly with your God. He requires this of you.[1] Show mercy and compassion to one another.[2] You are blessed if you are merciful and you will be shown mercy.[3]

It is hypocritical and not pleasing to God to make a show of keeping some parts of the law, but at the same time neglecting its more important matters: mercy, justice, and faithfulness.[4] God wants you to seek mercy and recognition of himself even more than he wants any sacrifice you could make.[5] He sent his Son to save sinners, not the righteous.[6]

Pray the humble sinner's prayer: "God, have mercy on me, a sinner."[7] He will save you because of his mercy, not because of any of the good things you may have done.[8] God's love for you is great and unfailing, rich in mercy and compassion. He will blot out your transgressions and freely pardon your every sin.[9-11] God delights in showing mercy.[12]

In view of God's mercy, offer your body as a living sacrifice, holy and pleasing to God. This is an act of true spiritual worship.[13] Now you can approach God with confidence and find his mercy and grace to help in your time of need.[14]

Be merciful just like God is merciful.[15] There will be no mercy for those who have not shown mercy to others. But if you have been merciful, God will be merciful when he judges you.[16]

Be merciful to those whose faith is wavering.[17] Rescue others by snatching them from the flames of judgment. Show mercy to still others, but do so with great caution, hating the sins that contaminate their lives.[18]

If your spiritual gift is showing mercy, do it cheerfully.[19]

MISSION

1   Luke 19:10

2   Luke 4:18

3   Luke 4:19

4   2 Cor. 5:18

5   2 Cor. 5:19

6   2 Cor. 5:20

7   Gal. 1:11

8   Rom. 1:16

9   1 Cor. 15:3

10   1 Cor. 15:4

11   Matt. 28:19

12   Matt. 28:20

13   Acts 1:8

14   2 Tim. 4:5

15   1 Peter 3:15

16   1 Peter 3:16

MISSION

Jesus came to seek and save those who are lost.[1] He came to preach the good news of the gospel to the poor, heal the brokenhearted, proclaim freedom for prisoners, restore sight for the blind and liberty for the oppressed. He began a new era in God's plan.[2,3]

God has given you the mission of bringing people back to himself.[4] The wonderful message of reconciliation is that because of Christ, God no longer counts our sins against us.[5] Be an ambassador for Christ. God makes his appeal to other people through you to come back to him.[6]

Do not be ashamed of your mission. This gospel you present to others is not based on human reasoning or made up by any mere person. It is God's powerful plan to save everyone who has faith in Jesus.[7,8] It tells us that Christ died for our sins; that he was buried; and that he was raised from the dead on the third day, exactly as predicted by the Scriptures.[9,10]

Go and make disciples in all the nations of the world. Baptize them in the name of the Father and the Son and the Holy Spirit. Teach these new disciples to obey all the commands Jesus has given.[11,12] The imperative, authority and power to do this come from Jesus and his Holy Spirit.[13]

Work at telling others the good news of the gospel, fully carrying out the mission God has given you.[14] Worship Christ as the Lord of your life and always be ready to explain your faith in a gentle and respectful way.

Live a good life to show that you belong to Christ.[15,16]

MOTIVATION

1	Eph. 2:4	29	Eph. 3:19	57	2 Cor. 5:11
2	John 3:16	30	2 Cor. 5:15	58	Heb. 11:6
3	Eph. 2:5	31	Phil. 2:6	59	Heb. 11:1
4	Matt. 22:37	32	Phil. 2:7	60	Heb. 10:35
5	Deut. 6:5	33	Phil. 2:8	61	Titus 2:11
6	Deut. 10:12	34	2 Cor. 5:9	62	Col. 3:1
7	Deut. 11:1	35	1 John 3:2	63	Eph. 4:1
8	Deut. 11:13	36	1 John 3:3	64	Col. 1:10
9	Deut. 11:22	37	2 Cor. 7:1	65	1 John 2:17
10	Deut. 19:9	38	2 Peter 1:5	66	1 Thess. 4:1
11	Deut. 30:16	39	Titus 2:13	67	2 Peter 1:3
12	Deut. 30:16	40	Titus 3:7	68	2 Peter 1:4
13	Deut. 30:20	41	2 Tim. 2:11	69	Eph. 5:10
14	Josh. 22:5	42	John 8:51		
15	Josh. 23:11	43	John 10:28		
16	Matt. 22:37	44	Heb. 6:18		
17	Mark 12:30	45	Heb. 6:19		
18	Luke 10:27	46	2 Cor. 5:10		
19	Matt. 22:38	47	Jer. 17:10		
20	1 John 5:3	48	Rom. 14:12		
21	John 14:15	49	Eph. 6:8		
22	John 15:10	50	Col. 3:24		
23	John 14:21	51	Matt. 16:27		
24	1 John 5:2	52	Col. 3:24		
25	1 John 4:21	53	1 Peter 1:4		
26	Matt. 22:39	54	Rom. 8:17		
27	Rom. 12:1	55	1 Peter 1:17		
28	Rom. 12:2	56	2 Peter 3:14		

MOTIVATION

God's love for you is greater than you can comprehend.[1] He gave his only Son so that you can inherit eternal life, even though you don't deserve it.[2,3] You must love him with all your heart, all your soul, all your mind, and all your strength. There is no greater motivation for your life.[4-19]

Genuine love for God must motivate you to obey his commandments.[20-24] The second greatest of these commandments is to love those who are around you.[25,26]

God's mercy for you should motivate you to offer yourself to him; body and mind. This is pleasing to God and will transform your whole life so that you can understand and do his will.[27,28]

Jesus's love for you is too great to fully understand, but it should motivate you to live your life for others.[29-30] He was humble and obedient to the point of death.[31-33] So make it your goal to please him in all you do.[34]

The blessed hope you have should motivate you to live a life of knowledge, faith, purity, and moral excellence.[35-38] Your hope is in the return of your Savior, Jesus Christ, and your secure and endless life with him.[39-43] Your hope is based on the unchanging character of God and is a strong and trustworthy anchor for your soul.[44,45]

Judgment day will come when you will have to appear before Christ in his courtroom to be judged on the basis of your works.[46,47] You will have to give a personal account of your life to God.[48] God has promised an inheritance, a rich reward to those who have loved and served him.[49-54] This should motivate you to live your life in reverent fear of him, persuading others by your godly life to do the same.[55-57]

Without faith, it is impossible to please God.[58] Faith is the confidence that our hope is going to become a reality.[59] Do not throw away this motivation; it will be richly rewarded.[60]

God's grace in bringing you salvation should motivate you to set your mind on heavenly issues rather than earthly ones.[61,62] Live your life worthy of the Lord and please him in every way.[63-66]

God gives you everything you need to live a godly life as you come to know him. He is powerful, glorious, and excellent and has made promises that enable you to share his divine nature and escape the corruption that is in the world caused by human desires.[67,68]

Carefully determine what pleases God, and then do it.[69]

MURDER

1   Ex. 20:13

2   Deut. 5:17

3   Prov. 6:16

4   Gen. 9:5

5   Gen. 9:6

6   Num. 35:31

7   Num. 35:30

8   Num. 35:6

9   Num. 35:12

10   Matt. 5:21

11   Matt. 5:22

12   1 John 3:15

13   John 8:44

14   Matt. 15:19

15   Mark 7:21

16   Rom. 1:29

17   Rom. 13:9

MURDER

You must not commit murder.[1,2] Murder is detestable to God; he hates it.[3]

Anyone who murders another human being must die. His life must be taken away by human hands. This is because God made human beings in his own image, and they are of supreme value to him.[4,5] There is no other acceptable punishment.[6] Evidence must always be presented by more than one witness.[7]

Cities of refuge are to be established to protect persons who have accidently killed someone.[8,9]

Don't curse another human being. Don't call anyone an idiot or any other derogatory name. Don't even be angry with them. Jesus included these actions all together with murder.[10,11]

Hate is the moral equivalent of murder.[12] It originates with the Devil and resides in the human heart.[13-16]

All of the commandments, including "do not murder," are summed up in this one rule: "Love your neighbor as yourself."[17]

NEIGHBORS

1   Rom. 13:9

2   Gal. 5:14

3   Mark 12:31

4   James 2:8

5   Ex. 20:16

6   Deut. 5:20

7   Prov. 24:28

8   Ex. 20:17

9   Prov. 3:29

10   Prov. 22:28

11   Lev. 19:13

12   Deut. 22:1

13   Ex. 22:14

14   Prov. 3:28

15   Luke 14:12

16   Deut. 27:24

17   Prov. 25:9

18   Lev. 19:16

19   Prov. 14:21

20   Ps. 15:3

21   Ps. 15:1

22   1 Peter 2:12

23   James 4:12

24   Luke 6:31

25   Luke 10:29

NEIGHBORS

Love your neighbor as yourself. Along with loving God, this summarizes all the commandments and is the second greatest of them all.[1-3] It is the "royal law" of Scripture.[4]

Do not testify falsely or without cause against your neighbor.[5,6] Don't lie about them.[7]

You must not covet anything that is your neighbor's: spouse, house, property, or possession.[8]

Do not plot harm against your neighbor.[9] Don't cheat your neighbor by moving an ancient boundary marker.[10] Don't rob or defraud your neighbor.[11] If you find your neighbor's lost property, take it back to them.[12] If you borow your neighbor's property and damage or lose it, you must make full restitution.[13]

Do not delay meeting your neighbor's need when you have the means to do so.[14] Don't just invite your rich neighbors when you give a party because they will invite you back and that will be your only reward.[15]

Do not attack your neighbor in secret.[16] Don't betray another person's secret when arguing with your neighbor.[17] Do not stand idly by when your neighbor's life is threatened.[18]

Do not belittle your neighbor. It is a sin.[19] Refuse to gossip about your neighbors or your friends.[20] It shows pride and conceit and hinders your ability to worship God.[21]

Be careful to live properly among your unbelieving neighbors so that they will see your honorable behavior.[22] Do not be judgmental of your neighbor—God alone has that right.[23]

Do to others as you would like them to do to you.[24]

And who is your neighbor?[25]

OATH/VOW

1   Zech. 8:16

2   Eph. 4:25

3   Zech. 8:17

4   Lev. 19:12

5   Ex. 20:7

6   Ps. 24:4

7   Matt. 5:33

8   Matt. 5:34

9   Matt. 5:35

10   Matt. 5:36

11   Matt. 5:37

12   James 5:12

13   Heb. 6:16

14   Ps. 76:11

15   Deut. 23:23

16   Num. 30:2

17   Eccl. 5:4

18   Deut. 23:21

19   Eccl. 5:5

20   Deut. 23:22

21   Deut. 23:23

OATH/VOW

You must tell the truth to each other.[1,2] Do not scheme against each other by taking an oath of truth when you know it is a lie. The Lord hates this.[3]

Do not profane the name of God by using it to swear a false oath.[4] You must not misuse the name of the Lord your God in this way.[5] Those who swear what is false cannot stand in the presence of God.[6]

Don't say anything you don't mean. If you intend honesty, there is no need for an oath and you should not swear one.[7-10] Simply let your "Yes" mean yes and your "No" mean no.[11,12] A written contract puts an end to all argument.[13]

Make vows to the Lord.[14] Since this is voluntary, you must be very careful to do everything you promise to the Lord.[15,16] Do not delay in fulfilling your vow; God has no pleasure in fools. He will certainly demand it of you and you will be guilty of sin if you delay.[17,18]

It is better not to make a vow than to make one and not fulfill it.[19] There is no guilt in not making a vow.[20]

You must be sure to do whatever you say you are going to do because you have made your vow freely to the Lord with your own mouth.[21]

OBEDIENCE

1	1 John 5:3	28	Deut. 6:8
2	1 John 2:3	29	Deut. 6:9
3	1 John 3:24	30	Num. 15:40
4	Acts 5:32	31	Matt 7.21
5	John 14:21	32	Matt. 19:17
6	John 14:23	33	Rom. 2:13
7	John 15:10	34	Rom. 3:20
8	1 John 2:5	35	Rom. 1:17
9	1 Peter 1:22	36	James 1:22
10	Phil. 2:12	37	Luke 11:28
11	John 14:15	38	Acts 4:19
12	John 14:24	39	Acts 5:29
13	Heb. 5:9	40	Eph. 6:1
14	Ps. 119:4	41	Col. 3:20
15	Lev. 18:4	42	Col. 3:22
16	Lev. 18:5	43	Eph. 6:5
17	Deut. 6:5	44	Eph. 6:6
18	Lev. 19:18	45	Heb. 13:17
19	Matt. 22:37	46	Matt. 28:19
20	Matt. 22:38	47	Matt. 28:20
21	Matt. 22:39		
22	Matt. 22:40		
23	Mark 12:30		
24	Mark 12:31		
25	Luke 10:27		
26	Deut. 6:6		
27	Deut. 6:7		

OBEDIENCE

Obedience to God's commandments is the way you show that you love him.[1] You can be sure you know God if you do this.[2] You live in God, and he lives in you when you obey his commandments. He gives his Holy Spirit as proof to those who obey him.[3,4]

Obedience is an essential part of loving God and experiencing his love in your life.[5-7] God's love is evident in your life when you obey his word.[8] You will also have sincere and deep love for others in your Christian community. Obeying the truth has a purifying effect on your life.[9] Obedience is key to working out the implications of salvation in your own life.[10]

You prove that you love Jesus by obeying his commandments.[11] If you do not obey them, you are showing that you do not really love him.[12] He is the source of eternal salvation for all who obey him.[13]

The Lord has laid down precepts and commandments, which must be fully obeyed.[14-16] The two most important of these are to love the Lord with all your heart, soul, mind, and strength, and to love your neighbor as much as you love yourself.[17-25] Constantly remind yourself of his commandments by keeping them on your heart and mind. Impress them on your children. Talk about them when you are at home. Place reminders in places where they will often be seen.[26-29] They will help you remember to obey all the commandments of God and your commitment to him.[30]

You must know and obey the commandments of the Lord if you want to enter the kingdom of heaven.[31,32] Those who merely know about the word of God are not righteous.[33] Only those who obey it can be righteous, and that comes by faith.[34,35] Don't just listen to God's word. You must do what it says. Otherwise, you are only fooling yourself.[36] Those who both hear and obey the word of God are blessed.[37]

Obedience to the laws of God is more important than obedience to the laws of man.[38,39]

Children must obey their parents because this right and pleases the Lord.[40,41] Employees must obey their employers, not just when they are watching, but with a sincere heart just as they would obey Christ and do the will of God from the heart.[42-44] Obey your spiritual leaders so that their work will be a joy and not a burden.[45]

Teach new disciples of Christ to obey all his commands.[46,47]

ONE ANOTHER

1	John 13:34	30	Eph. 5:19
2	1 John 3:23	31	Heb. 10:24
3	1 John 4:7	32	Heb. 10:25
4	1 John 4:11	33	1 John 1:7
5	1 John 3:11	34	1 Peter 4:9
6	John 13:35	35	Rom. 16:16
7	Rom. 12:10	36	2 Cor. 13:12
8	1 Peter 1:22	37	1 Cor. 16:20
9	1 John 4:12	38	1 Peter 5:14
10	Eph. 4:32	39	Matt. 22:37
11	James 5:16	40	Matt. 22:38
12	Col. 3:13	41	Matt. 22:39
13	Gal. 6:2		
14	Phil. 2:3		
15	Eph. 4:2		
16	Rom. 12:16		
17	Rom. 12:10		
18	John 13:14		
19	Gal. 5:13		
20	1 Peter 4:10		
21	1 Peter 3:8		
22	Rom. 15:7		
23	James 4:11		
24	Eph. 5:21		
25	1 Peter 5:5		
26	1 Cor. 1:10		
27	Heb. 3:13		
28	1 Thess. 5:11		
29	Col. 3:16		

ONE ANOTHER

Love one another. Love just like Jesus loves you.[1,2] This kind of love comes from God and compels us to love one another.[3-5] Loving one another like this will show the world that you are a follower of Jesus Christ.[6] Be devoted to one another in brotherly love.[7] Let it be sincere, deep, and from your heart.[8] Since no one has ever seen God, loving one another in this way shows that he lives in you and makes you a tangible expression of his love.[9]

Be kind and compassionate to one another and forgive each other just as God has forgiven you because of Christ.[10] Confess your sins to each other and pray for each other.[11] Bear with each other and forgive whatever grievances you may have against one another. Forgive as the Lord has forgiven you.[12] Carry each other's burdens and in this way fulfill the law of Christ.[13]

Be completely humble and gentle, bearing with one another in love.[14] Do not be proud, but be willing to associate with people of low position. Do not be conceited.[15] Don't be selfish or try to impress others. Be humble, thinking of others as better than yourself.[16] Be devoted to one another and honor one another above yourself.[17] Follow Jesus's example of humble service and serve one another in love.[18,19] Use whatever gift you have received to serve others as a faithful minister of God's grace.[20]

Live in harmony with one another and be sympathetic, compassionate, and humble.[21] Accept one another just like Jesus has accepted you because this brings praise to God.[22] Don't speak poorly or be critical of one another as it is judgmental and brings dishonor on the gospel.[23] Submit to one another out of reverence for Christ.[24,25] Come to agreement with one another so that there are no divisions within the church.[26]

Encourage and build one another up daily so that no one will be hardened by sin's deceitfulness.[27,28] Let the rich message and word of Christ fill your life so that you can teach and counsel one another with all his wisdom.[29] Use the words of psalms and hymns as you speak with one another and sing and make music in your heart to the Lord.[30] Think about ways to motivate one another to acts of love and good works.[31]

Don't neglect meeting together with one another.[32] In this way, you have fellowship with others as you walk in God's light.[33]

Offer hospitality to one another cheerfully.[30] Greet one another with a holy kiss.[34-38]

Love one another as much as you love yourself. It is just as important as loving God.[39-41]

PATIENCE

1	Eph. 4:2
2	Col. 3:12
3	Gal. 5:22
4	Gal. 5:23
5	Col. 1:10
6	Ps. 37:7
7	Rom. 2:4
8	Rom. 9:22
9	2 Peter 3:9
10	Ps. 37:8
11	Ps. 37:9
12	James 5:7
13	James 5:8
14	Rom. 2:6
15	Rom. 2:7
16	Rom. 12:12
17	James 1:2
18	James 1:3
19	2 Cor. 1:6
20	James 5:10
21	Heb. 12:1
22	2 Tim. 4:2
23	1 Thess. 5:14
24	James 5:9
25	Prov. 19:11
26	Prov. 14:29
27	Prov. 15:18
28	Prov. 25:15
29	1 Cor. 13:4

PATIENCE

Be patient and gentle with each other. Always make allowances for each other's faults.[1] God's people must be known for their patience, kindness, compassion, and humility.[2]

Patience is one evidence that the Holy Spirit is working in your life to develop other characteristics that are pleasing to God: love, joy, peace, kindness, goodness, faithfulness, gentleness, and self-control. These virtues help you live a life pleasing to him.[3-5]

Be patient with God and wait for him to act.[6] Do not show contempt for his patience by thinking he does not care about suffering and evil.[7] He tolerates them for now because he is giving everyone time to come to repentance.[8,9] So do not be anxious or angry about this perceived unfairness because it only leads you to sin.[10] Evil persons will be punished in the end, and you will receive an inheritance in heaven because you have placed your hope in the Lord.[11]

Be patient and stand firm while you wait for the Lord's return, which will happen at any time.[12,13] He will judge everyone according to what they have done in this life and grant eternal life to those who have patiently sought the glory, honor, and immortality that God offers.[14,15]

Be patient when the going is tough.[16] In fact, be happy when you face trials of all kinds because they are a test of faith and develop patient endurance.[17-19] Remember the prophets of old as examples of patience in the face of suffering and affliction.[20]

Run with patience and perseverance the race of life set out for you. There is a great crowd watching and cheering for you.[21]

Be prepared to explain the Scriptures whenever you have opportunity, using them to correct, rebuke, and encourage others with great patience and careful instruction.[22]

Be patient with everyone.[23] Don't grumble against each other or you will be judged.[24]

A wise person is patient and overlooks an offense.[25] A patient person shows great understanding and calms a quarrel, but a hot-tempered person is foolish and stirs up trouble.[26,27] Patience is persuasive.[28]

Love is patient.[29]

PEACE

1	Isa. 9:6	30	2 Peter 3:14
2	Luke 1:35	31	Matt. 5:9
3	Luke 1:31	32	Matt. 5:9
4	Matt. 1:23	33	James 3:18
5	Isa. 9:7	34	Eph. 6:13
6	Col. 3:15	35	Eph. 6:14
7	John 14:27	36	Eph. 6:15
8	John 16:33	37	Heb. 12:11
9	Rom. 8:38	38	Ps. 122:6
10	Rom. 8:39	39	Ps. 122:9
11	Phil. 4:6		
12	Phil. 4:7		
13	Isa. 26:3		
14	Rom. 15:13		
15	Rom. 5:1		
16	Acts 10:36		
17	2 Tim. 2:22		
18	Ps. 34:14		
19	1 Peter 3:11		
20	Rom. 8:6		
21	Gal. 5:22		
22	Gal. 5:23		
23	Heb. 12:14		
24	Rom. 12:18		
25	1 Thess. 5:13		
26	Mark 9:50		
27	Rom. 14:19		
28	Eph. 4:3		
29	Rom. 14:17		

PEACE

The Prince of Peace was born into the world as a baby boy.[1] He is the Son of God, also called the Mighty God, Everlasting Father, Wonderful Counselor, and Immanuel (God with us).[2-4] The peace he brings, peace with God, will never end.[5]

Let the peace of Christ rule in your heart.[6] Do not let your heart be troubled, and do not be afraid.[7] You can expect to have trouble in this world, but he has overcome the world.[8] Nothing can separate you from his love.[9,10]

Pray about everything and don't worry about anything. Then you will experience the peace of God, which far exceeds anything anyone else can understand. Prayer is the antidote for anxiety. It will guard your heart and mind as you live your life for Jesus. Present the deepest requests of your heart to God in sincere petition with a thankful heart.[11,12]

Keep your mind steadfastly fixed on God and you will be filled with perfect peace because you have put your trust in him.[13,14] You have peace with God if you have faith in his Son, Jesus Christ who is Lord of all.[15,16]

Pursue peace and righteousness and faith and love with a pure heart.[17-19] Let your mind be controlled by God's Spirit and you will experience true life and peace.[20] He will also produce character traits in you that please God: peace, love, joy, patience, kindness, goodness, faithfulness, gentleness, and self-control.[21,22]

Spare no effort to live in peace with everyone.[23-26] Do whatever leads to peace and mutual edification.[27] Work hard to keep unity in God's Spirit through the bond of peace.[28] After all, the kingdom of God is about more than what you eat or drink but is about living a life of goodness and peace and joy.[29] So make every effort to be found spotless, blameless, and at peace with each other.[30]

Work for peace, and you will experience God's blessing.[31,32] Peacemakers do the hard work of getting along with each other; treating each other with dignity and honor; and developing a healthy, robust community that lives right with God.[33]

Peace that comes from the gospel is an important defense God has given you in resisting the devil in a time of temptation. Make sure to use it.[34-36.]

Endure the unpleasantness and pain of adversity or discipline because it produces righteousness and peace for those who have been trained by it.[37]

Pray for the peace of Jerusalem for the sake of the house of the Lord.[38,39]

PERSECUTION

1	Matt. 5:44
2	Rom.12:14
3	Matt. 5:12
4	Luke 6:23
5	Luke 6:22
6	Matt. 5:11
7	Matt. 5:10
8	1 Peter 4:12
9	1 Peter 4:13
10	Heb. 12:3
11	Heb. 12:2
12	1 Peter 4:16
13	1 Peter 4:14
14	1 Peter 4:19
15	Rev. 14:12
16	James 1:12
17	Matt. 5:39
18	Luke 12:4
19	Luke 12:5
20	John 16:33
21	Rom. 8:38

PERSECUTION

Pray for those who persecute you.[1] Bless those who persecute you, and do not curse them.[2]

Be very happy when you suffer persecution, because then you will experience God's blessing.[3,4] A great reward awaits you in heaven when people persecute you, lie about you, hate you, exclude you, mock you, or curse you as evil because you follow Jesus.[5,6] The kingdom of heaven belongs to those who are persecuted for doing right.[7]

Do not be surprised, as if it is something strange, when you have to endure painful persecution.[8] Instead, be happy that in this way, you participate now in the sufferings of Christ and will be ecstatic when he returns.[9]

Think of Jesus who endured persecution and opposition from sinful men.[10] Focus and fix your eyes on him, the author and perfecter of our faith, who endured the cross, scorning its shame for the joy of reconciling us to God.[11]

Do not be ashamed if you suffer persecution or are insulted because you follow Jesus Christ. Instead, praise God that you bear his name and that his Spirit rests on you.[12,13] Commit yourself to your faithful Creator and continue to do good, maintaining your faith in Jesus.[14,15] Persevere under your trials, and when you have stood the test of time, you will receive the Crown of Life, which God has promised to those who love him.[16]

Do not resist an evil person. If someone strikes you on the right cheek, turn the other one also.[17] Do not be afraid of anyone who can kill the body only, but fear the one who also has the power to throw you into hell.[18,19]

Expct persecution here on earth, but be encouraged by the fact that Jesus has overcome the world.[20] No persecution or any other calamity can ever separate you from the love God has for you.[21]

PERSEVERANCE

1	Eph. 6:18		28	Gal. 6:9
2	Rom. 12:12		29	Heb. 6:11
3	Matt. 7:7		30	Rom. 2:7
4	2 Peter 3:8		31	Rom. 12:12
5	2 Peter 3:9		32	Rom. 5:3
6	Heb. 10:23		33	Rom. 5:4
7	2 Thess. 2:15		34	James 1:3
8	1 Cor. 16:13		35	James 1:4
9	2 Cor. 1:21		36	Heb. 12:7
10	2 Cor. 1:24		37	Heb. 10:36
11	Rom. 11:20		38	James 1:12
12	1 Cor. 10:12			
13	1 Tim. 6:12			
14	Heb. 12:2			
15	Heb. 12:3			
16	1 Tim. 6:11			
17	2 Peter 1:5			
18	2 Peter 1:6			
19	2 Peter 1:7			
20	2 Peter 1:8			
21	Heb. 12:1			
22	1 Cor. 9:24			
23	Phil. 3:14			
24	Heb. 12:3			
25	2 Thess. 3:13			
26	2 Thess. 3:13			
27	Rom. 12:11			

PERSEVERANCE

Persevere in your prayers.[1,2] Ask and keep on asking, and it will be given to you; seek and keep seeking, and you will find; knock and keep knocking, and the door will be opened to you.[3]

Remember that with the Lord, one day is like a thousand years and a thousand years is like one day.[4] He is not slow in keeping his promises in the way we normally think. He is patiently waiting for everyone to come to repentance; not wanting anyone to perish.[5]

Persevere in holding on to the hope you profess in Jesus and stand firm in the faith.[6,7] Your faith in God is what makes you strong to stand, but be on your guard so that you don't fall.[8-12]

Fight the good fight of faith, and fix your eyes on Jesus who persevered in the face of evil men and is a role model for you.[13-15]

Persevere in the pursuit of a righteous and godly life.[16] Your character should show perseverance, knowledge, faith, gentleness, kindness, goodness, and love.[17-19] These qualities will make you effective and productive in your knowledge of the Lord.[20]

Persevere in running the race that is set out for you. Run to win! Get rid of everything that tangles you up and slows you down. Remember that there is a large crowd cheering for you.[21,22] Persevere to reach the finish line and receive the prize of heaven to which Jesus is calling you.[23] Think of Jesus who persevered under great opposition and you will not grow weary and lose heart.[24]

Never grow tired of or lose your zeal for doing what is right.[25-27] Persist with diligence in doing good works to the very end and you will receive the gift of eternal life.[28-30]

Be patient when you are not doing or feeling well, because suffering produces perseverance.[31,32] Perseverance and endurance produce a mature character, which strengthens your confident hope of salvation.[33-35] Endure hardship as discipline from God.[36]

Persevere in faith so that when you have done the will of God, you will receive the reward he has promised to all those who love him.[37,38]

PLEASING GOD

1	Heb. 11:6	30	Josh. 22:5	59	1 Peter 2:20
2	Rom. 8:8	31	Deut. 11:1	60	1 Peter 4:19
3	Gal. 6:8	32	Deut. 11:22	61	1 Tim. 2:1
4	Matt. 7:21	33	1 Kings 2:3	62	1 Tim. 2:2
5	Matt. 19:17	34	Deut. 30:10	63	1 Tim. 2:3
6	1 John 2:17	35	Deut. 12:28	64	Rom. 15:1
7	Deut. 6:5	36	Mic. 6:8	65	Rom. 14:17
8	Matt. 22:37	37	Deut. 30:20	66	Rom. 14:18
9	Matt. 22:38	38	Mic. 6:7	67	Col. 3:20
10	Matt. 22:39	39	Ps. 40:6	68	1 Tim. 5:4
11	Matt. 22:40	40	Heb. 10:6	69	1 Tim. 5:4
12	Mark 12:30	41	Heb. 10:8	70	Ps. 104:34
13	Mark 12:31	42	Ps. 51:17	71	Ps. 19:14
14	Luke 10:27	43	Rom. 12:1		
15	Ps. 115:3	44	Rom. 12:2		
16	Ps. 135:6	45	Heb. 12:28		
17	Job 23:13	46	Ps. 69:30		
18	Isa. 42:21	47	Ps. 69:31		
19	Ezek. 18:23	48	Prov. 21:3		
20	Matt. 3:17	49	Heb. 13:16		
21	Matt. 17:5	50	1 Chron. 29:17		
22	Mark 1:11	51	Prov. 20:23		
23	Luke 3:22	52	Prov. 15:26		
24	Luke 3:22	53	Eph. 5:10		
25	Isa. 53:10	54	Phil. 2:13		
26	Col. 1:19	55	Col. 1:9		
27	1 Cor. 1:21	56	Col. 1:10		
28	Deut. 10:12	57	Eph. 5:2		
29	Deut. 30:16	58	1 Peter 2:19		

PLEASING GOD

Without faith, it is impossible to please God.[1] Those controlled by their sinful nature cannot please God.[2,3] Not everyone who says, "Lord, Lord" will enter the kingdom of heaven; only those who actually do the will of God.[4-5] The person who pleases God will live forever.[6]

Love the Lord your God with all your heart and all your mind and all your soul and all your strength. Love your neighbor as yourself. These are the two greatest commandments of all and summarize the way to please God.[7-14]

God is in heaven and does whatever pleases him.[15-17] It pleased him to make his law great and glorious.[18] He does not take pleasure in the death of the wicked, but is pleased when they turn from their ways.[19] He is very pleased with his Son, Jesus Christ, who was made to bear the sin of the world.[20-25] God is pleased to have him be the full expression of himself.[26] He is pleased to save all those who put their faith in his Son.[27]

God requires that you fear him and live in a way that pleases him, loving and serving him with all your heart and soul.[28-29] Carefully obey his commandments at all times, walk in all his ways, hold fast to him, and serve him with all your heart and soul.[30-34] In this way, you will be doing what is good and pleasing to God.[35] He requires you to act justly, love mercy, and to walk humbly with your God.[36] Choose to love the Lord and commit yourself firmly to him. This is the key to a life that pleases God.[37]

God does not desire nor is he pleased with sacrifice or anything you can give him, even though he required it in days past.[38-41] The sacrifice he wants is a broken and contrite heart.[42] Offer your body as a living sacrifice to God, a spiritual act of worship that pleases him. Let him transform you into a new person by changing the way you think and you will learn how to please God.[43-44]

Please God by worshiping him with holy fear and awe.[45] Please him with praise and thankful songs.[46-47] Please him by doing what is right.[48] Please him by doing good deeds and sharing with others.[49] Please him with purity and integrity.[50-52]

Carefully determine what pleases the Lord.[53] He will give you the desire and the power to do what pleases him.[54] He will fill you with the knowledge of his will through all spiritual wisdom and understanding so that the way you live will honor and please the Lord.[55-56] Live a life of love, following the example of Christ who was pleasing to God.[57]

God is pleased when you do what you know is right, and patiently endure unfair treatment for doing so.[58-60] Pray for those in authority over you because this is pleasing to God.[61-63] Share in the failures of those weaker than you in faith and defer to their conscience in controversial issues. You serve Christ in this way and please God.[64-66]

Children are to obey their parents because this pleases God.[67] They should also put their religion into practice by taking care of them in their old age because this also pleases God.[68-69]

Make the words of your mouth and the meditation of your heart pleasing to God, your Rock and your Redeemer.[70-71]

POVERTY

1   Deut. 15:11

2   Deut. 15:10

3   Deut. 15:9

4   Prov. 17:5

5   Prov. 19:17

6   Prov. 22:22

7   Deut. 15:7

8   Deut. 15:8

9   Zech. 7:10

10   Deut. 24:14

11   Mal. 3:5

12   Deut. 24:19

13   Deut. 24:21

14   Lev. 19:10

15   Ex. 22:22

16   Ex. 22:23

17   Ezek. 22:29

18   Isa. 10:2

19   Isa. 58:6

20   Isa. 58:7

21   Luke 3:11

22   Matt. 6:3

23   Matt. 5:3

POVERTY

There will always be poor people in your world. Be openhanded toward them.[1] Give generously to them without a grudging heart.[2] Be careful not to harbor any wicked thoughts that you can defraud them by some "legal" scheme.[3]

Whoever mocks the poor shows contempt for their Maker and whoever gloats over disaster will be punished.[4]

He who is kind to the poor lends to the Lord and will receive a reward.[5]

Do not exploit the poor because they are needy or crush the poor in court.[6] Do not be hardhearted toward the poor, but rather be compassionate and freely donate whatever is needed.[7,8] Do not oppress the poor nor think evil of them.[9]

Do not take advantage of an employee who is poor and needy.[10] Otherwise you will be accountable on Judgment Day for defrauding them of their wages.[11]

When you are harvesting your crops, leave some for the poor and needy.[12-14]

Do not take advantage of a widow or an orphan.[15] If you do, God will hear their cry and be angry.[16] Do not oppress anyone who is poor nor deprive them of their rights.[17,18]

Share your food with the hungry and provide poor wanderers with shelter and clothing. The person who has extra clothing should share with anyone who has none and the person who has food should do the same.[19] This is the kind of religious practice that pleases God.[20-21]

When you give to the poor, do not let your left hand know what your right hand is doing.[22]

God blesses those who are poor and satisfies their need for him.[23]

PRAISE

1	Ps. 100:4	29	Ps. 52:9	57	Heb. 13:15
2	Ps. 100:1	30	Ps. 92:1	58	Eph. 2:10
3	Ps. 100:2	31	Ps. 135:3	59	Matt. 5:16
4	Isa. 42:10	32	Ps. 66:2	60	Ps. 150:6
5	Jer. 20:13	33	Ps. 72:18		
6	Ps. 95:6	34	Ps. 66:3		
7	Ps. 95:7	35	Ps. 66:5		
8	Ps. 106:1	36	Ps. 96:3		
9	Jer. 33:11	37	Ps. 26:7		
10	Ps. 107:1	38	Ps. 105:2		
11	Ps. 136:1	39	Ps. 103:22		
12	Ps. 71:22	40	Ps. 89:5		
13	Ps. 117:2	41	Ps. 89:5		
14	Ps. 100:5	42	Ps. 148:3		
15	Lam. 3:22	43	Ps. 148:4		
16	Lam. 3:23	44	Ps. 148:5		
17	Ps. 48:1	45	Ps. 148:6		
18	Ps. 145:3	46	Ps. 148:7		
19	Ps. 150:2	47	Ps. 148:8		
20	Ps. 104:1	48	Ps. 148:9		
21	Ps. 33:1	49	Ps. 148:10		
22	Ps. 96:4	50	Ps. 148:11		
23	Ps. 103:1	51	Ps. 148:12		
24	Ps. 97:12	52	Ps. 148:13		
25	Ps. 99:3	53	Ps. 139:14		
26	Ps. 148:13	54	Ps. 71:6		
27	Ps. 47:7	55	1 Peter 1:3		
28	Ps. 146:10	56	Rev. 5:12		

PRAISE

Come into the presence of the Lord with praise and thanksgiving. Shout for joy to the Lord, all the earth. Worship him with gladness and joyful songs.[1-5] Bow down and kneel in worship before the Lord, your Maker.[6,7]

Praise the Lord and give him thanks because he is good, and his love endures forever.[8-11] His faithfulness continues through all generations.[12-14] His compassions never fail; they are new every morning. Great is his faithfulness.[15,16]

The Lord is worthy of praise. No one can comprehend his surpassing geatness.[17-19] His splendor and majesty are very great.[20] It is fitting for the righteous to praise him.[21] He is to be feared above all others.[22]

Praise the holy name of the Lord.[23,24] His name is great and awesome.[25] His name alone is exalted above the earth and heavens.[26] He is King of all the earth and reigns forever.[27,28] Put your hope in his name, and praise him because he is good.[29] Praise the Lord with music; sing glorious praises to his name.[30-32]

Praise the Lord who alone does miraculous and marvelous things.[33] His power and deeds are awesome on your behalf.[34-38] His works praise him.[39] The heavens declare the glory of God; the skies proclaim the work of his hands.[40,41] All of creation brings praise to God.[42-52] Praise him because you are one of his works, fearfully and wonderfully made, starting in your mother's womb.[53,54]

Praise God, the Father of our Lord Jesus Christ. Because of his great mercy, he has given you a new birth and a living hope through the resurrection of Jesus Christ from the dead.[55] He is worthy to receive glory and honor and power and praise.[56] Offer a continuous sacrifice of praise to God by confessing his name.[57]

You have been given this new life so that you can do good works.[58] Let them be visible so that others can see them and praise your heavenly Father.[59]

Let everything that has breath praise the Lord.[60]

PRAYER, Part 1

1	Matt. 6:9	30	Mark 14:38
2	Matt. 6:10	31	James 1:6
3	Matt. 6:11	32	Mark 11:24
4	Matt. 6:12	33	Luke 11:9
5	Matt. 6:13		
6	Matt. 6:5		
7	Matt. 6:6		
8	Matt. 6:7		
9	Matt. 6:8		
10	Mark 11:25		
11	James 4:8		
12	Heb. 10:22		
13	Ps. 134:2		
14	Jer. 33:3		
15	Ps. 37:7		
16	Ps. 55:22		
17	John 16:24		
18	John 14:6		
19	John 14:13		
20	John 15:5		
21	Eph. 3:12		
22	Heb. 4:16		
23	Heb. 4:15		
24	Heb. 4:14		
25	Col. 4:2		
26	1 Peter 4:7		
27	Rom. 12:12		
28	1 Thess. 5:17		
29	1 Tim. 2:8		

PRAYER, Part 1

Pray like this: "Our Father in heaven, may your name be kept holy. May your kingdom come soon. May your will be done on earth, as it is in heaven. Give us today the food we need, and forgive us our sins, as we have forgiven those who sin against us. And don't let us yield to temptation, but rescue us from the evil one."[1-5]

Don't be like hypocrites who love to pray publicly where everyone can see them.[6] Go away by yourself and pray to your Father in private and he will reward you.[7] Don't babble on and on as people of other religions do, thinking their prayers will be answered merely because of repetition.[8] Don't be like them, because your Father knows exactly what you need even before you ask him.[9]

When you are praying, if you realize that you hold anything against anyone, forgive them, so that your Father in heaven may forgive you for your sins.[10]

Come near to God and he will come near to you. Commit to him in your heart and do not be double-minded.[11] Draw near to him with a sincere heart, a clear conscience, and in the full assurance of your faith.[12]

Lift up your hands and praise the Lord.[13] Call out to God, and he will answer you and tell you great and mighty things you do not know.[14] Be still before the Lord and wait patiently for him. Do not fret when the wicked succeed in their wicked schemes.[15] Cast your cares on the Lord and he will sustain you. He will never let the righteous fall.[16]

Pray in Jesus's name. Ask and you will receive.[17] He is the way, the truth, and the life. No one can come to God except through him.[18] Ask in his name so that he can glorify his Father, God.[19] Jesus is like a vine, and you are like a branch. Separated from him, you can do nothing. Stay connected to him and you will produce a good crop of fruit.[20]

Approach God in prayer with freedom and confidence through Jesus so that you can receive mercy and grace to help in your time of need.[21,22] You have a high priest in heaven, Jesus, who is able to sympathize with your weaknesses. He was tempted in every way, just like you are—yet without sin.[23] So hold firmly to the faith you profess.[24]

Devote yourself to prayer with an alert mind and a thankful heart.[25] Be earnest and disciplined in your prayers. The end of the world is coming soon.[26] Rejoice in your confident hope, be patient in trouble and keep on praying.[27] Pray without ceasing.[28] Pray with uplifted hands, free from anger and controversy.[29] Watch and pray so that you do not give in to temptation. The spirit is willing, but the flesh is weak.[30] You must believe and not doubt and your prayers will be answered.[31,32]

Ask and it will be given to you; seek and you will find; knock and the door will be opened.[33]

PRAYER, Part 2

1   1 Tim. 2:1

2   Luke 6:28

3   Matt. 5:44

4   Eph. 6:18

5   Col. 4:3

6   2 Thess. 3:1

7   Luke 10:2

8   James 5:14

9   James 5:15

10   James 5:16

11   1 John 5:16

12   James 5:20

13   1 Tim. 2:2

14   Ps. 122:6

15   James 4:8

16   Ps. 66:18

17   Phil. 4:6

18   Phil. 4:7

19   Matt. 26:41

PRAYER, Part 2

Pray for all people. Intercede for them and ask God to help them. Be thankful for them.[1] Bless those who curse you. Pray for those who hurt you.[2] Love your enemies and pray for those who persecute you.[3] Pray in the Spirit at all times and on every occasion with all kinds of prayers and requests. Stay alert and be persistent in your prayers for all believers everywhere.[4]

Pray for those who proclaim the mystery of Christ.[5] Pray that the Lord's message will spread rapidly and be honored wherever it goes.[6] Pray that the Lord will send more workers into the fields for his harvest.[7]

Call the elders of the church to pray over anyone sick and anoint them with oil in the name of the Lord.[8] Prayer offered in faith will make the sick person well.[9] Confess your sins to each other and pray for each other so that you may be healed. The prayer of a righteous person is powerful and effective.[10] Pray for a Christian brother or sister who is wandering into sin. Whoever brings them back will save that person from death and bring about the forgiveness of many sins.[11,12]

Pray for kings and all those in authority so that we can live peaceful and quiet lives with religious freedom marked by godliness and dignity.[13] Pray for peace in Jerusalem.[14]

Come near to God, and he will come near to you.[15] Do not hold sin in your heart or the Lord will not hear your prayers.[16]

Pray about everything and don't worry about anything. Tell God what you need and thank him for all he has done.[17] You will experience the peace of God, which transcends all human understanding, and it will guard your heart and mind as you live your life with Jesus.[18]

Pray with an alert mind so that you do not wander off into temptation without even knowing it.[19]

PRIDE

1   Prov. 16:5
2   Prov. 8:13
3   Ps. 101:5
4   Prov. 21:4
5   Prov. 6:16
6   Prov. 6:17
7   Ps. 5:5
8   James 4:6
9   Prov. 3:34
10 Mic. 6:8
11 Phil. 2:3
12 James 4:7
13 James 4:10
14 Prov. 3:7
15 Prov. 3:34
16 Deut. 8:11
17 Deut. 8:12
18 Deut. 8:13
19 Deut. 8:14
20 Prov. 27:1
21 James 4:16
22 James 4:15
23 Prov. 16:18
24 Matt. 23:12
25 James 4:10
26 1 Peter 5:5
27 Rom. 12:16
28 1 John 2:15

29 1 John 2:16
30 James 4:7
31 1 Cor. 13:4

PRIDE

The Lord detests proud people and will surely punish them.[1] He hates pride and arrogance, evil behavior and perverse speech.[2] He will not tolerate those with haughty eyes and a proud heart. Both are sins.[3-7]

God opposes the proud.[8,9] He requires humility.[10] Be humble, always thinking of others as better than yourself.[11-13] Do not be wise in your own eyes. Fear the Lord and shun evil.[14] He resists the proud but gives grace to the humble.[15]

Be careful in your time of prosperity that you do not become proud and forget the Lord and what he has done for you. Then you will almost certainly disregard his commandments.[16-19]

Do not brag about what you are going to do tomorrow. You have no idea what will happen.[20] Such boasting is evil.[21] Instead, you ought to say, "If it is the Lord's will, I will do this or that."[22]

Pride goes before destruction and a haughty spirit before a fall.[23] Whoever builds themselves up will be humbled, and those who humble themselves will be built up.[24]

Humble yourself before the Lord, and he will lift you up.[25] Clothe yourself with humility toward one another because "God opposes the proud, but gives grace to the humble."[26] Live in harmony with one another. Do not be proud but willing to associate with people of low position. Do not be conceited.[27]

Do not love the world or anything in it because it displaces love for God.[28] Pride, lust, and greed characterize the worldly system, which is opposed to God.[29]

Humble yourself before God. Resist the Devil, and he will flee from you.[30]

Love is not proud and does not boast.[31]

PRIORITIES

1	Ex. 20:3		30	Rom. 12:16
2	Deut. 6:5		31	Eph. 4:2
3	Matt. 22:37		32	Eph. 4:32
4	Luke 10:27		33	Col. 3:13
5	Mark 12:31		34	1 Thess. 5:11
6	1 John 5:3		35	Col. 3:23
7	1 John 2:15		36	Col. 3:22
8	Matt. 6:33		37	Eph. 6:7
9	Rom. 14:17		38	Eph. 6:6
10	Luke 12:29		39	Eph. 6:5
11	Matt. 28:19		40	Col. 3:24
12	Prov. 4:23			
13	1 Thess. 4:3			
14	Rom. 12:2			
15	Col. 3:2			
16	Gal. 5:22			
17	Gal. 5:23			
18	Ps. 119:37			
19	Eph. 6:10			
20	Luke 12:15			
21	Mark 8:36			
22	1 Tim. 5:8			
23	Eph. 6:2			
24	Eph. 5:25			
25	Eph. 5:33			
26	Eph. 5:21			
27	Col. 3:20			
28	Matt. 22:39			
29	John 13:34			

PRIORITIES

GOD: You must have no greater priority than God.[1] You must love him with all your heart and all your soul and all your mind and all your strength.[2-4] There is no greater commandment than this.[5] Loving God means keeping his commandments.[6] Do not love the things of the world; they displace love for God.[7]

KINGDOM OF GOD: Seek the kingdom of God above everything else, and live in his righteous ways.[8] This kingdom is not about eating and drinking, so don't set your heart on these kinds of things, but instead on righteousness, justice and peace.[9,10] Go and make disciples for Jesus and his kingdom everywhere in your world.[11]

CHARACTER: Guard your heart above all else because it determines the course of your life.[12] God wants you to live a pure life.[13] Do not conform to the norms of the world, but become a transformed person by gaining a renewed mind that desires to understand and do God's will.[14] Set your mind on God's priorities.[15] Let the Holy Spirit develop virtues in your character that please God: love, joy, peace, patience, kindness, goodness, faithfulness, gentleness, and self-control.[16-17] Turn away from worthless pursuits.[18] Be strong in the Lord.[19] Beware of greed. Your life cannot be measured by the abundance of your possessions.[20] What good would it be to gain the whole world and forfeit your own soul?[21]

FAMILY: You must not neglect your family as that would be a repudiation of genuine faith.[22] Honor your father and mother.[23-24] Husbands must love their wives and wives must respect their husbands.[25] They must both be willing to submit to each other.[26] Children must obey their parents because this pleases the Lord.[27]

ONE ANOTHER: Love your neighbor as yourself.[28] Love one another just as Jesus has loved you.[29] Live in harmony with one another. Do not be proud, but be willing to associate with people of low position. Do not be conceited.[30] Be humble, gentle and patient, bearing with one another.[31] Be kind and compassionate.[32] Forgive whatever grievances you have just as God forgives you.[33] Encourage one another and build each other up in faith and character.[34]

WORK: Work willingly at whatever you do as though you were working for the Lord rather than for people.[35] Respectfully carry out your employers' duties at all times, not just when they are watching, because of your reverent fear of the Lord.[36] Keep a positive attitude and don't do just the minimum required.[37] Work heartily, keeping in mind that you are really working for Christ and doing what he wants you to do.[38] Serving your earthly master is a way of serving your heavenly Master who will give you a heavenly inheritance as a reward.[39-40]

PRISONERS

1   Isa. 61:1

2   Luke 4:18

3   Ps. 146:7

4   Heb. 13:3

5   Matt. 25:36

6   Matt. 25:35

7   Matt. 25:40

8   Matt. 25:34

9   Gal. 3:22

10 Gal. 3:23

11 Gal. 3:24

12 Gal. 3:25

13 Rom. 6:14

14 John 8:36

PRISONERS

Jesus's mission on earth was to release prisoners from darkness, preach the gospel to the poor, bind up the brokenhearted, restore sight to the blind, and release the oppressed.[1,2] The Lord sets prisoners free and upholds the cause of the oppressed.[3]

Remember those in prison as if you were a fellow prisoner.[4]

Visit those in prison; give clothing to the poor; care for the sick; feed the hungry; give drink to the thirsty.[5,6] Whenever you do anything like this for the least and lowest of society, you do it for Jesus.[7] He promises you a reward for this in the kingdom of heaven[8]

We were all prisoners of sin at one time. We can be set free only by believing in Jesus Christ.[9] Before the way of faith in Christ was available to us, we were under guard by the Law of Moses.[10,11] But now that faith in Christ has come, we are no longer prisoners of the Law.[12] Instead, we live by faith in the freedom of God's grace.[13]

When Jesus sets you free, you are truly free.[14]

PURITY

1	Matt. 5:8		28	1 John 3:1
2	Prov. 15:26		29	1 John 3:2
3	Ps. 119:9		30	1 John 3:3
4	Ps. 19:9		31	James 1:27
5	Ps. 19:10		32	1 Tim. 4:12
6	Ps. 24:3		33	2 Cor. 6:6
7	Ps. 24:4		34	1 Peter 3:2
8	1 Tim. 5:22		35	2 Cor. 6:6
9	Phil. 2:14		36	1 Peter 3:1
10	Phil. 2:15		37	1 Peter 3:2
11	1 Tim. 1:5		38	Col. 3:2
12	Phil. 1:9		39	Phil. 4:8
13	Phil. 1:10		40	James 3:17
14	1 Thess. 4:3		41	Ps. 51:10
15	1 Thess. 4:4			
16	1 Thess. 4:5			
17	1 Cor. 6:18			
18	Col. 3:5			
19	2 Tim. 2:22			
20	Eph. 5:3			
21	Heb. 13:4			
22	Matt. 5:27			
23	Matt. 5:28			
24	Mark 7:20			
25	Mark 7:21			
26	Mark 7:22			
27	Mark 7:23			

PURITY

Blessed are the pure in heart for they shall see God.[1] The thoughts of the pure are pleasing to him, but he detests the thoughts of the wicked.[2]

Live your life according to God's Word. It is the way to keep your life pure.[3] The fear of the Lord is pure and will endure forever. His commandments are sure and righteous and more precious than pure gold.[4,5] Only those with a pure heart and clean hands can ever stand in the presence of God.[6,7]

Keep yourself pure.[8] Do everything without complaining or arguing so that you may be blameless and pure in these cooked and perverse times.[9,10] Let your love for others come from a pure heart, a good conscience and a sincere faith.[11] Grow in your knowledge and insight so that you become able to discern what is best and live a pure and blameless life until Jesus returns.[12,13]

It is God's will that you live a pure life. Keep yourself from sexual immorality.[14] Learn to control your body in a way that is pure, holy, and honorable, not in passionate lust like those who do not know anything about God.[15,16] Flee sexual immorality. It is a sin against your own body.[17] Put to death whatever belongs to your earthly nature and instead pursue righteousness, faith, love, and peace out of a pure heart.[18,19] Do not allow even a hint of sexual immorality or any kind of impurity or greed because these are improper for God's holy people.[20] Marriage should be honored by all and the marriage bed kept pure because God will judge the adulterer and the sexually immoral.[21] Keep your thought life pure as it is the source of actions that follow.[22-27]

Keep your life pure by reminding yourself that you are a child of God now, known by him, with unimaginably good things to come.[28-30] Pure religion is to look after anyone in distress and to keep yourself from being polluted by the world.[31]

Be an example of a pure life to others. This includes faith, holiness, reverence, speech, patience, understanding, kindness, gentleness, a clear head, steady hand, and sincere love for others.[32-35] A pure life is a powerful witness.[36,37]

Set your mind and affections on heavenly virtues; not on earthly values.[38] Think about what is pure, true, noble, right, lovely, admirable, excellent, or praiseworthy.[39] The wisdom that comes from God is pure.[40]

Create in me a pure heart, O God.[41]

RECONCILIATION

1   Col. 1:21

2   Col. 1:22

3   Col. 1:20

4   2 Cor. 5:19

5   2 Cor. 5:18

6   2 Cor. 5:20

7   Eph. 4:32

8   Col. 3:13

9   Luke 17:3

10 Luke 17:4

11 Matt. 5:23

12 Matt. 5:24

13 Luke 12:58

14 Rom. 5:8

15 Rom. 5:9

16 Rom. 5:10

17 Rom. 5:11

RECONCILIATION

God has reconciled you to himself by means of the physical death of Jesus Christ. You are no longer alienated from him. He now sees you as holy, without blemish, and free from accusation.[1-3] He no longer counts your sins against you. You have been reconciled with God by faith in Jesus.[4]

Now God gives you the message and ministry of reconciliation.[5] You are an ambassador for Christ. God makes his appeal to others through you: "Be reconciled to God."[6]

Be kind and compassionate to one another.[7] Bear with each other and forgive whatever grievances you may have with each other, just like God has forgiven you.[7,8]

Confront a person who has harmed you. If they sincerely apologize, you must forgive them.[9] If they repeat the offense multiple times and they apologize each time, you must forgive them each time.[10]

If in the midst of your worship of God, you suddenly recall that you have an issue with another person, break off your worship and go and be reconciled to that person. Then you can resume your worship in good conscience before God.[12]

Make every effort to be reconciled to your adversary if you find yourself in a lawsuit. Otherwise, you may face an even worse outcome.[13]

Think of God's great love for you. While you were still his enemy, he sent Christ to die in your place. This has brought about your reconciliation with God. Since he did this while you were his enemy, think of what he will do now that you are his friend![14-16]

Celebrate the new relationship you have with him.[17]

REMINDERS

1   Num. 15:38

2   Num. 15:40

3   Num. 15:39

4   Deut. 6:5

5   Deut. 6:6

6   Deut. 6:7

7   Deut. 6:8

8   Deut. 6:9

9   Deut. 8:11

10 Deut. 8:12

11 Deut. 8:13

12 Deut. 8:14

13 Ps. 105:5

14 John 14:26

15 Heb. 13:16

REMINDERS

Set up visible reminders in your life of God's commandments so that you will remember to obey all of them and be fully devoted to him.[1,2] Doing so protects you from following your own desires as we are all so prone to do.[3]

Keep God's commandments prominent in your own heart. Impress them upon your children. Talk about them when you sit around the dinner table, when you are driving on the freeway, when you go to bed at night, and when you get up in the morning. Put them on your cellphone. Hang plaques on the walls of your house, and paint symbols on your gate.[4-8]

Be careful that you do not forget the Lord and fail to do what pleases him.[9] This often happens when things are going well because pride takes over and we think it's all due to our own efforts.[10-13]

God sent his Holy Spirit to be a reminder to you of all that Jesus taught and said.[14]

Remember to do good works. These are pleasing to God.[15]

REPENTANCE

1   Matt. 4:17

2   Luke 13:3

3   Acts 2:38

4   Acts 3:19

5   Acts 17:30

6   2 Chron. 7:14

7   Joel 2:12

8   Joel 2:13

9   Hos. 12:6

10 Isa. 1:16

11 Ezek. 18:30

12 Zech. 1:3

13 Ezek. 18:31

14 Luke 13:3

15 1 John 1:8

16 1 John 1:9

17 2 Peter 3:9

18 Luke 15:7

19 Matt. 3:8

20 Acts 26:20

REPENTANCE

Repent of your sins and believe the gospel because the kingdom of heaven has now arrived.[1] Jesus began his preaching ministry with this command. Unless you repent, you will all perish.[2] Repent and be baptized in the name of Jesus Christ for the forgiveness of your sins. And you will receive the gift of the Holy Spirit.[3,4]

God commands all people everywhere to repent.[5] Humble yourself before the Lord and pray, seek his presence, repent and turn away from your wicked ways. Then he will hear from heaven and forgive your sins.[6]

Return to the Lord now, while there is still time. Give him all your heart. Go to him with fasting, weeping, and mourning. Don't tear your clothing in your grief, but tear up your hearts instead. Return to the Lord your God, for he is merciful and compassionate, slow to become angry, and filled with unfailing love. he is eager to forgive and not to punish.[7,8]

You must return to God, maintain love and justice, and always wait for God.[9] Stop doing wrong.[10] Repent! Turn away from all your offenses. Then sin will not be your downfall.[11] Put all your rebellion behind you and find yourselves a new heart and a new spirit.[12,13] You will perish unless you repent of your sins and turn to God.[14]

If you say you are not guilty of sin, you are only deceiving yourself and not facing reality. You are living in denial.[15] If you confess your sins to God, he will be faithful to his own nature and satisfy justice. He will forgive you and cleanse you from all unrighteousness.[16] He does not want anyone to perish but wants everyone to repent.[17]

There is more joy in heaven over even one lost sinner who repents and returns to God than over ninety-nine others who have remained righteous and not strayed away.[18]

Prove by the way you live that you have repented of your sins and turned to God.[19,20]

RESPECT

1   1 Peter 2:17

2   1 Peter 2:13

3   Rom. 13:7

4   Zech. 7:10

5   1 Tim. 5:10

6   Deut. 28:50

7   Lev. 19:3

8   Ex. 20:12

9   Heb. 12:9

10   Titus 2:2

11   1 Tim. 5:17

12   1 Tim. 3:4

13   1 Tim. 3:2

14   1 Tim. 3:8

15   1 Tim. 3:11

16   1 Peter 2:18

17   1 Tim. 6:1

18   Acts 10:34

19   Acts 10:35

20   1 Sam. 16:7

RESPECT

Show proper respect to everyone. Love your community of believers, fear God and honor the president.[1] Respect all human authority for the Lord's sake.[2,3]

Respect the rights of the widow and orphan, the alien and the poor. Do not think of them in your heart as second-class citizens.[4] Widows deserve special respect if they have raised their children well, been kind to strangers, served other believers humbly, helped those in trouble and always been ready to do good.[5]

It is a fierce and heartless nation that does not show respect for the old or pity for the young.[6]

Respect your parents.[7] Honor them so that you may have a long life.[8] They taught you discipline, and just as you submitted to their discipline, you should also submit to the discipline of your heavenly Father so that you can live forever.[9]

Respect older men who have exercised self-control and lived wisely. They must have sound faith and be filled with love and patience.[10]

Respect the elders of your church, especially those who work hard at both preaching and teaching.[11] Each of them must manage their own family well and have children who respect and obey them.[12,13] Deacons and their wives must be well respected and have integrity.[14,15]

Employees must accept and respect the authority of their employers not only if they are kind and reasonable, but even if they are not.[16] Disrespect brings shame on the name of God.[17]

God has no special respect for anyone. He does not look at outward appearances, but at the heart. He accepts everyone who knows and does his will.[18-20]

REST

1   Ex. 23:12
2   Ex. 34:21
3   Ex. 34:22
4   Gen. 2:2
5   Ex. 20:11
6   Gen. 1:31
7   Gen. 2:3
8   Deut. 5:14
9   Mark 2:27
10 Ex. 31:17
11 Ps. 37:7
12 Ps. 116:7
13 Ps. 16:9
14 Ps. 16:8
15 Isa. 30:15
16 Jer. 6:16
17 Matt. 11:28
18 Matt. 11:29
19 Heb. 4:2
20 Heb. 4:9
21 Heb. 4:4
22 Heb. 4:10
23 Heb. 4:3
24 Heb. 4:11
25 Heb. 4:1
26 Ps. 62:5
27 Ps. 62:1
28 Ps. 91:1

REST

Do all your work in six days of the week and rest on the seventh. Give rest to all in your household including employees and even your working animals. Do this even during your busiest seasons so that all may be refreshed.[1-3] This must be a day of complete rest from your labor and one of enjoyment of what you have accomplished, even as God rested after the six days of creation and admired his own work.[4-6] Furthermore, God blessed this day and declared it holy because it was the day he rested from all his work of creation.[7,8]

You must observe a special day of rest each week because God commanded it. It is for your benefit,not his.[9] It is meant to be a permanent sign of the special relationship between God and his people.[10]

Rest in the Lord and wait patiently for him. Do not fret about those who prosper unjustly or in wicked ways.[11] Rest in the Lord because he has been good to you.[12] Rest in the hope he offers because he is always with you.[13,14] You will you find confidence and strength by resting in him.[15] When you stand at a crossroads in your life, ask God which is the good way and then walk in it and you will find rest for your soul.[16]

Go to Jesus when you are frustrated or burned out, and he will give you true rest.[17] Walk with him, work with him, and learn from him, and he will give you rest for your troubled soul.[18]

Good news: God has prepared a "rest" for his people.[19,20] Just as he rested after creation, so will you rest in him after your work in this life is complete.[21,22] However, you must have faith in him to enter that rest.[23] You must not disobey him, or you will fail to experience his rest.[24,25]

Find rest for your soul in God alone because your salvation and hope come from him.[26,27]

The person who dwells in the shelter of the Most High God safely rests in the shadow of the Almighty.[28]

REVENGE

1   Lev. 19:18

2   Prov. 24:29

3   Prov. 20:22

4   Deut. 32:35

5   Heb. 10:30

6   Rom. 12:19

7   Nah. 1:2

8   Jer. 51:56

9   Ezek. 7:3

10   Ezek. 7:4

11   Hos. 12:14

12   Col. 3:25

13   Rom. 12:17

14   1 Thess. 5:15

15   1 Peter 3:9

16   Luke 6:28

17   Matt. 5:44

18   Luke 6:27

19   Luke 6:35

20   Rom. 12:20

21   Rom. 12:21

REVENGE

Do not seek revenge or hold a grudge against anyone.[1] Do not say that you intend to pay back someone for what they did to you.[2,3]

Vengeance belongs to the Lord; he will repay.[4,5] Do not take revenge, but leave room for God to act.[6] He is a God of retribution and will execute his wrath and vengeance on his enemies[7,8] He will judge bad conduct, detestable practices, and contempt.[9-11] Anyone who has done wrong will be repaid for their wrong, and there will be no favoritism.[12]

Do not pay back evil for evil or wrong for wrong. Always try to be kind to others and do what is right in the eyes of everybody.[13,14]

Do not repay an insult with an insult, but with a blessing. You are called to do this so that you may inherit a blessing.[15] Bless those who curse you and pray for those who despise you.[16,17] Do good to those who hate you.[18] Offer help to your enemy. Your reward in heaven will be very great because in this way, you will truly be acting as children of the Most High who is kind to those who are wicked and ungrateful.[19,20]

Do not be overcome by evil, but overcome evil with good.[21]

SABBATH

1	Gen. 1:1	25	Col. 2:16
2	Gen. 2:1	26	Col. 2:17
3	Gen. 2:2	27	Rom. 14:5
4	Gen. 2:3	28	Rom. 14:6
5	Gen. 2:4	29	Heb. 4:9
6	Ex. 20:8	30	Heb 4:11
7	Ex. 23:12		
8	Ex. 31:15		
9	Ex. 35:2		
10	Lev. 23:3		
11	Deut. 5:14		
12	Ex. 20:10		
13	Ex. 31:13		
14	Ezek. 20:12		
15	Ezek. 20:20		
16	Lev. 19:30		
17	Isa. 56:2		
18	Jer. 17:22		
19	Jer. 17:24		
20	Isa. 58:13		
21	Isa. 58:14		
22	Mark 2:28		
23	Mark 2:27		
24	Matt. 12:12		

SABBATH

In the beginning, God created the heavens and the earth and everything in them in six days.[1,2] When the work of creation was complete, he rested from all his work on the seventh day.[3] He blessed that day and declared it holy because it was the day when he rested from all his work of creation.[4] This is the account of the creation of the heavens and the earth.[5]

Remember the Sabbath day by keeping it holy.[6] Do your work in six days, but do not work on the seventh day so that you and your household may rest and be refreshed.[7-10] This day is to be dedicated to the Lord. No one is to work, not even your animals.[11,12]

Observing the Sabbath will be a sign between you and the Lord your God so that you may know that He is the one who makes you holy.[13-15]

Observe the Sabbath and have reverence for God's place of worship. He is the Lord.[16] You will be blessed if you adhere to this command and do not desecrate it.[17,]

Keep the Sabbath day holy. Don't work at your business or career on that day. Don't pursue your own interests on that day or spend time in idle and foolish talk. Enjoy the Sabbath and speak of it with delight as the Lord's holy day. Honor the Sabbath in everything you do on that day. Then the Lord will be your delight.[18-21]

Jesus is Lord even over the Sabbath.[22] The Sabbath was made for the benefit of people, not for people to meet the requirements of the Sabbath.[23] It is permissible to do good on the Sabbath.[24]

Do not pass judgment on one another in matters of diet, worship services, religious holidays, or Sabbaths. These issues are only a shadow of things to come. The real substance is found in Christ.[25,26] Some believers think one day is more holy than another day and others think every day is alike. Both worship the Lord on a special day to honor him and should be fully convinced that whichever day they choose is acceptable to God.[27,28]

There is a Sabbath rest waiting for God's people.[29] Do your best to enter that rest.[30]

SACRIFICE

1   Ps. 51:17

2   Prov. 21:3

3   Heb. 13:16

4   Ps. 50:14

5   Ps. 50:23

6   Hos. 6:6

7   Prov. 21:27

8   Eph. 5:2

9   1 John 4:10

10   Heb. 9:28

11   Mark 14:24

12   Heb. 9:14

13   Rom. 12:1

SACRIFICE

The sacrifice that God wants is a broken spirit, a broken and contrite heart.[1] He is more pleased when you do what is right than when you offer him sacrifices.[2] Don't forget to do good and to share with those in need. These are sacrifices that please God.[3]

Make gratitude your sacrifice to God and keep the vows you have made to him.[4] Giving thanks to God is a sacrifice that truly honors him.[5]

Show love to others rather than offering sacrifices. God wants you to know him more than he wants your sacrifices.[6]

The sacrifice of an evil person is detestable to the Lord.[7]

Live a life filled with love following the example of Christ who loved you and offered himself as a sacrifice pleasing to God.[8] This is real love, not that you loved God, but that he loved you and sent his Son as a perfect sacrifice to take away your sins.[9] He died once for all time to take away the sins of the world.[10] His blood was poured out as a sacrifice for many and confirms a new covenant between God and his people.[11] His sacrifice purifies you so that you can truly worship God.[12]

Give your body to God as a living and holy sacrifice; one that is pleasing to him. This is a true way to worship him.[13]

SALVATION

1	John 3:7	28	Rom. 10:10	55	Rom. 8:38
2	John 3:3	29	Rom. 10:11	56	Rom. 8:39
3	Rom. 3:23	30	2 Cor. 5:17	57	Jude 24
4	Rom. 6:23	31	Acts 13:39	58	Heb. 7:25
5	Acts 16:31	32	Rom. 8:3	59	Rom. 1:16
6	Acts 2:21	33	John 11:25	60	Rom. 1:17
7	Rom. 10:13	34	John 11:26	61	Phil. 2:12
8	Acts 4:12	35	Heb. 11:6	62	Phil. 2:13
9	John 14:6	36	Gal. 5:6		
10	John 3:16	37	Heb. 11:1		
11	John 3:17	38	Rom. 3:28		
12	1 John 5:11	39	Rom. 5:1		
13	John 3:36	40	Rom. 4:5		
14	1 John 5:12	41	James 2:14		
15	John 5:24	42	James 2:17		
16	Matt. 7:21	43	James 2:20		
17	Eph. 2:9	44	Eph. 2:10		
18	Gal. 2:16	45	2 Cor. 5:17		
19	Rom. 3:20	46	2 Cor. 5:18		
20	Gal. 3:11	47	1 John 4:13		
21	Gal. 2:21	48	1 John 3:24		
22	Eph. 2:8	49	Eph. 1:13		
23	Titus 3:5	50	Eph. 1:14		
24	Rom. 11:6	51	Eph. 4:30		
25	Rom. 6:23	52	Rom. 8:35		
26	1 John 1:9	53	Rom. 8:36		
27	Rom. 10:9	54	Rom. 8:37		

SALVATION

You must be born again.[1] No one can enter the kingdom of God unless they are born again.[2] Everyone is guilty of sin and falls short of God's standards.[3] The result of sin is death.[4]

Believe in Jesus Christ and you will be saved.[5] Everyone who calls on the name of Jesus will be saved.[6,7] There is no other name under heaven revealed to mankind by which you must be saved.[8] Jesus is the way and the truth and the life. No one can come to God except through him.[9]

God loves you so much that he sent his one and only Son to earth so that if you believe in him, you will never die but live forever.[10-12] If you believe in him, you have life; if you do not believe in him, you will perish.[13-15] Be sincere when you call on the hame of the Lord. Only those who commit to know and do the will of God will enter the kingdom of heaven.[16]

Salvation is not a reward for the good things you have done, so there is no room for pride.[17-21] It is only because of God's grace that you are offered salvation.[22-24] It is a free gift from God[25]

Confess your sins to God. He will forgive you for all of them.[26] Confess with your mouth that "Jesus is Lord"—this affirms your commitment. Truly believe in your heart that God raised him from the dead, and you will be saved.[27-30] Good works and adherence to the Law of Moses cannot put you in good standing with God. Only belief in Jesus will do that.[31,32] If you believe in him, you will never die. You will live even after your physical death.[33-34]

It is impossible to please God without faith. You must believe that he exists and that he rewards those who sincerely seek him.[35] Faith is the only thing that counts.[36,37] You are justified before God by faith alone and not by your good works.[38-40] True faith will motivate you to do good works. Otherwise, it is not genuine.[41-43] You are God's masterpiece, created to do the good things he has planned for you to do.[44] You are a new person.[45] God has reconciled you to himself and now gives you a ministry of reaching others with this message.[46]

This is how you can know that Christ lives in you. He puts the Holy Spirit in you.[47] He is God's mark on you, his guarantee of your salvation.[48-50] Do not betray him by the way you live.[51] Nothing in creation can separate you from God's love.[52-56] He will keep you from falling and bring you into his glorious presence without a single fault. He can do this because Jesus is already there to intercede on your behalf.[57,58]

Do not be ashamed of the gospel, because it is the story of God's powerful way of salvation for everyone who believes it.[59] It tells of the righteousness of God and how he makes you righteous in his sight.[60]

Work hard to show the results of your salvation, obeying God with deep reverence and fear. He is working in you and will give you the desire and power to do what pleases him.[61-62]

SANCTIFICATION

1	1 Thess. 4:3		30	2 Cor. 7:1
2	1 Peter 1:16		31	2 Peter 1:4
3	1 Peter 1:15		32	2 Peter 1:5
4	Heb.10:10		33	2 Peter 1:6
5	Heb.10:14		34	2 Peter 1:7
6	1 Cor. 1:2		35	Rom. 12:2
7	1 Thess. 4:7		36	Phil. 2:13
8	1 Cor. 6:11		37	Phil. 2:12
9	Rom. 6:11		38	Heb.12:14
10	Rom. 6:18		39	1 Thess. 4:3
11	Rom. 6:22		40	1 Cor. 6:18
12	Rom. 8:29		41	1 Thess. 4:4
13	2 Cor. 3:18		42	1 Cor. 6:19
14	Phil. 1:6		43	1 Cor. 6:20
15	2 Thess. 2:13		44	Rom. 6:13
16	Rom.15:16		45	Gal. 5:24
17	1 Cor. 1:30		46	Rom. 12:1
18	2 Peter 1:3		47	1 Thess. 5:23
19	John 17:17		48	2 Cor. 7:1
20	John 17:19		49	2 Peter 1:11
21	Rom. 15:4		50	Acts 20:32
22	Rom. 5:3		51	2 Peter 1:4
23	Rom. 5:4			
24	Phil. 2:13			
25	1 Peter 1:2			
26	Gal. 5:22			
27	Gal. 5:23			
28	Heb. 12:2			
29	Phil. 3:12			

SANCTIFICATION

It is God's will that you should be sanctified.[1] You must be holy because he is holy.[2,3]

It is God's will to make you holy by the once-for-all-time sacrifice of the body of Jesus Christ,.[4-6] You are called to live a holy life.[7] You were justified and sanctified in the name of Jesus Christ.[8] You should consider yourself dead to the power of sin—no longer its slave—and alive to God through Jesus as a slave to righteous living.[9-11]

It is God's will that you be transformed into the likeness of his Son, Jesus. This process of sanctification makes you a reflection of God's glory.[12,13] It is accomplished by God working in your life through the Holy Spirit from this time forward.[14-16] Everything you need for a fresh start, right thinking and right living, comes from him.[17,18] He uses the truth expressed in Scripture to accomplish this.[19,20] He also uses the difficult circumstances in your life.[21-23]

God works in your life to give you the desire and ability to do what pleases him.[24] His Spirit makes you holy and develops character that is in favor with everyone.[25-27]

Keep your eyes on Jesus, the founder of your faith. Watch how he lived it.[28] Press on toward complete holiness—a lifetime process—because you fear God.[29,30] Make every effort to add to your faith: goodness, knowledge, self-control, perseverance, godliness, kindness, and love.[31-34]

Do not adopt or copy the patterns of worldly culture. Instead, be transformed into a completely new mindset. Then you will be able to understand and do what is pleasing to God.[35] God will change your desires and enable you to be and do what pleases him.[36] Live a holy life and work hard to demonstrate the results of your salvation.[37,38]

Since it is God's will for you to be holy, you must stay away from all sexual sin.[39] It is clearly a sin against your own body.[40] You must control your body and live in holiness and honor.[41] You must realize that your body is not your own. God purchased it at great price. It is now a temple of the Holy Spirit, and he lives in you. Do not do anything to disgrace or harm your body.[42-45] Instead, offer your body to God as a living sacrifice, a spiritual act of worship that pleases him.[46]

God can make you holy in every way and keep your whole body, soul and spirit blameless until Jesus returns.[47] Get rid of everything that can defile your body, soul or spirit and press on toward complete sanctification.[48] You will receive a rich welcome and inheritance in the eternal kingdom of Jesus and escape the corruption of the world caused by evil desires.[49-51]

SCRIPTURE

1	2 Tim. 2:15		30	2 Tim. 3:17
2	2 Tim. 3:16		31	Col. 3:16
3	2 Pet. 1:20		32	Ps. 119:11
4	2 Peter 1:21		33	Ps. 119:16
5	2 Sam. 22:31		34	Ps. 119:15
6	Ps. 18:30		35	Ps. 119:36
7	Prov. 30:5		36	Ps. 119:37
8	Deut. 4:2		37	Ps. 119:105
9	1 Cor. 4:6		38	Eph. 6:17
10	Eccl. 12:12		39	Luke 11:28
11	Rev. 22:18		40	James 1:22
12	Rev. 22:19		41	Isa. 40:8
13	2 Peter 1:19			
14	Rom. 15:4			
15	Rom. 1:2			
16	1 Cor. 15:3			
17	1 Cor. 15:4			
18	1 Cor. 15:5			
19	1 Cor. 15:6			
20	1 Cor. 15:7			
21	1 Cor. 15:8			
22	John 20:31			
23	Acts 18:28			
24	John 5:39			
25	2 Tim. 3:15			
26	2 Tim. 3:16			
27	Heb. 4:12			
28	1 Thess. 2:13			
29	Rom. 12:2			

SCRIPTURE

Study the Scriptures so that you can correctly understand and explain them to others and gain God's approval.[1]

All Scripture is a direct message from God.[2] It never had its origin in the human mind or the writer's own understanding or initiative. Holy men of God were moved by the Holy Spirit and spoke directly from and for God.[3,4] The Word of God is flawless and a protection for those who seek to please him.[5-7]

Do not add to or take away from anything that is written.[8] To do so is a sign of pride[9] and will bring severe judgment upon yourself.[10-12]

Pay attention to what the prophets have written since their predictions about Jesus Christ have proven to be true.[13] This is a strong reason to have confidence in Scripture.[14] The gospel tells us that he died for our sins, was buried, and raised back to life on the third day exactly as the Scriptures predicted. He appeared to hundreds of living people including the apostles.[15-21] Scripture was written so that you can believe that Jesus is the Christ, the Son of God, and that by believing you can have eternal life in his name.[22-25]

Every part of Scripture is useful in one way or another: showing us truth, exposing our rebellion, correcting our mistakes and training us to live God's way.[26] It is living and active, sharper than a surgeon's scalpel, incising the deepest parts of our inner being and revealing the thoughts and attitudes of our hearts.[27] If you believe it, your life will be transformed.[28-29] You will be prepared and equipped to face every life challenge and do good works.[30]

Let Scripture, in all its richness with its message about Christ, fill your life. Teach and counsel each other with all its wisdom.[31] Hide the Scripture in your heart. It will help you avoid sin.[32] Do not neglect it, but meditate on and take delight in its instruction.[33,34] Turn your heart toward its statutes and away from worthless things and selfish gain.[35,36] It is a light for your journey, a lamp on your path.[37]

Use the Scripture to fight your spiritual battles. It is the "sword" of the Spirit.[38]

Read and obey the Scripture and you will be blessed.[39] You must not only know, but also do what it says. Otherwise, you are only fooling yourself and you live in denial.[40]

The summer grass and flowers of the field wither and fall, but the Word of God will stand forever.[41]

SERVICE

1	Josh. 24:15	30	1 Peter 2:21
2	Deut. 13:4	31	Matt. 20:26
3	Matt. 4:10	32	Matt. 20:27
4	Luke 4:8	33	Matt. 23:11
5	Ps. 2:11	34	Mark 10:43
6	Deut. 11:13	35	Luke 22:26
7	Ps. 100:2	36	Gal. 6:10
8	1 Sam. 12:24	37	Mark 9:35
9	1 Cor. 15:58	38	1 Peter 4:10
10	Rom. 12:11	39	Rom. 12:6
11	John 12:26	40	Rom. 12:4
12	Matt. 7:21	41	1 Cor. 12:12
13	Matt. 25:34	42	1 Cor. 12:25
14	Matt. 25:35	43	1 Cor. 12:26
15	Matt. 25:36	44	1 Cor. 12:27
16	Matt. 25:40	45	Rom. 12:7
17	Rom. 14:16	46	Gal. 5:13
18	Rom. 14:13	47	1 Peter 4:11
19	Rom. 14:15	48	Gal. 6:2
20	Rom. 14:16	49	Heb. 13:3
21	Rom. 14:17	50	Heb. 13:2
22	Rom. 14:18	51	Heb. 13:16
23	Col. 3:23	52	Gal. 6:9
24	Col. 3:24	53	Matt. 6:24
25	Matt. 20:28	54	Luke 16:13
26	Mark 10:45	55	Col. 3:17
27	Phil. 2:7		
28	Phil. 2:8		
29	John 13:15		

SERVICE

Choose for yourself whom you will serve, either the false gods of the world or the Lord God Almighty.[1]

Serve only the Lord, and worship him with reverence and fear.[2-5] Carefully obey his commands and listen to his voice. Think of all the wonderful things he has done for you. Serve him gladly with all your heart and soul.[6-8] Serve him enthusiastically because nothing you do for him is ever wasted.[9,10]

You must follow Jesus and obey his teachings if you want to serve him.[11] Not everyone who says they follow him will enter the kingdom of heaven, only those who do the will of God.[12] You serve Jesus when you meet the needs of the destitute.[13-16] You serve Jesus when you defer to someone with a weak conscience; this is pleasing to God.[17-22] Work willingly at whatever you do because the Master you are serving is actually Christ. You will receive an inheritance as your reward.[23,24]

Jesus came to serve—not to be served—and to give his life as a ransom for many.[25,26] He was humble and obedient to his Father, taking on the role of a servant and even going to the extent of suffering an unjust and humiliating death.[27,28] He should be your example to follow.[29,30]

You must be the servant of all if you want to become great in God's kingdom.[31-35] Serve anyone whenever you have an opportunity, especially those in God's family.[36] You must put yourself last and be the servant of all here on earth if you want to be first in the kingdom of heaven.[37]

Use whatever gifts you have to serve others. It is your way of spreading around the grace of God.[38] We all have different gifts.[39] Just like the human body has many parts and all are necessary, so the body of Christ, the Church, is made up of many members with different gifts and all are necessary.[40-44] If your gift is serving, serve one another well and with love.[45-47] Carry each other's burdens.[48] Remember those in prison.[49] Be hospitable even to strangers.[50] Serve and share with others because this pleases God.[51] Don't get tired of serving because you will receive a reward if you don't quit.[52]

Don't try to serve two masters at the same time. You will create irreconcilable conflicts.[53,54]

In whatever way you serve, do it all as a representative of Jesus.[55]

SEXUALITY, Part 1

1	Gen. 2:7		30	Lev 18:7-16
2	Gen. 2:22		31	Lev. 18:17
3	Mark 10:6		32	Lev. 18:22
4	Gen. 2:24		33	Lev. 20:13
5	Mark 10:7		34	Rom. 1:20
6	Mark 10:8		35	Rom. 1:21
7	Matt. 19:6		36	Rom. 1:24
8	Mark 10:9		37	Rom. 1:28
9	Ex. 20:14		38	Rom. 1:26
10	Deut. 5:18		39	Rom. 1:27
11	Luke 18:20		40	Rom. 1:25
12	Lev. 18:20		41	Rom. 1:22
13	1 Thess. 4:6		42	Rom. 1:32
14	Prov. 6:32		43	1 Cor. 6:9
15	Matt. 19:9		44	Jude 7
16	Mark 10:11		45	Matt. 18:6
17	Luke 16:18		46	Mark 9:42
18	Matt. 5:27		47	Lev. 18:23
19	Matt. 5:28		48	Deut. 27:21
20	Prov. 5:8			
21	Prov. 6:24			
22	Prov. 6:25			
23	Prov. 7:25			
24	Prov. 5:9			
25	Prov. 5:10			
26	Prov. 5:11			
27	Prov. 6:33			
28	Prov. 4:23			
29	Lev. 18:6			

SEXUALITY, Part 1

God made human beings male and female at the beginning of creation.[1-3] This explains why a man leaves his father and mother and is joined to his wife, and the two are united into one.[4-6] They are no longer two, but one. Do not let anyone split apart what God has joined together.[7,8]

You must not commit sexual sin.[9-11] Do not have sexual relations with anyone else's wife or husband.[12] Never harm or cheat a fellow Christian in this matter because the Lord avenges all such sins.[13] Persons who commit sexual sin lack judgment and destroy themselves.[14] Anyone who divorces their spouse, except for marital unfaithfulness, and marries another person, commits adultery.[15,16,17] Looking at another person lustfully means you have already committed adultery in your heart.[18,19]

Stay far away from the immoral or promiscuous person.[20,21] Do not let yourself be seduced by lust or good looks and smooth words.[22,23] Many who do, squander their youth, lose their wealth, and end up in cruel relationships, which come to a miserable end filled with regret.[24-27] Be proactive. Guard your heart above all else because it determines the course of your life.[28]

You must never have sexual relations with a close relative.[29] This includes a parent, sibling, step-sibling, grandchild, aunt or uncle, and your in-laws.[30] Sexual relations with a close relative is a wicked act.[31]

Homosexual acts are detestable to God.[32,33] They contradict what should be obvious. They originate with rejection of God and dark and confused minds.[34,35] They are vile and degrading to the body and should never be done.[36,37] Women with women and men with men turn against the natural way for sex and do shameful things with each other.[38,39] They have traded the truth of God for a lie. They claim to be wise but instead have become utter fools.[41,42] You must realize that those who do such wrong will not have a place in the kingdom of God.[43] Sodom and Gomorrah are examples of God's severe punishment for this sin.[44]

Do not bully a child or take advantage of their simple trust to lead them into sin.[45] It would be better for you to be thrown into the sea with a large millstone hung around your neck.[46]

Do not have sexual relations with an animal whether you are a man or woman.[47] You would defile yourself and put yourself under God's curse.[48]

SEXUALITY, Part 2

1	1 Cor. 6:18		29	1 Cor. 7:4
2	1 Cor. 6:19		30	Eph. 5:28
3	1 Cor. 6:20		31	Eph. 5:33
4	Eph. 5:3		32	Eph. 5:32
5	1 Thess. 5:22			
6	1 Thess. 4:3			
7	1 Thess. 4:4			
8	Gal. 5:19			
9	Col. 3:5			
10	Rom. 6:12			
11	Gal. 5:17			
12	Gal. 5:22			
13	Gal. 5:23			
14	Rom. 8:8			
15	Gal. 5:16			
16	Heb. 13:4			
17	Gen. 2:24			
18	Eph. 5:31			
19	Mal. 2:15			
20	Mal. 2:14			
21	Mal. 2:16			
22	Prov. 5:18			
23	Prov. 5:18			
24	Prov. 5:19			
25	Prov. 5:15			
26	Prov. 5:17			
27	Prov. 7:18			
28	1 Cor. 7:3			

SEXUALITY, Part 2

Flee sexual immorality. Every other sin you commit is outside your body, but sexual sins harm your body.[1] As a follower of Christ, your body is a temple of the Holy Spirit. It is not your own because it has been bought with a price. So honor God with your body.[2,3] Do not allow even a hint of sexual immorality.[4] Stay away from even the appearance of evil.[5] It is God's will that you should avoid sexual immorality.[6]

You must learn to control your body in a way that is holy and honorable.[7] Sexual immorality follows when you give in to the desires of your basic human nature.[8] Do not let sin control the way you live; do not give in to its desires.[9,10] Your sinful nature wants you to do just the opposite of what the Holy Spirit wants.[11] The Holy Spirit in you will give you power for virtue and self-control.[12,13] You cannot please God if you are controlled by your sinful nature.[14] So let the Holy Spirit guide your life and you won't be doing what your sinful nature craves.[15]

Keep your marriage honorable and remain faithful to your spouse.[16] A man is to leave his parents and be joined to his wife, and the two are united into one.[17,18] The Lord is your witness and makes two of you into one—body and spirit. Do not break faith with the husband or wife of your youth.[19,20] God hates divorce.[21]

Let your marriage be a fountain of joy and blessing for you both.[22,23] Remain captivated by love and share its pleasures only with your spouse.[24-27] Husbands and wives should meet each other's sexual needs by mutual consent.[28-29] Husbands ought to love their wives as they love their own bodies.[30] Wives must respect their husbands.[31]

Marriage is an illustration of a great mystery: the way Christ and the Church are one.[32]

SIN, Part 1

1	Ex. 20:1	29	Rom. 8:3	57	Lev. 6:2	85	Gal. 5:21
2	Ex. 20:3	30	Rom. 3:20	58	Lev. 6:3	86	Heb. 10:26
3	Ex. 20:4	31	Rom. 8:3	59	James 2:9	87	1 John 1:8
4	Ex. 20:5	32	1 Tim. 1:15	60	1 Cor. 8:12	88	1 John 1:10
5	Ex. 20:7	33	Rom. 8:2	61	Job 1:22	89	1 John 1:6
6	Ex. 20:8	34	Acts 10:43	62	Amos 2:4	90	John 8:34
7	Ex. 20:9	35	Acts 13:38	63	Amos 2:6	91	Gal. 3:22
8	Ex. 20:10	36	Eph. 1:7	64	Amos 1:6	92	1 Cor. 15:56
9	Ex. 20:11	37	Col. 1:14	65	Amos 1:9	93	Rom. 6.23
10	Ex. 20:12	38	Gal. 1:4	66	Amos 1:11	94	John 8:24
11	Ex. 20:13	39	2 Cor. 5:19	67	Hos. 13:2		
12	Ex. 20:14	40	2 Cor. 5:21	68	2 Kings 21:11		
13	Ex. 20:15	41	Rom. 5:8	69	2 Tim. 3:2		
14	Ex. 20:16	42	Heb. 11:6	70	2 Tim. 3:3		
15	Ex. 20:17	43	Rom. 5:12	71	2 Tim. 3:4		
16	Matt. 22:37	44	Rom. 5:19	72	2 Tim. 3:5		
17	Matt. 22:38	45	Ps. 51:5	73	2 Tim. 3:2		
18	Matt. 22:39	46	Jer. 17:9	74	2 Tim. 3:3		
19	Matt. 22:40	47	Matt. 15:18	75	2 Tim. 3:4		
20	Rom. 13:9	48	Matt. 15:19	76	2 Tim. 3:5		
21	1 John 3:4	49	Rom. 3:23	77	Matt. 12:31		
22	1 John 5:17	50	Gal. 5:19	78	Matt. 12:32		
23	James 2:10	51	Gal. 5:20	79	Mark 3:28		
24	Lev. 4:27	52	Gal. 5:21	80	Mark 3:29		
25	Lev. 5:17	53	1 Peter 2:1	81	Luke 12:10		
26	James 4:17	54	Prov. 21:4	82	1 John 3:9		
27	Gal. 3:11	55	Prov. 17:19	83	1 John 3:6		
28	Gal. 2:16	56	Prov. 14:21	84	1 John 5:18		

SIN, Part 1

God spoke all these words to Moses:

- Do not look to any other god but me.
- Do not make any idol in the form of anything on earth or in the sea or sky.
- Do not misuse the name of the Lord.
- Remember the Sabbath by keeping it a holy day.
- Honor your father and your mother.
- Do not commit murder.
- Do not commit adultery.
- Do not steal.
- Do not tell a lie.
- Do not covet anything that is not yours.[1-15]

God's entire law and all its demands are summarized by two commandments: Love the Lord with all your heart, soul, mind, and strength. Love your neighbor in the same way you love yourself.[16-20]

Sin is the breaking of God's laws.[21] All wrongdoing is sin.[22] Breaking even one of God's laws makes you guilty of breaking the entire law.[23] Unintentional sins[24] and sins done in ignorance of God's laws are not excused.[25] It is even a sin to fail to do what you know you ought to do.[26] It is humanly impossible to please God even by sincerely trying to keep these laws.[27-41] Faith in Jesus is the only way to please God.[42]

Sin and its consequence, death, entered the human race through one man, Adam.[43,44] Consequently, you inherited a sinful nature at birth.[45] Sin is deeply imbedded in your heart, and can easily deceive you.[46-48] Every human being is guilty of sin and fails to meet God's expectations.[49]

The actions of a sinful nature are myriad. Some are obvious like sexual immorality, selfish ambition, drunkenness, anger, narcissism, greed, and slander. Many are not obvious, such as pride, hatred, jealousy, greed, and hypocrisy.[50-81]

You cannot go on deliberately sinning and at the same time claim to be born again.[82] No one who maintains a relationship with God lives a sinful lifestyle.[83,84] Those who live in that way will not inherit the kingdom of God[85] There is no remedy for anyone who deliberately keeps on sinning after learning the truth of the gospel.[86]

If you claim to be without sin, you are in denial, deceiving yourself, and contradicting God.[87,88] You cannot truthfully claim to have fellowship with God and live in denial of your own guilt at the same time.[89] Everyone who sins is a slave to sin.[90] In fact, the whole world is a prisoner of sin.[91] The result of sin is death, but the gift of God is eternal life through faith in Jesus Christ.[92-94]

SIN, Part 2

1	1 John 2:1	30	1 Cor. 6:18
2	Heb. 4:15	31	1 Cor. 10:13
3	1 Peter 3:18	32	Ps. 119:11
4	Heb. 9:28	33	Ex. 20:20
5	1 John 1:9	34	Num. 32:23
6	Rom. 4:8	35	Luke 17:2
7	1 John 1:9	36	1 John 5:16
8	Ps. 103:10	37	Gal. 6:1
9	Heb. 8:12	38	James 5:20
10	Ps. 103:12	39	1 Peter 4:8
11	Mark 11:25	40	Heb. 12:1
12	Luke 11:4	41	Gal. 6:7
13	Matt. 6:15	42	Gal. 6:8
14	Ps. 66:18		
15	Rom. 6:12		
16	Rom. 6:14		
17	Eph. 4:26		
18	1 Thess. 5:22		
19	Mark 9:43		
20	Mark 9:45		
21	Mark 9:47		
22	1 Peter 2:11		
23	Col. 3:5		
24	2 Tim. 2:22		
25	James 1:21		
26	1 Peter 2:1		
27	Gal. 5:16		
28	1 Thess. 4:3		
29	James 1:14		

SIN, Part 2

When you do sin, you have an advocate with God in your defense, Jesus Christ the Righteous One.[1] He can sympathize with your weaknesses because he was tempted in every way just like you—only without sin.[2] He died for your sins once and for all—the righteous for the unrighteous—to bring you to God's salvation.[3,4] If you confess your sins, God will forgive them all and purify you from all unrighteousness.[5] He will never count your sin against you.[6] If you confess your sins, God is faithful to his own nature and just and will forgive your sins and give you a full pardon for them all.[7] He does not treat us as our sins deserve.[8] He will forgive your sins and never bring them up again.[9] He puts them away from us as far as the east is from the west.[10]

Pray for the forgiveness of your own sins, always forgiving those who have sinned against you.[11,12] God will not forgive you if you do not forgive others.[13] He will not hear your prayers if you hold sin in your heart.[14]

Do not let your sin nature control your life.[15] Sin is always waiting just around the corner to ruin you, especially when you are angry.[16,17] Avoid every kind of sin.[18] Get rid of anything that causes you to sin.[19-21] Abstain from indulging sinful desires.[22-26] Live in the power of the Holy Spirit and you will not gratify the desires of your sinful nature.[27] It is God's will that you be sanctified.[28]

Temptations arise from your own evil desires.[29] They often result in sin against your own body as well as against God.[30] These temptations in your life are no different than what others experience and not more than you can resist. Remember that God will show you a way to escape them if you ask.[31]

Keep away from sin by hiding God's Word in your heart.[32] Fear the Lord; it will keep you from sinning.[33] You can be sure that your sin will find you out.[34]

You must not cause a child to sin. It would be better for you to be thrown into the sea with a millstone around your neck than to lead a child into sin.[35]

Pray for a member of your congregation if you see them committing sin.[36,37] Turn a sinner from the error of their way and you will have saved them from death.[138] Above all, love each other deeply because love covers a multitude of sins.[39]

Get rid of everything that hinders you and the sins that so easily distract and entangle you, and run with perseverance the race that God has marked out for you to run.[40]

Do not be deceived; you cannot mock God. You will reap what you sow. If you live for your sinful nature, you will reap your own destruction, but if you live to please God, you will reap eternal life.[41,42]

SLANDER

1	Lev. 19:16	29	James 1:26
2	Ex. 20:16	30	Matt. 22:39
3	Prov. 24:28	31	1 Peter 3:10
4	Prov. 3:30		
5	Ps. 34:13		
6	Prov. 12:22		
7	Ps. 101:5		
8	Prov. 6:17		
9	Prov. 6:19		
10	Ps. 15:1		
11	Ps. 15:2		
12	Ps. 15:3		
13	Prov. 13:3		
14	Titus 3:		
15	1 Peter 2:1		
16	Eph. 4:31		
17	Col. 3:8		
18	1 Cor. 5:11		
19	James 4:11		
20	Matt. 15:19		
21	Mark 7:22		
22	Matt. 12:34		
23	Matt. 12:35		
24	Matt. 12:36		
25	James 3:6		
26	James 3:8		
27	James 3:5		
28	Luke 12:3		

SLANDER

Do not spread slander or do anything to upset another's life.[1] Do not be a false witness against your neighbor.[2,3] Do not accuse anyone without good reason when they have done you no harm.[4]

Keep your tongue from evil and your lips from speaking lies.[5] God detests those who tell lies, but delights in all who tell the truth.[6] He will not tolerate those who tell lies and slander others, nor will he tolerate conceit, pride, violence, a false witness who pours out lies, or anyone who stirs up trouble.[7-9]

God welcomes those whose walk is blameless, who do righteous acts and speak the truth from their heart. They never speak slander or cast a slur on anyone. They guard their lips and do no wrong to others.[10-13]

Do not slander anyone. On the contrary, be peaceable and considerate, showing true humility to all.[14] Get rid of slander of every kind. Also get rid of its associated vices: malice, deceit, hypocrisy, envy, bitterness, rage, anger, brawling, and filthy language.[15-17] Don't even associate with anyone who calls themselves a Christian, but in fact is a slanderer.[18]

Do not slander or judge a Christian brother or sister. To do so would be speaking against God's law and showing that you are not doing what you know is God's will.[19]

Slander and all other vices come from the human heart. The things you say come from your heart; good from a good one and evil from an evil one.[20-23] You will have to give account on judgment day for every idle word you speak.[24]

Your tongue can be a fire, set by hell itself![25] It is a restless evil, full of poison. It can corrupt your whole person and destroy the course of your whole life.[26] Think of it as a spark in a dry forrest.[27] Remember that whatever you whisper to another in a secret room is likely to be shouted from the housetop![28] So if you consider yourself to be a follower of Christ, but can't or don't control your tongue, your Christianity is worthless.[29]

Love your neighbor in the same way you want them to love you.[30]

Keep your tongue from speaking slander.[31]

SOLITUDE

1	Ps. 37:7	29	Mark 1:45	57	1 Peter 5:7
2	Ps. 46:10	30	Mark 6:31	58	Phil. 4:6
3	Ps. 62:5	31	Mark 6:32	59	Phil. 4:7
4	Ps. 62:1	32	Isa. 46:9	60	Ps. 46:1
5	Ps. 130:7	33	Isa. 46:10	61	Deut. 8:3
6	Lam. 3:26	34	Ps. 46:10	62	Ps. 4:7
7	Lam. 3:25	35	Ps. 95:6	63	Isa. 32:17
8	Isa. 30:15	36	Isa. 55:9	64	Ps. 4:8
9	Ps. 62:2	37	Jer. 33:3	65	2 Peter 3:18
10	Ps. 62:6	38	Ps. 119:15		
11	Ps. 62:7	39	Col. 3:2		
12	Eccl. 3:7	40	Phil. 4:8		
13	Ps. 131:2	41	Ps. 100:2		
14	Ps. 46:10	42	Ps. 97:12		
15	1 Kings 19:11	43	Ps. 118:1		
16	1 Kings 19:12	44	Ps. 107		
17	John 15:4	45	1 John 1:9		
18	Matt. 11:28	46	Isa. 43:25		
19	Matt. 11:29	47	Ps. 66:18		
20	Matt. 11:30	48	James 4:8		
21	Luke 5:16	49	Heb. 10:22		
22	Mark 1:35	50	Eph. 3:12		
23	Luke 4:42	51	Heb. 4:15		
24	Luke 6:12	52	Heb. 4:16		
25	Matt. 14:23	53	Col. 4:2		
26	Mark 6:46	54	Matt. 6:5		
27	Matt. 14:13	55	Matt. 6:6		
28	John 6:15	56	Ps. 55:22		

SOLITUDE

Get alone and be quiet before the Lord and wait patiently for him. Do not fret when others succeed in their wicked ways.[1] Be still, and learn to know God. Everyone on the face of the earth will eventually be forced to look up to him.[2]

Find rest for your soul in God alone. Your hope and salvation come from him. Put your hope in him because of his unfailing love and redemption.[3-5] It is good to sit alone in silence and wait quietly for him because he is good to those who place their hope in him.[6,7] Your strength comes from quietness and trust and your salvation from repentance and rest.[8] He alone is your rock and refuge.[9-11]

There is a time to be silent and alone, just as there is a time to speak to others.[12] Allow your soul to be quiet and still.[13] This is the way to get to know God.[14] He rarely speaks in dramatic ways, but often in a quiet and gentle whisper.[15,16]

Spend time alone with Jesus and stay connected to him. You are like a branch that will wither and die unless it remains connected to its vine.[17] Spend time with him when you are tired and feeling burned out. He will provide rest for your soul. Learn how to live life from him.[18-20]

Jesus often made time to be alone to pray.[21] Sometimes it was early morning, sometimes all night, and regularly after dealing with large crowds of people.[22-29] Sometimes he included his disciples so they too could be alone with him.[30,31]

Meditate on God when you are alone. There is no one more worthy of your time. He is your Creator, and he alone is sovereign over the universe.[32-35] His thoughts and methods are much higher than yours.[36] Call out to him, and he will show you great and mighty things you have never even thought about.[37] Fill your mind with those things that are excellent and worthy of praise.[38-40] Worship him with a glad heart and joyful songs.[41] Give praise and thanks to the Lord because he is good, and his love for you endures forever.[42-44] Honestly confess your sins, knowing that he will forgive them and never bring them up again.[45-47] Come near to God with confidence and freedom because you have a sincere heart and faith in Jesus. You will find grace and mercy to help in your time of need.[48-52] Devote yourself to prayer and do so in solitude.[53-55] Cast your cares and anxiety on the Lord because he cares for you.[56-59]

God will be your refuge and strength.[60] You will come to realize that God, rather than food, is the primary sustaining force in your life.[61] He will fill you with great joy.[62] He will grant you peace, calmness, and confidence forever.[63,64]

Grow in grace and knowledge of Jesus Christ, your Savior.[65]

SPEECH

1	Col. 3:8	28	1 Peter 3:9
2	Eph. 4:29	29	1 Peter 3:10
3	Prov. 4:24	30	Prov. 15:1
4	Eph. 5:4		
5	Prov. 8:13		
6	1 Peter 2:1		
7	James 4:11		
8	Matt. 12:34		
9	Matt. 12:35		
10	Matt. 12:36		
11	Matt. 12:37		
12	Prov. 26:4		
13	Prov. 9:8		
14	Prov. 17:5		
15	Eph. 5:6		
16	Eph. 5:5		
17	1 Tim. 6:20		
18	1 Tim. 6:21		
19	2 Tim. 2:23		
20	2 Tim. 2:24		
21	Eph. 4:15		
22	Ps. 15:2		
23	Eph. 5:19		
24	1 Tim. 4:12		
25	James 1:26		
26	James 3:5		
27	Prov. 17:28		

SPEECH

Get rid of anger, rage, malice, slander, and filthy language.[1] Don't use foul or abusive language.[2] Don't engage in perverse or corrupt talk.[3] Don't let foolish talk, obscene language, or coarse jokes be part of your speech because the Lord hates perverse speech and corruption along with pride and arrogance.[4,5] So get rid of all deceit, malice, hypocrisy, envy, and slander of every kind.[6] Do not slander one another. Doing so puts you in judgement of God's law, an indication that you are not keeping it.[7]

The thoughts in your mind determine what you say. A pure heart is a treasury of good words and an evil heart is the source of evil words. Your speech reveals the contents of your heart. You will be required to give an account on judgment day for every idle word you speak.[8-11]

Don't respond to the stupidity of a fool or you will only look foolish yourself.[12] Do not rebuke a mocker or they will hate you. Rebuke a wise person and they will love you.[13] Do not mock the poor for in so doing you show contempt for their Maker. Do not gloat over the disaster of another or you will not go unpunished.[14]

Don't let anyone deceive you with empty words because you can be sure that God's wrath comes on those who are immoral, impure, or greedy (such a person is an idolater). They have no inheritance in the kingdom of God.[15,16]

Turn away from godless chatter and foolish discussions with those who oppose you with their fake knowledge.[17] Some have wandered away from the faith by following such foolishness.[18] Furthermore, such discussions often cause quarrels.[19] You must not quarrel, but be kind to everyone and not resentful.[20]

Speak the truth in love and thus grow up in Christ.[21] You show your walk is blameless and righteous in this way.[22] Speak to one another in psalms, hymns and spiritual songs, making music in your heart to the Lord.[23] Let your speech be an example to others.[24]

Keep a tight rein on your tongue. Although a small part of your body, it is like a spark in a tinder-dry forest. Anyone who considers themselves religious but does not control their tongue is a hypocrite and makes their religion worthless.[25,26]

Hold your tongue and you will be regarded as discerning. Even a fool is thought wise if he keeps silent.[27]

Don't retaliate with insults when people insult you. Instead, pay them back with a blessing.[28]

Keep your tongue from evil and your lips from lying if you want to have a good life.[29]

Use gentle words to turn away wrath. Harsh words stir up anger.[30]

SPIRITUAL GIFTS

1	Acts 2:38	30	1 Cor. 14:12
2	Eph. 5:18	31	1 Cor. 12:31
3	1 John 3:24	32	1 Cor. 12:8
4	Eph. 1:13	33	1 Cor. 12:9
5	Eph. 1:14	34	1 Cor. 12:10
6	Rom. 6:23	35	Eph. 4:11
7	Eph. 2:8	36	Eph. 4:12
8	Rom. 5:16	37	Eph. 4:13
9	Rom. 5:17	38	1 Cor. 14:1
10	1 Cor. 7:7	39	1 Cor. 13:2
11	Rom. 12:6	40	1 Peter 4:8
12	Rom. 12:3	41	Rom. 12:9
13	1 Tim. 4:14	42	2 Cor. 9:15
14	2 Tim. 1:6		
15	1 Cor. 12:11		
16	1 Cor. 12:7		
17	1 Cor. 12:1		
18	1 Cor. 12:4		
19	1 Cor. 12:5		
20	1 Cor. 12:6		
21	1 Cor. 12:11		
22	1 Cor. 12:27		
23	1 Cor. 12:12		
24	1 Peter 4:10		
25	1 Peter 4:11		
26	Rom. 12:7		
27	Rom. 12:8		
28	Rom. 12:13		
29	1 Peter 4:9		

SPIRITUAL GIFTS

The Holy Spirit is God's gift to you when you repent of your sins and are baptized.[1] Be preoccupied with him![2] He is God's guarantee of your salvation.[3-5]

Salvation leading to eternal life is a gift from God.[6,7] The result of the sin of Adam and Eve was and is death, but the result of Jesus's death is your justification and righteousness before God.[8,9]

Your unique gifts and talents are gifts from God.[10,11] Carefully evaluate your abilities to do certain things well so that you can wisely choose how and where to use these gifts.[12] Do not neglect or underutilize them, but develop and enhance them by every means.[13,14] They are a demonstration of the work of the Holy Spirit in your life, and are not just for you, but for the common good.[15,16]

Make sure you understand your own spiritual gifts.[17] There are many different kinds of gifts, but all originate with God's Holy Spirit who distributes these gifts as he pleases.[18-21] In the same way that the human body has many different parts, all of which are essential and of equal importance for a complete body, so too the church, the body of Christ, has many parts, and you are an essential one of them.[22,23]

Use whatever gift you have been given to serve others. This is the way for you to bring God's grace in into the lives of other people.[24] If your gift is service, do it with all the strength God gives you. If it is speaking or teaching, do it as one speaking the very words of God.[25,26] If it is encouraging others, be positive. If it is contributing to the needs of others, be generous. If it is leadership, govern diligently. If it is showing kindness and mercy to others, do it cheerfully.[27] If it is hospitality, offer it willingly.[28,29]

Try especially hard to develop gifts that build up the church.[30,31] The Holy Spirit has given some the gift of wisdom. Others have special knowledge. Some have remarkable faith, miraculous powers of healing, preaching, discernment, and speaking or interpreting language.[32-34]

God gave gifts to the church: apostles, prophets, evangelists, pastors, and teachers.[35] Their job is to prepare you to do good works and help you become more like Jesus, so that the body of Christ may be built up and united. The ultimate goal is that you reach maturity in faith and knowledge of the Son of God.[36,37]

Don't forget to show love in the use of your gifts.[38] Regardless of which ones you have or how well you use them, you are nothing without love.[39] Above all else, love one another deeply and without pretense because love covers a multitude of sins.[40,41]

Thanks be to God for his indescribable gift![42]

SPIRITUAL WARFARE

1   Eph. 6:12

2   1 Peter 5:8

3   2 Cor. 11:14

4   2 Cor. 11:15

5   1 John 5:19

6   Eph. 2:2

7   John 8:44

8   2 Cor. 4:4

9   Heb. 2:14

10   2 Thess. 2:3

11   2 Thess. 2:4

12   2 Thess. 2:9

13   2 Thess. 2:10

14   2 Cor. 10:3

15   2 Cor. 10:4

16   2 Cor. 10:5

17   Eph. 6:11

18   Eph. 6:10

19   Eph. 6:14

20   Eph. 6:15

21   Eph. 6:16

22   Eph. 6:17

23   Eph. 6:18

24   Eph. 6:13

25   1 Tim. 6:12

26   Josh. 1:9

27   2 Chron. 20:15

28   Zech. 4:6

29   James 4:7

SPIRITUAL WARFARE

Your real enemies in life are not the flesh-and-blood type. They are spiritual powers and authorities and spiritual forces of evil.[1]

Stay alert and watch out for your archenemy, the Devil. He prowls around like a hungry lion, looking for someone to devour.[2] Sometimes he disguises himself as an angel of light, and so it is no wonder that his servants also disguise themselves as ministers of righteousness.[3,4] The whole world is under his control.[5,6] He is a murderer and a liar—actually the father of lies.[7] He has blinded the minds of unbelievers so that they cannot see or understand the gospel of Christ.[8] He has held the power of death over every human being that has ever lived.[9] He will someday appear as the antichrist, calling himself God and deceiving many with counterfeit powers and signs and miracles.[10-13]

This is a war unlike any other, and you can't fight it like human warfare.[14] You must use God's mighty weapons to knock down strongholds of human reasoning and destroy false arguments and obstacles that keep people from knowing God.[15-16]

Use all of God's armor so that you will be able to stand firm against all the strategies of the Devil.[17] Be strong in the Lord and in his mighty power.[18] Stand your ground. Put on God's righteousness as your body armor. Truth is your belt. Your shoes will be the peace that comes from the gospel, making you fully prepared. Faith is a shield that will stop the fiery arrows of the Devil. Salvation will be your helmet. The Word of God will be your offensive weapon. Let prayer be your strategic planning.[19-23] When you have done all of this, you will be able to resist the enemy and still be standing after the battle.[24]

Fight the good fight of faith.[25] Be strong and courageous. Do not be terrified or discouraged because of this challenge.[26] This battle is not yours—it is God's.[27] You cannot win it by might or power, but only by his Spirit.[28]

Submit yourself to God. Resist the Devil and he will flee from you.[29]

SUBMISSION

1   James 4:7

2   Rom. 8:5

3   Rom. 8:6

4   Rom. 8:7

5   Rom. 8:8

6   Rom. 8:9

7   1 Peter 2:13

8   1 Peter 2:14

9   Rom. 13:1

10   Rom. 13:5

11   Rom. 13:6

12   1 Peter 2:15

13   Heb. 13:17

14   Eph. 5:21

15   Rom. 12:10

16   1 Cor. 1:10

17   1 Cor. 16:16

18   Eph. 5:24

19   Col. 3:18

20   Eph. 5:25

21   1 Peter 2:18

SUBMISSION

Submit yourself to God. Resist the devil and he will flee from you.[1]

Set your mind on the things of God and live accordingly.[2] A mind submitted to the Spirit is life and peace; a sinful mind means death.[3] A sinful mind is hostile to God because it will not submit to his law.[4] You cannot please God unless you submit control of your sinful nature to him.[5,6]

Submit yourself for the Lord's sake to every governing authority instituted among mankind. They are sent by God to maintain justice and order.[7,8] Submit to them because they are established by God.[9] Submit to them and pay your taxes because of conscience and to avoid punishment.[10,11] This is God's will and doing so will silence the ignorant talk of foolish people.[12]

Submit to the authority of your congregational leaders because they are accountable for keeping watch over your soul. Obey them so that their work will be a joy and not a burden.[13]

Submit to one another out of reverence for Christ.[14] Honor one another above yourself.[15] Come to agreement with others in order to avoid divisions and factions, especially fellow workers in the church.[16,17]

Wives, submit to your husbands in the same way the church submits to Christ.[18] Understand and support them in ways that honor the Lord.[19]

Husbands, love your wives in the same way that Christ loves the church and gave himself up for it.[20]

Employees submit to your boss with all respect, not only to those who are good and considerate, but also to those who are harsh.[21]

SUFFERING

1	Heb. 12:7	30	2 Cor. 4:10
2	Heb. 12:10	31	1 Peter 4:1
3	James 1:2	32	2 Tim. 1:8
4	Rom. 12:12	33	1 Peter 4:12
5	Rom. 8:18	34	Rom. 8:17
6	1 Peter 1:6	35	1 Peter 2:21
7	2 Cor. 4:17	36	1 Peter 4:13
8	2 Cor. 4:18	37	1 Peter 4:19
9	1 Peter 1:5	38	1 Peter 2:19
10	1 Peter 1:3	39	1 Peter 2:19
11	1 Peter 1:4	40	1 Peter 2:20
12	1 Peter 1:7	41	1 Peter 4:16
13	Isa. 48:10	42	1 Peter 4:1
14	James 1:2	43	1 Peter 4:2
15	James 1:3	44	Isa. 38:17
16	James 1:4	45	2 Cor. 1:9
17	Rom. 5:3	46	Job 36:15
18	Rom. 5:4	47	Gal. 6:2
19	James 1:12	48	Ps. 119:71
20	1 Peter 1:8	49	Ps. 119:67
21	1 Peter 1:9		
22	Phil. 3:10		
23	Phil. 3:11		
24	Rom. 8:17		
25	Col. 1:24		
26	2 Cor. 12:7		
27	2 Cor. 12:8		
28	2 Cor. 12:9		
29	2 Cor. 12:10		

SUFFERING

Endure suffering and hardship because it is God's method of training and discipline for those who follow him.[1] Just like an earthly father trains his children, God disciplines you for your good so that you may share in his holiness.[2]

Think of suffering in the most positive terms.[3] Be patient and joyful.[4] Your present hard times are temporary and do not deserve to be compared with the good times that God will reveal later on that will last forever.[5-8] Rejoice in the midst of your suffering and fix your mind on things that are unseen: God's protection, your new birth, your living hope, and an inheritance kept safe in heaven for you.[9-11]

Suffering is a test to prove that your faith is genuine. It is like a fire that refines precious metals. Your purified and tested faith is more precious than gold or silver and brings glory to Jesus.[12,13] Testing leads to endurance, perseverance, strong character, confident hope and mature faith.[14-18] You will receive the reward of eternal life if you pass the test.[19-21]

Suffering helps you understand the suffering of Christ and identifies you with him and all those who have suffered with and for him.[22-25] It keeps you humble. It is an opportunity to experience God's grace and see his power demonstrated through your weakness.[26-29] It is a way to demonstrate the life of Jesus in your own body.[30]

Have the same attitude as Christ who suffered physical pain.[31] Be willing to suffer for his sake and the gospel and don't be surprised when it happens to you.[32-34] It is your calling.[35] It is a way for you to participate in his suffering.[36]

Commit yourself to God and continue to do good when you suffer.[37] God is pleased when you know and do the right thing and then suffer unfair treatment and injustice for doing so.[38-40] Don't ever be ashamed if you suffer as a Christian, but praise God that you bear his name.[41]

Anyone who has endured suffering tends to abandon self-interest and earthly pursuits, and focus the rest of their life on doing the will of God.[42-44] It reduces self-reliance and increases your dependence on him.[45] It is often a time when he speaks.[46]

Support each other when suffering and in this way you will obey the law of Christ.[47]

Suffering is good because it teaches us to know and do God's will.[48,49]

TEACHING

1	2 Tim. 2:15	28	Matt. 28:20
2	2 Tim. 3:16	29	Rom. 12:7
3	Deut. 6:5	30	Col. 3:16
4	Deut. 6:6	31	Titus 2:1
5	Deut. 6:7	32	1 Tim. 3:2
6	Deut. 6:8	33	2 Tim. 2:24
7	Deut. 6:9	34	Titus 1:9
8	Deut. 11:19	35	Titus 2:7
9	Deut. 4:9	36	James 3:1
10	Prov. 1:8		
11	Prov. 6:20		
12	Prov. 6:23		
13	Prov. 13:14		
14	Prov. 4:2		
15	Prov. 4:4		
16	Ps. 86:11		
17	Ps. 32:8		
18	Isa. 48:17		
19	Ps. 119:66		
20	Ps. 119:33		
21	Ps. 143:10		
22	Ps. 90:12		
23	John 14:23		
24	John 14:24		
25	John 7:16		
26	John 8:31		
27	Matt. 28:19		

TEACHING

Study so that you can be a teacher for God who does not need to be ashamed and who can correctly understand and explain Scripture.[1] It is inspired by God and useful for teaching and training in the right way to live your life.[2]

You must teach your children to love the Lord with all their hearts, all their souls, all their minds, and all their strength. Teach them to be wholeheartedly committed to his commandments. Repeat them over and over. Talk about them when you are at home and away, when you are going to bed and when you are getting up. Write them on the palm of your hand and the doorpost of your house as reminders.[3-8] Be careful yourself that you do not forget your own life experiences. Teach these lessons to your children and grandchildren.[9]

Listen to your father's instruction and do not forsake your mother's teaching.[10,11] Their instruction gives light and their corrections and discipline prepare you for life.[12] They are a fountain of life, turning you away from the snares of death.[13] They give sound teaching and are the path to life.[14,15]

Teach me your way, O Lord, and I will walk in your truth with an undivided heart.[16] Instruct and teach me with your counsel in the way I should go and what is best for me.[17,18] Teach me knowledge and good judgment,[19] to follow your decrees,[20] and to do your will.[21] Teach me to realize the brevity of life so that I might grow in wisdom.[22]

Obey the teachings of Jesus if you want to demonstrate that you love him and want to experience the love of God.[23] His teachings come from God, his Father, who sent him into the world.[24,25] Obey his teaching and prove you really are his disciple.[26] Go and make disciples wherever you can and teach them to obey all he taught.[27,28]

Teach in the church if that is your spiritual gift.[29] Let the message of Christ, in all its richness, fill your life as you teach and counsel each other.[30] Teach what is in accordance with sound doctrine.[31] Leaders in the church must be able to teach[32,33] and have a strong belief in the trustworthy message they have been taught.[34] Show integrity and seriousness in your teaching by setting a good example in doing good works.[35]

Few of us should become teachers, because those who teach will be judged more strictly.[36]

TEMPTATION

1	James 1:13	25	James 5:19
2	James 1:14	26	James 5:20
3	1 Tim. 6:9		
4	Matt. 5:29		
5	2 Tim. 2:22		
6	Matt. 4:7		
7	1 Cor. 10:9		
8	Heb. 3:12		
9	Ps. 95:9		
10	Heb. 3:13		
11	Matt. 6:9		
12	Matt. 6:13		
13	Matt. 26:41		
14	Mark 1:13		
15	Heb. 2:18		
16	Heb. 4:15		
17	2 Peter 2:9		
18	Cor. 10:12		
19	1 Cor. 10:13		
20	1 Peter 5:8		
21	James 4:7		
22	Eph. 6:11		
23	Eph. 6:10		
24	Gal. 6:1		

TEMPTATION

Never say that God is tempting you. God does not tempt anyone, nor can he be tempted by evil.[1]

Temptation comes from your own desires, which seduce you and drag you away from God.[2] For example, people who want to get rich often fall into temptation's trap and into many foolish and harmful desires that plunge them into ruin and destruction.[3] So if your eye, even your good eye, causes you to lust, gouge it out and throw it away. It is better to lose a body part than for your whole body to be thrown into hell.[4] Flee the temptations of youth, and pursue righteousness, faith, love, and peace.[5]

Do not tempt the Lord or put him to the test.[6,7] Do not let your heart turn away from God especially after seeing all he has done for you.[8,9] Encourage each other daily so that none of you may be seduced by sin's subtle temptations.[19]

Pray like this: "Don't let me yield to temptation, but rescue me from the evil one."[11,12] Watch and pray so that you don't fall into temptation, because the spirit is willing, but the body is weak.[13]

Jesus was tempted by Satan in the desert for forty days.[14] Because he suffered through this temptation, he is able to help you when you are being tempted.[15] He is able to sympathize with your weaknesses because he was tempted in every way just like you are.[16] So he knows how to rescue you from temptation.[17]

Be especially careful not to fall when you think you are standing strong against temptation.[18] The temptations in your life are no different from what others experience. God is faithful and will not allow any temptation to be more than you can stand. He will always show you a way out so that you can stand up under it.[19]

Be self-controlled and alert. Your enemy, the Devil, prowls around like a hungry lion looking for someone to devour.[20] Resist the Devil, and he will flee from you.[21] Use all of the defenses God has given you to stand against his evil schemes.[22] Be strong in the mighty power of the Lord.[23]

If someone wanders off into sin, restore them gently. Watch out or you may also be tempted.[24] Go after them, and bring them back. You will have saved them from death.[25,26]

THANKSGIVING

1   1 Thess. 5:18
2   Eph. 5:20
3   Ps. 92:1
4   Ps. 100:4
5   Ps. 105:1
6   1 Chron. 16:34
7   Ps. 107:1
8   Ps. 118:1
9   Ps. 118:29
10 Ps. 136:26
11 Ps. 119:7
12 Ps. 50:23
13 Matt. 15:36
14 Col. 1:12
15 Heb. 12:28
16 2 Cor. 9:15
17 1 Cor. 15:57
18 Col. 3:16
19 Col. 4:2
20 Phil. 4:6
21 Col. 3:17
22 James 1:17
23 Job 1:21
24 Rev. 7:12

THANKSGIVING

Be thankful in all circumstances because this is God's will for you.[1] Continually give thanks to God the Father for everything in the name of Jesus.[2]

It is good to give thanks to the Lord.[3] Come into his presence with thanksgiving. Give thanks to him, and praise his name.[4] Give thanks to the Lord, and proclaim his greatness. Let the whole world know what he has done.[5]

Give thanks to the Lord because he is good, and his faithful love endures forever.[6-10] Thank him by living as you should.[11] Giving thanks is something that truly honors God.[12] Jesus gave thanks before serving a meal.[13]

Give thanks to God who has qualified you through Jesus to share in the kingdom of light, which is unshakable. Be thankful for this privilege, and please God by worshiping him with holy fear and awe.[14,15]

Thank God for the gift to us of his Son. This gift is too wonderful for words.[16] Thank God for giving us victory over sin and death through our Lord Jesus Christ.[17] Let the message about Christ, in all its richness, fill your life, and it will make you thankful.[18]

Devote yourself to prayer with an alert mind and a thankful heart.[19] Do not be anxious about anything, but present all your requests to God in prayer along with thanksgiving.[20]

Do whatever you do, whether in word or deed, in the name of the Lord Jesus, giving thanks to God the Father through him.[21]

Every good gift comes from God, and he never changes.[22] You came into the world with nothing, and you will leave it in the same way. The Lord gives, and the Lord takes away. Blessed be his name.[23]

Thanksgiving is due our God forever and ever.[24]

THEFT

1   Ex. 20:15

2   Deut. 5:19

3   Lev. 19:11

4   Ex. 22:1

5   Ex. 22:4

6   Ex. 22:12

7   Deut. 19:14

8   Ps. 62:10

9   Hab. 2:6

10   Prov. 10:2

11   Prov. 30:8

12   Prov. 30:9

13   Eph. 4:28

14   Titus 2:10

15   Matt. 19:18

16   Mark 10:19

17   Luke 18:20

18   Rom. 13:9

19   Matt. 6:19

20   Matt. 6:20

THEFT

Do not steal. Do not lie or deceive one another.[1-3]

You must make restitution for stolen goods. You must also make restitution for borrowed goods that are stolen or ruined while in your possession.[4-6]

Do not move your neighbor's boundary marker.[7]

Do not engage in extortion to increase your wealth. Do not take pride in stolen goods. Do not hoard them.[8-9] Ill-gotten wealth has no lasting value. Do not set your heart on it.[10]

Beware both poverty and riches. The latter may make you arrogant and disown the Lord. The former may force you to steal and dishonor the name of God.[11,12]

You must not steal, but work, doing something useful with your own hands, so that you may have something to share with those in need.[13] Do not steal from your employer, but show that you can be fully trusted. This makes the gospel attractive to others.[14]

All of the commandments—do not steal, do not murder, do not commit adultery, do not lie, do not defraud, do not covet, honor your parents, may be summed up in this one single rule—"Love your neighbor as yourself."[15-18]

Do not store up treasures on earth where they may be stolen. Put your treasure in heaven where it is ensured against theft.[19,20]

TIME

1	Eph. 5:16	30	Heb. 1:1
2	1 Chron. 12:32	31	1 Peter 1:20
3	Rom. 13:11	32	Gal. 4:4
4	Luke 12:56	33	Gal. 4:5
5	Matt. 16:3	34	Rom. 5:6
6	Isa. 33:6	35	1 Peter 3:18
7	Hos. 10:12	36	2 Tim. 1:9
8	Ps. 62:8	37	Heb. 10:10
9	Ps. 9:9	38	Mark 1:15
10	Heb. 4:16	39	Acts 3:19
11	2 Cor. 12:9	40	2 Cor. 6:2
12	Ps. 130:5	41	Heb. 9:28
13	Ps. 40:1	42	Mark 13:33
14	2 Peter 3:8	43	Luke 12:40
15	Ps. 31:15	44	John 5:25
16	Eccl. 3:11	45	John 5:28
17	Eccl. 3:1	46	John 4:23
18	Eccl. 3:2	47	Gal. 6:9
19	Eccl. 3:3	48	1 Peter 5:6
20	Eccl. 3:4		
21	Eccl. 3:5		
22	Eccl. 3:6		
23	Eccl. 3:7		
24	Eccl. 3:8		
25	Ps. 34:1		
26	Phil. 4:4		
27	1 Thess. 5:17		
28	Eph. 6:18		
29	Ps. 34:1		

TIME

Make the best use of your time. Make the most of every opportunity because the times are evil.[1]

You need to understand the times in which you live.[2,3] Just as you know how to interpret the signs of changing weather in the sky, you need to know how to interpret the signs of the times.[4,5]

Trust God to be the sure foundation for your times. He is a rich store of salvation and wisdom and knowledge. The fear of the Lord is the key to this treasure.[6] So plow up the hard ground of your heart, and plant good seeds of righteousness. Now is the time to seek the Lord.[7]

Trust in the Lord at all times. Pour out your heart to him because he is a refuge for the oppressed and a stronghold in times of trouble.[8,9] Go to him with confidence for help in times of need.[10] His grace is all you need. His power is demonstrated best in times when you are weak.[11]

Wait patiently for the Lord, and put your hope in his word.[12,13] Remember that with the Lord, a day is like a thousand years and a thousand years are like a day.[14] Your times are in his hands.[15]

God has made everything beautiful in its time and has imprinted eternity in your heart, even though it is impossible to fully comprehend.[16] There is a time and a season for every activity under heaven, from birth to death.[17-24]

Praise the Lord at all times.[25] Rejoice in the Lord always.[26] Pray all the time and on every occasion.[27] Stay alert, and be persistent in your prayers.[28] Speak the praises of the Lord at all times.[29]

In the past, God spoke through the prophets at many different times about Christ, who was chosen before the creation of the world and revealed at just the right time to redeem us from the demands of the law.[30-33] Although sinless, he suffered and died for our sins, and was miraculously raised from the dead.[34-36] It is God's will for you to be made holy by his once-for-all-time sacrifice.[37]

So the time has come to repent and believe the Good News that God will wipe out your sins.[38-40] Christ will appear a second time to bring salvation to those who are waiting for him.[41] Be alert and on your guard because no one knows when that time will come.[42-45]

The time has come when true worship of God must be a spiritual exercise in the pursuit of truth.[46]

Do not become weary in doing good, for you will reap a harvest in due time if you do not give up.[47]

Humble yourself under God's mighty hand so he may lift you up in due time.[48]

TRUST

1	John 14:1		30	Ps. 37:5
2	John 14:6		31	Ps. 84:12
3	Prov. 3:5		32	Ps. 31:14
4	Prov. 3:6		33	Ps. 56:3
5	Isa. 26:4		34	Ps. 56:4
6	Nah. 1:7		35	Ps. 33:21
7	Jer. 17:7		36	Ps. 40:4
8	Isa. 26:3		37	Prov. 28:26
9	Isa. 41:10		38	Isa. 2:22
10	Isa. 30:15		39	Ps. 146:3
11	Isa. 43:4		40	Prov. 29:25
12	Isa. 43:1		41	Prov. 11:28
13	Isa. 43:2		42	1 Cor. 13:7
14	Ps. 37:3			
15	Titus 3:8			
16	Rom. 4:5			
17	Eph. 2:9			
18	Rom. 5:1			
19	Rom. 5:2			
20	Eph. 2:8			
21	John 12:36			
22	Eph. 2:10			
23	Rom. 15:13			
24	Isa. 12:2			
25	Ps. 91:2			
26	Ps. 28:7			
27	Ps. 32:10			
28	Ps. 13:5			
29	Ps. 9:10			

TRUST

Put your trust in Jesus, just as you have trusted God.[1] He is the way and the truth and the life. No one gets to God except through him.[2]

Trust in the Lord with all your heart and do not lean on your own understanding.[3] Acknowledge him in all your ways, and he will make your paths straight.[4] Trust in the Lord forever—he is the eternal Rock.[5] The Lord is good, a refuge for those in trouble. He cares for those who trust him.[6] He blesses those who put their confident trust in him.[7]

Put your steadfast trust in the Lord, and he will keep your mind in perfect peace.[8] Do not be fearful or upset, because he is with you. He will strengthen and help you. He will hold you up with his right hand.[9] Your salvation is found in repentance and rest and your strength in quietness and trust, not in anything you can do for yourself.[10] God loves you, and you are precious and honored in his eyes.[11] He created and formed you and called you by name. You are his own.[12] He will protect you when you pass through the deep waters and fiery trials of life.[13]

Trust in the Lord and devote yourself to doing good.[14,15] However, you are not justified before God because of your good works, but because of your faith.[16] Salvation is not a reward for the good things you have done.[17] You are made right with God by faith in what Jesus Christ has done for you.[18] Because you put your trust in Christ, he has brought you into a place of undeserved privilege where you can confidently and joyfully look forward to sharing God's glory.[19] Salvation is a gift from God; you can't take any credit for it.[20] So put your trust in God in light of all this.[21] You are his masterpiece, a new creation in Christ Jesus so that you can do good works for him.[22] Put your trust in him, and he will fill you with joy and peace and hope.[23]

Trust in God for your salvation. He will be your strength and song.[24] Trust in the Lord; he is your refuge and fortress.[25] Let your heart trust him, and he will fill it with joy.[26] Trust him and you will be surrounded by his unfailing love.[27] Rejoice in your salvation because you trust his unfailing love![28] Trust in the Lord; he has never forsaken those who seek him.[29]

Commit yourself to the Lord and trust in him.[30] Trust the Lord, and he will bless you.[31,32] Trust him when you are afraid.[33] Praise his name, and do not be afraid.[34] Trust in his holy name, and let your heart rejoice.[35]

Trust in the Lord, and do not look to the proud or progressive.[36] Trusting yourself is foolish; trusting God's wisdom is safe.[37] Do not trust mankind who has but a breath in his nostrils and is of little account.[38] Don't put your trust in princes or mortal men who cannot save you.[39] The fear of man will prove to be a snare, but trusting the Lord ensures your safety.[40]

Do not put your trust in wealth or you will fall.[41]

Love always trusts.[42]

TRUTH, Part 1

1	Ps. 119:30	30	Rom. 1:25
2	Jer. 10:10	31	Rom. 2:2
3	Psa. 31:5	32	Rom. 2:8
4	Isa. 45:19	33	2 Thess. 2:10
5	Ps. 33:4	34	2 Thess. 2:12
6	Ps. 119:151	35	2 Tim. 4:4
7	Ps. 119:142	36	Heb. 10:26
8	Ps. 119:160	37	John 4:23
9	Ps. 51:6	38	John 4:24
10	Prov. 30:5	39	1 Cor. 2:13
11	Rev. 15:3	40	1 Cor. 2:14
12	Rev. 16:7	41	1 Cor. 2:12
13	Rev. 19:2	42	2 Tim. 3:7
14	John 17:17	43	1 Tim. 3:9
15	2 Tim. 3:16	44	1 Peter 1:22
16	2 Tim. 2:15	45	1 John 4:20
17	John 16:13	46	1 John 1:6
18	1 Tim. 2:4	47	1 John 1:8
19	John 14:6	48	1 John 2:4
20	1 John 5:20	49	1 John 3:18
21	John 17:3	50	1 John 3:19
22	Rom. 1:16	51	Eph. 4:15
23	Col. 1:5	52	1 Cor. 13:6
24	Gal. 2:5		
25	Gal. 2:14		
26	Eph. 1:13		
27	Col. 1:6		
28	John 8:32		
29	Rom. 1:18		

TRUTH, Part 1

Choose the way of truth. Set your heart on God's ways.[1] He is the true and living God, the eternal King.[3] He is the God of truth.[3] He has not spoken in secret but has spoken the truth and declared what is right.[4] His word is right and true.[5] All his commandments are true.[6] His righteousness is everlasting, and his righteous laws are true and never change.[7,8]

Surely God desires truth in your inner being.[9] Every word of his is truth.[10] True and just are his ways and his judgments.[11-13] His word is truth.[14] He has inspired all Scripture to teach us the truth and what is right and what is wrong.[15] Study it so that you will be able to understand and explain it correctly.[16] God's Spirit will guide you into all truth.[17]

God wants all people to be saved and come to a knowledge of the truth.[18] Jesus is the Truth, the Way and the Life. No one can come to God except through him.[19] He came to bring us an understanding of the true God and eternal life.[20] This is eternal life: to know the only true God and Jesus Christ whom He has sent.[21] The gospel of Christ is the powerful plan of God to bring you salvation.[22] The gospel is truth.[23-27] This truth can set you free.[28]

The wrath of God will be revealed against wicked persons who suppress the truth.[29] They have exchanged the truth of God for a lie, worshipping created things rather than the Creator.[30] His judgment against these people will be based on truth.[31] Those who are self-seeking and reject the truth, turning aside rather to man-made myths will perish because they refuse to love the truth and be saved.[32-35] Those who have knowledge of the truth but deliberately keep on sinning will likewise perish.[36]

God wants your worship to be based on truth and spiritual in nature, coming from your inner self.[37] This is because God himself is a spiritual being.[38]

Spiritual truth cannot be expressed in words taught by human wisdom but only those spiritual words taught by the Holy Spirit.[39] Furthermore, the person without the Holy Spirit does not accept these truths because they are foolishness to him or her. They can only be understood by spiritual discernment.[40] God will give you his Spirit so that you can understand the truth of the salvation, which he has freely given you.[41] Those who do not accept these truths are always learning but never able to come to a knowledge of truth.[42] Hold on to these deep truths with a clear conscience.[43]

Obeying the truth leads you to love others. Do so deeply, from your heart.[44] If you say you love God but harbor hatred for a another follower of Jesus, you are not telling the truth.[45] If you claim to have fellowship with God but live in darkness, claim to be without sin, or do not follow his commands, you are not telling the truth—not even to yourself.[46-48] You know you belong to the truth if you love others with actions and not just words.[49-50] Speak the truth in love.[51] Love rejoices in the truth.[52]

TRUTH, Part 2

1	John 1:14	30	Ex. 20:16
2	John 1:17	31	Ex. 20:16
3	John 8:58	32	Zech. 7:9
4	John 3:3	33	Titus 3:2
5	John 3:5	34	Ps. 51:6
6	John 5:24	35	Prov. 12:22
7	John 6:47	36	Phil. 4:8
8	John 5:25		
9	John 8:51		
10	Matt. 10:42		
11	Mark 9:41		
12	Matt. 25:40		
13	Matt. 25:45		
14	Matt. 17:20		
15	Matt. 18:3		
16	Mark 10:15		
17	Luke 18:17		
18	Matt. 18:13		
19	Matt. 19:23		
20	Mark 10:29		
21	Luke 18:29		
22	Luke 21:3		
23	Matt. 6:2		
24	Matt. 6:5		
25	John 8:34		
26	John 12:24		
27	Eph. 4:25		
28	Zech. 8:16		
29	Ps. 34:13		

TRUTH, Part 2

Jesus brought grace and truth from God.[1,2] He often said, "I tell you the truth:"

- • ...I was in existence long before Abraham was born.[3]
- • ...You must be born again to enter the kingdom of God.[4,5]
- • ...You have eternal life if you believe in Jesus[6,7]
- • ...You will hear the call of Jesus after your death if you believe him now.[8]
- • ...You will never see death if you keep his word.[9]
- • ...You will receive a reward for assisting a disciple of Christ.[10,11]
- • ...Anything done for the least of his followers is the same as doing it for Christ.[12,13]
- • ...Faith as small as a grain of mustard seed can move mountains.[14]
- • ...Unless you become like a little child, you will never enter the kingdom of God.[15-17]
- • ...There is great joy in heaven over every repentant sinner.[18]
- • ...It is hard for a rich person to enter the kingdom of God.[19]
- • ...You will be rewarded for denying yourself for the sake of the gospel.[20,21]
- • ...Proportional giving to charity is commendable.[22]
- • ...Charity should be private and not for public display.[23]
- • ...Prayer should be in secret.[24]
- • ...Everyone who sins is a slave to sin.[25]
- • ...A kernel of wheat produces many seeds only if it falls into the ground and dies first.[26]

Tell the truth to your neighbors because you are part of the same community.[27,28] Keep your lips from telling lies.[29,30] Do not lie or give false testimony against your neighbor.[31,] Administer true justice.[32] Slander no one, but be humble, peaceable and considerate to everyone.[33] God desires honesty and delights in people who are truthful. He detests lying.[34,35]

Think about truth, righteousness, purity, beauty, excellence, and whatever is noble and admirable.[36]

UNITY

1	Deut. 6:4	30	1 Cor. 12:19	59	Phil. 2:7
2	Rom. 3:30	31	1 Cor. 12:20	60	Phil. 2:8
3	1 Cor. 8:4	32	1 Cor. 12:26	61	Rom. 12:16
4	James 4:12	33	1 Cor. 12:27	62	1 Peter 3:8
5	Matt. 28:19	34	1 Cor. 12:13	63	Rom. 15:5
6	John 10:30	35	Eph. 2:14	64	Heb. 12:14
7	John 17:21	36	Eph. 2:15	65	Rom. 15:6
8	John 3:16	37	Eph. 2:16	66	Col. 3:15
9	John 14:24	38	Eph. 2:18	67	Eph. 5:21
10	1 Tim. 2:5	39	Eph. 3:6	68	Heb. 10:25
11	John 14:26	40	1 Peter 4:10	69	1 Thess. 5:11
12	John 15:26	41	Rom. 12:6	70	Heb. 3:13
13	John 16:7	42	1 Cor. 12:30	71	Gal. 6:10
14	Deut. 6:5	43	1 Cor. 12:8	72	Rom. 12:10
15	Mark 12:29	44	1 Cor. 12:9	73	1 John 4:11
16	Mark 12:30	45	1 Cor. 12:10	74	John 13:34
17	Eph. 4:3	46	Rom. 12:7	75	1 John 3:23
18	Eph. 4:4	47	Rom. 12:8	76	John 13:35
19	Eph. 4:5	48	1 Peter 4:11	77	Col. 3:14
20	Eph. 4:6	49	1 Cor. 12:31		
21	Eph. 4:12	50	John 17:21		
22	Eph. 4:13	51	John 17:22		
23	John 17:23	52	John 17:23		
24	Gen. 2:24	53	1 Peter 3:8		
25	Eph. 5:31	54	1 Cor. 1:10		
26	Matt. 19:6	55	Phil. 2:2		
27	1 Cor. 12:12	56	2 Cor. 13:11		
28	1 Cor. 12:14	57	Phil. 2:5		
29	1 Cor. 12:18	58	Phil. 2:6		

UNITY

The Lord your God is one.[1] There is only one God.[2-4] He has a three-fold name: Father, Son, and Holy Spirit.[5] Jesus and God are one.[6,7] God sent his Son to be the Savior of the world.[8,9] There is one God and one mediator between you and God, the man Christ Jesus.[10] Jesus sent the Holy Spirit to be your Helper in knowing and doing what he taught.[11-13] Love him with all your heart, soul, mind, and strength.[14-16]

Make every effort to keep yourself united in the Holy Spirit, binding yourself together with other believers with peace.[17] There is one Spirit, one Church, one glorious hope for the future, one Lord, one faith, one baptism, and one God and Father who is over all, in all, and living through all.[18-20]

Church leaders have the responsibility to equip God's people to do his work and build up the Church, the body of Christ. The goal is unity and maturity in your faith and knowledge of God's Son.[21,22] God in Christ, and Christ in you creates an important unity. It validates Christ's mission on earth and lets the world know how much you are loved by God.[23]

Marriage is an example of unity. A man is united with his wife and the two become one.[24,25] Since they are no longer two, but one, let no one split apart what God has joined together.[26]

The human body is an example of unity.[27] It is made up of many different parts, but they all work together to form one body. If one part suffers, the whole body suffers.[28-32]

You are a part of the body of Christ, his Church.[33] In it, God has unified access to himself for both Jews and Gentiles through Jesus Christ.[34-39] You have a part to play in this body of believers. God has given you a gift for doing certain things well. Use it willingly to serve one another. [40-49]

You can experience perfect unity with God and others when Christ lives in you.[50-52] Have the same mindset with all believers, being united in spirit and purpose.[53-56] Have the mind of Christ who was humble and obedient.[57-60]

Live in unity and harmony with one another. This pleases God.[61-65] Let the peace of Christ rule your heart since you are a part of his body.[66] Submit to one another out of reverence for Christ.[67]

Do not give up meeting together, but encourage each other.[68-70] Take every opportunity to do good to everyone—especially those united in your faith family.[71] Love others with genuine affection as a reflection of God's love for you and evidence that you are a follower of Christ.[72-76]

Practice love for each other. It is the virtue that binds all other virtues together in perfect unity.[77]

WAITING

1	Ps. 37:7	28	Heb. 9:28
2	Zeph. 3:8	29	1 Thess. 1:10
3	Ps. 130:6	30	James 5:7
4	Ps. 5:3	31	Luke 12:36
5	Ps. 37:34	32	Luke 12:35
6	Ps. 119:166	33	Rom. 8:25
7	Isa. 26:8	34	Rom. 8:23
8	Ps. 130:5	35	Rom. 8:19
9	Isa. 8:17	36	Jude 21
10	Ps. 25:5	37	2 Peter 3:8
11	Hos. 12:6	38	Isa. 40.31
12	Ps. 62:5		
13	Ps. 33:20		
14	Ps. 59:9		
15	Ps. 40:1		
16	Mic. 7:7		
17	Isa. 30:18		
18	Isa. 33:2		
19	Lam. 3:25		
20	Lam. 3:24		
21	Isa. 64:4		
22	Ps. 37:34		
23	Prov. 20:22		
24	Titus 2:13		
25	Lam. 3:26		
26	Ps. 119:166		
27	1 Cor. 1:7		

WAITING

Wait patiently and be quiet before the Lord.[1,2] Wait intensely, more intensely than a night watchmen waits for the morning.[3] Wait in expectation after you have made your requests known to God.[4]

Wait for the Lord, and keep his ways.[5] Follow his commands, and walk in his ways.[6,7] Put your hope in his Word.[8] Put your trust in him.[9] Learn from him as you wait for him, the God of your salvation.[10] Maintain love and justice as you wait for him.[11]

Wait in silence for God alone and put your hope in him.[12] He is your help and defense.[13,14] Wait patiently and hopefully, and he will hear your prayers.[15,16] Blessing and contentment are to be found in waiting for him.[17] He longs to be gracious to those who wait for him. He will be your strength every morning and salvation in time of distress.[18] He is good to those who put their hope in him and wait for him.[19]

Wait for God because he is your inheritance.[20] No one has ever heard; no eye has ever seen; no mind has perceived any other God who acts on behalf of those who wait for him.[21] He will exalt you in due time.[22] Wait for him, and he will deliver you from your distress.[23]

Wait eagerly and quietly for your most anticipated and blessed hope: the glorious appearing of our great God and Savior, Jesus Christ.[24-27] He died once to take away your sins, and will appear a second time to bring salvation to those who are waiting for him.[28,29] Wait patiently for this day, like a farmer waiting for spring rains and his land to yield a good crop.[30] Be like groomsmen waiting for the groom. Be prepared for this day.[31,32] Wait for it patiently with hope for what you do not yet have: the redemption of your body.[33,34] All of creation waits for this day![35] Keep yourself in God's love as you wait for this day.[36]

Do not forget this one thing as you wait: With the Lord one day is like a thousand years and a thousand years are like one day.[37]

Those that wait on the Lord shall renew their strength; they shall mount up with wings like eagles; they shall run and not be weary; they shall walk and not faint.[38]

WEALTH

1	Deut. 8:18	30	1 Tim. 6:7
2	Prov. 3:9	31	1 John 2:15
3	Prov. 23:4	32	1 John 2:16
4	Prov. 27:23	33	1 Cor. 7:31
5	Prov. 27:24	34	1 Cor. 7:30
6	Prov. 23:5	35	James 1:9
7	Deut. 8:11	36	James 1:10
8	Deut. 8:12		
9	Deut. 8:13		
10	Deut. 8:14		
11	Luke 12:15		
12	Col. 3:5		
13	1 Tim. 6:9		
14	1 Tim. 6:10		
15	Matt. 6:24		
16	Luke 12:15		
17	Matt. 16:26		
18	Mark 8:36		
19	Luke 9:25		
20	Matt. 6:19		
21	Luke 12:33		
22	Prov. 19:17		
23	Matt. 6:20		
24	Matt. 6:21		
25	1 Tim. 6:17		
26	1 Tim. 6:18		
27	1 Tim. 6:19		
28	Heb. 13:5		
29	1 Tim. 6:6		

WEALTH

Remember that it is God who gives you the ability to create wealth.[1] Honor the Lord with your wealth.[2] Do not wear yourself out to get rich. Have the wisdom to show restraint.[3] Be sure to know the condition of your financial resources because riches do not endure forever.[4,5] Your wealth can disappear in the blink of an eye.[6]

Be careful that you do not forget the Lord when things are going well by failing to know and do his commands. Otherwise in your prosperity, your heart will become proud and you will forget him.[7-10]

Watch out and be on your guard against all kinds of greed.[11] Greed is a form of idolatry. Do not let it be any part of your life.[12] People who want to get rich fall into the temptations of many foolish and harmful desires that lead to ruin and destruction.[13] The love of money is at the root of all kinds of evil. Many people eager for money have wandered away from the faith and caused themselves much grief.[14]

Do not try to serve two masters at the same time. You will inevitably be devoted to one and despise the other. You cannot serve God and money.[15] Do not attempt to measure the value or quality of your life by the quantity of your possessions.[16] Suppose you could gain the whole world, but at the cost of your own soul. Would it be worth it?[17-19]

Do not store up treasures for yourself on earth where moth, rust, and thieves threaten to destroy or steal them.[20] Sell some of your possessions and give to the poor. In this way, you are lending to the Lord and storing up treasures for yourself in heaven where they will be eternally safe and never exhausted.[21-23] Your heart will surely follow wherever you put your treasure.[24]

Do not be arrogant or put your hope in wealth, which is so uncertain. Instead, put your hope in God who richly provides us with everything for our enjoyment.[25] Do good, and be rich in good deeds, generous and willing to share.[26] This is the way to lay up treasure for yourself in heaven as a firm foundation for the coming age and eternal life.[27]

Keep yourself free from the love of money and be content with what you have. God will never leave or forsake you.[28] Godliness with contentment is great wealth.[29] You brought nothing into this world, and you can take nothing out of it.[30]

Do not love the world nor the things it has to offer. Love of worldly goals and values—sex, money, power, and position—is incompatible with love for God.[31,32] Don't let yourself be attached to your business or absorbed in the joy of your possessions.[33,34]

Take pride in your high position in Christ if you are a Christian who lives in humble circumstances.[35] Rich Christians should take pride in their low position, knowing that they and their riches will pass away like a wildflower in the heat of summer.[36]

WILL OF GOD

1	Mark 12:30	30	1 Peter 1:15
2	Mark 12:31	31	Rom. 12:2
3	Deut. 10:12	32	2 Cor. 3:18
4	Ezek. 20:19	33	Col. 1:9
5	Mic. 6:8	34	Eph. 5:16
6	Jer. 22:3	35	Eph. 5:17
7	Jer. 9:24	36	Heb. 13:21
8	John 6:40	37	Eph. 3:10
9	Col. 1:15	38	1 Tim. 3:15
10	Col. 1:19	39	Eph. 1:9
11	John 3:16	40	Col. 1:18
12	John 3:17	41	Col. 1:15
13	Isa. 53:10	42	Col. 1:19
14	Isa. 53:4	43	1 Cor. 12:12
15	Isa. 53:5	44	1 Cor. 12:27
16	Isa. 53:6	45	Matt. 7:21
17	John 3:36	46	Luke 6:46
18	Acts 4:12	47	1 John 2:17
19	1 Tim. 2:4	48	1 Thess. 5:18
20	1 Peter 2:15		
21	James 2:17		
22	James 2:26		
23	Eph. 2:8		
24	Eph. 2:9		
25	Eph. 2:10		
26	1 Peter 2:15		
27	John 7:17		
28	1 Thess. 4:3		
29	1 Peter 1:16		

WILL OF GOD

Love the Lord your God with all your heart, soul, mind, and strength.[1] Love your neighbor as yourself. There is no greater expression of God's will for you than these two commandments.[2]

God's will for you is that you fear him, walk with him, love him, and serve him with all your heart and soul.[3] Respect and obey all of his commandments.[4] Act justly, love mercy, and walk humbly with him.[5] Do what is just and right for the alien, orphan, widow and those who are oppressed.[6] Tell others that you know the God who delights in kindness, justice and righteousness.[7]

God's will for you is to believe in his Son, Jesus, who was the physical image and full presence on earth of God himself.[8-10] He sent Jesus into the world to bring salvation and the hope of eternal life.[11,12] It was God's will to make him a sacrifice to blot out your sins.[13-16] If you believe in him, you will have this eternal life, but if you reject him, you will suffer the wrath of God.[17] There is no other name under heaven by which you can be saved. Salvation cannot be obtained in any other way.[18] He wants everyone to come to a knowledge of this truth.[19]

It is God's will that you should demonstrate your faith by doing good works.[20-22] It is your mission once you accept the gift of salvation.[23-25] It is God's will that you silence and shame the ignorant talk of foolish know-it-all's by doing good.[26] If you choose to do God's will, you will come to a deeper understanding of the teachings of Jesus.[27]

It is God's will that you be sanctified.[28-30] Don't copy the customs of your culture, but let God transform you into a new person and a way of thinking that is more like Jesus.[31,32] Let him fill you with the knowledge of his will and give you spiritual wisdom and understanding. Then you will learn to know God's will for you.[33]

Do your best to understand the will of God. Make the most of every opportunity to do what you know to be the will of God because the times you live in are evil.[34,35] God will equip you with everything you need for doing his will and becoming what is pleasing to him.[36]

It is God's will to make his wisdom known to the world through the Church.[37] This Church is the visible body of Christ in the world, the family of God, and the pillar and foundation of the truth.[38] God has revealed the mystery of his will through Jesus, who now is the head of the Church.[39-42] You are an important part of this body if you put your faith in him.[43,44]

You must know and do the will of God in order to enter the kingdom of heaven.[45,46] The world and everything it offers will pass away, but you will live forever if you do the will of God.[47]

Be thankful in all of your circumstances because this is the will of God for everyone who belongs to Jesus.[48]

WISDOM

1	Prov. 9:10	30	1 Cor. 2:16
2	Prov. 9:10	31	Prov. 3:7
3	Isa. 33:6	32	Jer. 9:23
4	Ps. 111:10	33	1 Cor. 2:5
5	Ps. 19:7	34	1 Cor. 2:13
6	Prov. 4:7	35	Jer. 9:24
7	Prov. 4:5	36	Col. 2:3
8	Prov. 2:2	37	Col. 3:16
9	Prov. 16:16	38	James 3:13
10	Prov. 8:11	39	Eph. 5:15
11	Prov. 23:4	40	Eph. 5:16
12	Prov. 19:20	41	Col. 4:5
13	Prov. 4:6	42	Eph. 5:17
14	Prov. 9:11	43	Prov. 29:15
15	Luke 7:35	44	James 1:5
16	Ps. 90:12	45	James 3:17
17	Job 9:4		
18	Job 12:13		
19	Rom. 11:33		
20	Jer. 10:12		
21	1 Cor. 3:19		
22	1 Cor. 1:27		
23	Rom. 1:20		
24	Rom. 1:21		
25	Rom. 1:22		
26	Rom. 1:25		
27	Col. 2:8		
28	1 Cor. 2:12		
29	1 Cor. 2:14		

WISDOM

The fear of the Lord is the beginning of wisdom and knowledge.[1,2] He will be the sure foundation for your times, a rich store of salvation and wisdom and knowledge. The fear of the Lord is the key to this treasure.[3] Follow his law and statutes, and they will make you wise.[4,5]

Focus your attention and apply yourself to gaining wisdom regardless of the cost; it is of supreme value.[6-8] Wisdom is worth more than gold, and understanding is worth more than silver. It is more precious than rubies, and nothing you desire can compare with it.[9,10] Do not wear yourself out to get rich, but have the wisdom to show restraint.[11]

Listen to good advice and accept instruction, and you will become wise.[12] Wisdom will protect you and add years to your life.[13,14] Wisdom is proven right in the end by all who follow her.[15] Learn to appreciate the brevity of your life, and you will gain a heart of wisdom.[16]

The wisdom of God is profound, and his power is vast.[17,18] The riches of his wisdom and understanding are deep and beyond our understanding.[19] He created the earth by his power and wisdom and stretched out the heavens by his understanding.[20]

The wisdom of the world is foolishness in God's sight.[21] He has chosen things the world considers foolish in order to shame those who think they are wise.[22] Many so-called wise people reject what can be known of God simply by looking at his marvelous creation and thus become foolish and confused in their thinking.[23-26] Be careful that you are not taken in by their hollow and deceptive philosophies, which are based on human understanding.[27]

Your wisdom should come from the Holy Spirit, who is from God, and who helps you understand what he has freely given us.[28] The person who does not have the Spirit does not accept what comes from God and cannot understand what can only be spiritually discerned.[29] You can begin to understand the mind of God if you have the mind of Christ.[30]

Do not be wise in your own eyes or boast of your wisdom, your strength or your riches.[31,32] Your faith does not rest on any of these, but only on God's power and words taught by the Holy Spirit.[33,34] Your only reason to boast is that you understand and know God.[35] All the treasures of wisdom and knowledge are to be found in Christ.[36] Let his wisdom and words fill and govern your life.[37]

Let your wisdom show by humbly doing good deeds.[38] Live wisely and make the most of every opportunity.[39-41] Do not be foolish but learn to understand God's will.[42]

Discipline your children. It instills wisdom in them and avoids disgrace to their parents.[43]

If you lack wisdom, ask God for it. He gives it generously and without finding fault.[44] It comes directly from heaven and is pure, peace loving, considerate, merciful, impartial, and sincere.[45]

WITNESS

1	Matt. 4:19	30	Eph. 5:16
2	Luke 19:10	31	2 Tim. 2:15
3	John 14:6	32	2 Tim. 4:2
4	Acts 4:12	33	Phil. 1:27
5	1 Tim. 2:4	34	1 Peter 3.16
6	Matt. 18:14	35	Philem. 6
7	Luke 15:7	36	Eph. 6:19
8	2 Thess. 1:8	37	2 Tim. 2:16
9	Rom. 1:16	38	Matt. 5:14
10	Rom. 1:17	39	Matt. 5:16
11	Gal. 1:11	40	James 5:20
12	2 Tim. 1:8	41	Dan. 12:3
13	2 Tim. 1:7		
14	John 14:26		
15	Rom. 8:26		
16	Matt. 10:32		
17	Mark 8:38		
18	Mark 16:15		
19	Matt. 28:19		
20	Matt. 28:20		
21	Matt. 28:18		
22	John 20:21		
23	Matt. 24:14		
24	Matt. 9:37		
25	Matt. 9:38		
26	Luke 10:2		
27	Rom. 10:14		
28	Rom. 10:15		
29	1 Peter 3:15		

WITNESS

Follow Jesus, and he will teach and enable you to be a good witness for him.[1] He came into the world to seek and to save those who are lost.[2] He is the Way, the Truth, and the Life. No one can come to God except through him.[3] Salvation is found in no one else, for there is no other name under heaven given to mankind by which we must be saved.[4] God is not willing that anyone should be lost but wants everyone to be saved and come to a knowledge of the truth.[5,6] There is great rejoicing in heaven over every single person who repents of their sin and turns to God.[7] However, he will punish those who reject him and do not obey the gospel of Jesus Christ.[8]

Do not be ashamed of this gospel, because it is God's powerful way of showing us his own righteousness and how we can be made righteous in his sight by faith in Jesus.[9,10] This is not something made up by the human mind but has been revealed to us by God himself through faith.[11] Present it boldly and powerfully to your world, tempered with love and self-discipline.[12,13] You can count on God's Spirit to enable you to do this and Christ who will proudly present you to his Father, God.[14-16] Anyone ashamed of this good news in the midst of our rebellious and perverse culture brings shame on Jesus and themselves.[17]

Go into all the world and spread the gospel to all nations.[18] Make disciples everywhere, baptizing them in the name of the Father and of the Son and of the Holy Spirit.[19] Teach them to obey everything Jesus commanded.[20] He has all authority over heaven and earth and commands us to go into all the world and present this good news to all nations.[21-23]

There are many people in the world who do not believe in Jesus. Although this "harvest" is plentiful, there are few workers.[24] Pray to God to send more workers.[25,26] No one can believe in someone of whom they have not heard. And no one can hear without someone telling them. And no one can go tell them without someone to send them. It is a beautiful thing to be part of this process.[27,28]

Prepare yourself to be a witness for Christ at any time.[29] Make the most of every opportunity because time is short and the culture is evil.[30] Study so that you can correctly explain the Scriptures.[31] Use them to correct, rebuke, and encourage others with great patience and careful instruction.[32] Conduct yourself in a manner worthy of the gospel of Christ.[33,34] Be active in sharing your faith so that you will have a full understanding of every good thing you have in Christ.[35] Pray for others who are sharing their faith.[36] Avoid godless chatter as it is a distraction from meaningful conversation and leads to ungodly character.[37]

You are the light of the world.[38] Let your light shine so that others can see your good works and glorify God.[39] Remember this: If you turn a sinner from the error of their way, you will save a soul from death.[40]

Those who lead many to righteousness will shine like the stars for ever and ever.[41]

WORK

1   Col. 3:23

2   Eph. 6:7

3   Eccl. 9:10

4   1 Thess. 5:14

5   2 Thess. 3:6

6   2 Thess. 3:10

7   2 Thess. 3:12

8   John 6:27

9   Jer. 17:22

10   Ex. 20:8

11   Deut. 5:12

12   Ex. 20:10

13   Ex. 20:11

14   Ex. 31:15

15   Ex. 35:2

16   Lev. 23:3

17   Matt. 12:12

18   Matt. 5:16

19   Isa. 58:13

20   Mark 2:27

21   Ezek. 20:20

22   Ezek. 20:12

23   Ex. 31:13

24   Matt. 12:8

25   Mark 2:28

26   Luke 6:5

27   John 6:29

WORK

Work willingly and enthusiastically at whatever you do, as though you were working for the Lord rather than other people.[1,2] Whatever your hand finds to do, do it with all your might, for in the grave, where you are going, there is neither working nor planning nor knowledge nor wisdom.[3]

Warn those who will not work.[4] Keep away from anyone who is idle.[5] A person must work if they wish to eat.[6] Urge everyone to work for their living.[7]

Don't work with concern about the perishable things of this world, like food. Spend your energy seeking the eternal life that Jesus can give you. This is guaranteed by God to last forever.[8]

Do not do your work on the Sabbath, but make it a holy day.[9-11] No one in your household should do their work on this day.[12] The Lord created the universe in six days but rested from his work on the seventh day. That is why it is to be a day set aside from work as a holy day.[13] You have six days each week for your ordinary work, but the seventh is to be a day of complete rest.[14-16]

Good works are permitted on the Sabbath.[17] Let others see these good works and praise your Father in heaven.[18]

Keep the Sabbath free from idle talk and doing as you please. Honor and take delight in this day by not going your own way or pursuing your own interests.[19] This special day of rest was meant for your benefit.[20]

A day of rest from all your labors is also meant to be a sign to remind you of the Lord your God.[21] This is a special and holy day set apart to honor him and remind you that he has set you apart from the world to be holy.[22,23] Jesus is Lord of this day.[24-26]

The only work God really wants from you is for you to believe in Jesus, the one he has sent to be the Savior of the world.[27]

WORKS

1	Eph. 2:8	28	Rom. 12:8
2	Eph. 2:9	29	Heb. 10:24
3	Rom. 4:5	30	2 Tim. 2:15
4	Rom. 11:6	31	Phil. 2:12
5	Rom. 5:1	32	Heb. 12:14
6	Rom. 6:23	33	Heb. 6:11
7	2 Cor. 9:15	34	Eph. 6:8
8	Heb. 11:6	35	Ps. 62:12
9	James 2:17	36	Jer. 17:10
10	James 2:18	37	Heb. 6:10
11	James 2:24	38	Gal. 6:9
12	James 2:20	39	Rom. 2:7
13	James 2:22	40	Phil. 2:13
14	Eph. 2:10	41	Col. 1:10
15	Matt. 5:14	42	John 6:29
16	Matt. 5:16		
17	1 Pet. 2:15		
18	Mark 9:35		
19	Gal. 6:10		
20	Titus 3:14		
21	Heb. 13:16		
22	1 Cor. 16:14		
23	Col. 3:17		
24	1 Cor. 15:58		
25	2 Cor. 5:11		
26	2 Tim. 1:14		
27	1 Peter 4:10		

WORKS

Good works cannot earn your salvation. That is a gift from God. It is not a reward for the good things anyone has done so that no one gets bragging rights.[1,2] You are saved by God's grace through your faith and belief in Jesus Christ. You are made acceptable to God because of your faith in the one who forgives sinners.[3]

If works could achieve salvation, it would no longer require grace. However, since salvation does come to us by grace, it cannot be earned by good works. Otherwise it would no longer be grace.[4] You are justified by faith.[5] Eternal life is a gift from God.[6] Thank God for this indescribable gift![7]

Without faith, it is impossible to please God.[8] But faith without works is dead.[9] Faith that pleases God produces good works.[10] The good works that you do demonstrate that you have faith in God.[11] Faith that does not produce good works is not the kind of faith that pleases God.[12] Your actions prove the sincerity of your faith.[13]

God has saved you so that you can do his good works on earth.[14] You are the light of the world. Let the light shine on your good works so that others will see them and glorify God in heaven.[15,16] It is God's will that by so doing, you will silence the ignorant talk of foolish people.[17]

You must be the servant of all if you want to be great in the kingdom of heaven.[18] Do good to everyone at every opportunity, especially those who belong to the family of believers.[19] Meet the urgent needs of others.[20] Share with those in need. This is the type of work that pleases God.[21] Whatever you do, do it in love and in the name of Jesus.[22,23]

Work enthusiastically for the Lord because nothing you do for him is useless.[24] Work hard to persuade others of the precious truth of the gospel.[25,26] Use whatever gifts and abilities you have to serve others, such as encouragement, generosity, leadership, compassion. In this way you extend God's grace to others.[27,28] Encourage and motivate each other to love others and do good works.[29]

Work hard so you can understand and explain God's Word.[30] Work hard to show the results of your salvation by obeying God with deep reverence and respect.[31] Work at living a holy life in peace and love with one another.[32,33]

The Lord will reward you for the good works you do.[34-36] He will not forget how hard you have worked for him and how you have shown your love for him by caring for other believers.[37] Do not tire of doing good works because he will reward you with honor and immortality.[38,39]

God works in you to give you the desire and the power to do what pleases him.[40] You please him by doing good works and increasing your knowledge of him.[41]

The one work God requires of you is that you believe in his Son, Jesus Christ.[42]

WORLDLINESS

1	1 John 2:15		30	1 John 5:4
2	1 John 2:16		31	1 John 5:5
3	1 John 2:17		32	1 John 4:4
4	James 4:4		33	James 1:27
5	Matt. 6:24		34	Titus 2:12
6	Luke 16:13		35	1 Peter 2:12
7	Col. 3:5			
8	Eph. 5:5			
9	Rom. 12:2			
10	Col. 2:8			
11	2 Cor. 4:4			
12	1 John 4:1			
13	1 John 4:2			
14	1 John 4:3			
15	1 Peter 1:13			
16	1 Peter 4:7			
17	Eph. 6:10			
18	Eph. 6:13			
19	Eph. 6:12			
20	1 Tim. 6:17			
21	1 Tim. 6:7			
22	1 Cor. 7:31			
23	Matt. 16:26			
24	Mark 8:36			
25	Luke 9:25			
26	1 John 3:13			
27	John 15:18			
28	John 15:19			
29	John 16:33			

WORLDLINESS

Do not love this world or any of the things that it offers you. Craving physical pleasures, coveting material possessions, and boasting about your accomplishments do not come from God but the world. Love for the world displaces love for God.[1,2] The world and its offerings will all disappear someday, but the person who does what pleases God will live forever.[3]

You need to know that friendship with the world is the same as hatred for God. If you choose to be a friend of the world, you become an enemy of God.[4] You cannot serve two masters. You will either hate one and love the other or be devoted to one and despise the other.[5,6]

Get rid of whatever belongs to your worldly nature: sexual immorality, impurity, lust, evil desires, and greed, which is the same as idol worship. Persons who live in these ways have no place in the kingdom of God.[7,8]

Do not conform to the progressive ideology of the world. Do not copy its lifestyles and customs. Let God transform you into a new person by changing your worldview and the way you think. Then you will learn God's perfect will for you and how to please him.[9]

Don't let the world capture you with empty philosophies and high-sounding nonsense that are not from Christ.[10] Satan, the god of this world, has blinded the minds of unbelievers so that they cannot understand the gospel or see the beauty of Christ, who is the exact likeness of God.[11] So, do not believe everyone who claims to speak for God, because many are fakes.[12] This is the litmus test: The ones you can trust acknowledge that Jesus Christ came to earth in a real body.[13,14]

Prepare your mind for action. Be clear minded, self-controlled, and confident in your hope that Jesus is coming again.[15,16] Be strong in the Lord and his mighty power.[17] Use every spiritual defense available to you to stand against evil.[18] Worldliness is a spiritual battle and not a flesh-and-blood enemy.[19]

Do not be arrogant about your wealth or put your hope in such an uncertain thing.[20] You brought nothing into the world and will take nothing out of it.[21] Use the things of the world for good without becoming attached to them.[22] What good would it do if you gained the whole world and in the end had to forfeit your soul?[23-25]

Do not be surprised if the world hates you.[26] Remember, it hated Jesus first.[27,28] You should expect many trials and sorrows in this world, but do not be discouraged, because Jesus has overcome the world.[29] Everyone who believes that Jesus is the Son of God and places their faith in him overcomes the world.[30,31] Jesus in you is greater than the one who is in the world.[32]

Keep yourself from being polluted by the world.[33] Say "no" to ungodliness and worldly passions and live a self-controlled, upright, and godly life in your world.[34] Such a good life with its good deeds will be visible to unbelievers and bring glory to God.[3]

WORSHIP

1	Luke 4:8	30	Ps. 100:2	59	Ps. 98:5
2	Matt. 4:10	31	Ps. 64:10	60	Ps. 98:6
3	Ex. 20:3	32	Ps. 97:12	61	Ps. 33:3
4	Ex. 20:4	33	Ps. 32:11	62	Isa. 12:6
5	Ex. 20:5	34	Ps. 37:4	63	Ps. 98:4
6	Rom. 1:25	35	Deut. 4:39	64	Ps. 98:1
7	Deut. 12:31	36	Ps. 66:3	65	Ps. 68:4
8	Jer. 25:6	37	Ps. 100:3	66	Ps. 66:2
9	Ex. 34:14	38	Ps. 46:10	67	Isa. 12:5
10	Deut. 6:5	39	Ps. 37:7	68	Ps. 95:6
11	Luke 10:27	40	Ps. 103:2	69	Luke 22:41
12	Mark 12:30	41	Ps. 48:9	70	Neh. 8:6
13	Ps. 96:9	42	Ps. 145:5	71	Ps. 134:2
14	Ps. 29:2	43	Ps. 143:5	72	Lam. 3:41
15	Ps. 99:5	44	Ps. 77:12	73	1 Tim. 2:8
16	Rev. 15:4	45	Ps. 119:15	74	Ps. 141:2
17	Ps. 100:5	46	Ps. 119:27	75	Heb. 12:28
18	Heb. 12:28	47	Ps. 119:23	76	1 Chron. 16:29
19	Ps. 29:1	48	Ps. 119:78	77	Rom. 6:13
20	Ps. 62:11	49	Ps. 119:148	78	Rom. 12:1
21	Ps. 62:12	50	Ps. 19:14		
22	Ps. 66:3	51	Ps. 100:4		
23	Neh. 9:6	52	Ps. 103:2		
24	Rev. 14:7	53	Ps. 100:5		
25	John 4:23	54	Ps. 118:1		
26	John 4:24	55	Jer. 33:11		
27	Isa. 29:13	56	Lam. 3:22		
28	Col. 2:23	57	Lam. 3:23		
29	Col. 2:22	58	Ps. 92:1		

WORSHIP

Worship the Lord your God, and serve him only.[1,2] You must have no other gods, no man-made objects, which you worship.[3-7] God will have it no other way.[8-9]

You must love the Lord your God with all your heart and with all your soul and with all your mind and with all your strength.[10-12]

Worship the Lord in the splendor of his holiness.[13-14] He alone is holy.[15,16] He is good, and his love endures forever. He is faithful to all generations.[17]

Worship him in reverence and awe.[18] He is glorious and strong as well as loving.[19-21] His deeds are awesome.[22] Worship him who created the universe and all that is in it.[23,24]

True worship must be spiritual, coming from your spirit, your inner being, because God is a spiritual being and not a physical being.[25,26] False worship comes only from the lips and not the heart, and is based on human commands and teachings, which are of no lasting spiritual value.[27-29]

Worship the Lord with rejoicing and a glad heart.[30-33] Delight yourself in the Lord, and remember that he is supreme. There is no other.[34,35] Acknowledge his awesome power and deeds and that he is your Creator.[36,37]

Be quiet in God's presence. Wait for him, and you will come to know him better.[38,39] Bless the Lord and meditate on all he is and has done: his unfailing love, the glorious splendor of his majesty, his mighty works, ways, wonders, laws, and promises.[40-49] Such meditation is pleasing to God.[50]

Come before the Lord with thanksgiving and praise. Recall all his benefits.[51,52] He is good, and his love and faithfulness endure forever.[53-55] His compassion never fails.[56,57]

It is good to worship the Lord with musical instruments.[58-60] Play skillfully and shout for joy.[61,62] Burst into jubilant song with music.[63] Sing a new song, sing praise to the Lord, sing the glory of his name, sing because he has done glorious things. Let this be known to the whole world.[64-67]

Bow down in worship; kneel before the Lord your Maker.[68-70] Lift up your hands, and praise the Lord.[71] Lift up your hands in prayer—it is a profound act of worship.[72-74]

Worship the Lord with reverence and awe.[75] Ascribe to him the glory due his name. Bring an offering and come before him.[76]

Offer your body as a living sacrifice to be an instrument of righteousness. In view of what God has done for you, this is an act of spiritual worship, which pleases God.[77,78]

YOU ARE...

1	Matt. 5:14	29	1 Peter 2:9
2	Eph. 5:8	30	1 Peter 2:10
3	Matt. 5:16	31	Luke 22:26
4	Matt. 5:13		
5	Matt. 5:11		
6	1 Peter 4:14		
7	Luke 6:22		
8	Luke 6:20		
9	Luke 6:21		
10	John 15:5		
11	1 Cor. 1:30		
12	John 15:14		
13	1 Cor. 12:27		
14	1 Cor. 6:19		
15	1 Cor. 3:16		
16	Rom. 6:14		
17	Rom. 8:9		
18	Gal. 5:18		
19	2 Cor. 5:20		
20	2 Cor. 3:3		
21	Gal. 3:26		
22	Eph. 2:19		
23	Gal. 3:29		
24	Matt. 25:34		
25	1 Peter 1:9		
26	1 Peter 1:8		
27	Rom. 10:9		
28	Rom. 10:10		

YOU ARE...

You are the light of the world.[1] Let it shine and live as a child of the light.[2,3]

You are the salt of the earth. Do not lose your saltiness.[4]

You are blessed when you are persecuted, insulted, or slandered because God's Spirit rests on you.[5,6] God also blesses when you are hated, excluded, and rejected because of his Son.[7]

You are blessed if you are poor because you have the kingdom of God.[8] You are blessed if you hunger for righteousness because you will be filled.[9]

You are dependent on Christ like a branch is dependent on a vine.[10,11]

You are a friend of Christ if you do what he commands.[12]

You are part of the body of Christ and have a vital part to play in its function.[13]

You are a temple of God, and his Holy Spirit lives in your body. Do not defile it.[14,15]

You are not to be controlled by your sinful nature but led by God's Holy Spirit.[16-18]

You are an ambassador for Christ, imploring people to be reconciled to God.[19]

You are a letter from Christ, written by the Holy Spirit on human hearts.[20]

You are a son or daughter of God because of your faith in Jesus Christ.[21]

You are a member of God's family and have an inheritance in the kingdom of heaven [22-24]

You are receiving the goal of your faith, which is the salvation of your soul because you love Jesus, even though you have never seen him.[25-26]

You are made right with God if you believe in your heart that Jesus is Lord and that God raised him from the dead. Tell someone else about your faith.[27,28]

You are a chosen person, a royal priest belonging to God so that you can show others the goodness of God who has called you out of darkness into his wonderful light.[29]

You are one of the people of God.[30]

You are not to be like the powerful of the world who use position to impose their ideas. Instead, the greatest of you should be a servant to all.[31]

EPILOGUE

I DID NOT WRITE THIS book alone. The whole idea for the book from conception to delivery was a gift of the Holy Spirit who also granted insight, supervision, and perseverance through every step of the process. I will forever be grateful for the privilege of doing this work.

There were many memorable moments and milestones on this journey. It began in the midst of a year-long illness, which followed on the heels of an unexpected divorce. I spent a lot of time reading through the Scripture that year. I remember the moment of awakening when I first realized the central importance of "pleasing God." He requires faith, and true faith motivates us to do his will. The greatest learning moment of all came when I realized that God's will for us is not a mystery but is objectively set forth in the imperative statements in the Bible. These commands are the only objective statements of God's will available to us. Living according to these principles is the way to please God.

Actually, I did not start out to write a book. The project unfolded one step at a time beginning with routine Bible reading during which I was impressed with the number of Scriptural imperatives. As I started marking them, I became aware of the direct link between obedience to the commands (imperatives) and pleasing God. I also became aware of the broad range of subjects and decided to catalog them by topic. Only then did I begin to feel a "commission" to use the words of the Bible to write this book as you see it.

I learned many lessons in bringing this project to completion. Many were objective, as you might expect from the nature of the work. But many were also subjective and personal. One of the most important insight relates to my own spiritual health, which I would have rated "pretty good" at the beginning. After all, I was a lifetime Christian who had tried to live life "by the Book" and was now working on a big project to honor God and his Word.

However, I was soon to become painfully aware of just how far away from God's standards I was. I began to see my "pretty good" as spiritual arrogance, poorly disguised pride, and hypocrisy. These attitudes are definitely not pleasing to God. They are not easy for me to overcome. It is a spiritual battle every day.

Once I started noticing the phrase "pleasing God" it seemed like it was everywhere in my reading. About seventy references that use the term explicitly are included in the section on "Pleasing God." I expected that most of these references would be found in the Old Testament, but that turned out not to be true. Pleasing God is very much imbedded in the theology and terminology of the New Testament as well.

It's quite amazing to see how many of life's problem issues are specifically addressed by these imperatives. I have included over 135 topics with over 5,000 references (including some repetitions). You might expect that most of these topics would be "theological" in nature. Only about thirty-five are. The large majority of biblical imperatives give straightforward instructions on issues relevant to our daily lives like anxiety, family, money, honesty, pride, suffering, and so on (see list of topics in the front of the book).

Because of their large number, I have always wondered how we could ever keep all these imperatives in our head at the same time. Even with a photographic memory, could we measure up to God's standards? The answer is no. No one can. The good news is that God has provided a way around this problem, the way of faith in his Son.

I've learned a new way to think of God's will. It's not some small target where hitting the bullseye is the only thing that counts. It's also not a maze in which God's will is at the center of multiple pathways, most of which are dead ends. It's not specific with regard to non-moral decisions, which make up a large part of life. God's will has to do primarily with our character and behavior, and he chooses to give us wisdom and freedom to make our own choices in non-moral issues. What a wonderful arrangement for living.

Many people reject Christianity because of the lifestyle restrictions imposed by its imperatives. I've come to view them like a backyard fence. It establishes important boundaries. As far as children are concerned, the fence is restrictive. Parents view it as protective. It allows them to play but not chase a loose ball into the street. God's imperatives are like a backyard fence, protecting us from disaster and directing us to a satisfying life that pleases him.

I have experienced God in several new ways since beginning this project. I learned to pray in a way I never did before the divorce. My prayers had been quite general and well structured but often limited to "thank you for this beautiful day and please bless the grandkids." Overnight, I lost the thoughtless formality and relinquished the reluctance to open up my heart and soul to God. I saw myself as I had not seen myself before. I met God as I had not before. He met me as he had been waiting to do for so long. I turned my cares and anxieties over to him. I stopped asking "why" questions, which frequently had no satisfying answers, and start asking "how" questions, like "how am I supposed to live this new chapter of my life?" I began to feel the transcendent peace of mind and soul that he promises when we refocus on him.

I endured suffering, something I have often observed in others but seldom experienced. I felt acute and harsh pain, anguish, fear, anger, betrayal, and misunderstanding. I could share these emotions without reservation with God who surely understood. I began to identify in some small way with the suffering of Christ and the great numbers of those who suffer with and for him, the "fellowship of his suffering."

Confession and forgiveness were familiar topics for me. I have known the Scriptures since my youth but not the deep, soul-cleansing freedom of mind and spirit that unreserved confession brings to the true penitent. Every transgression, thought, attitude, word, and action is totally forgiven. God disposes them "as far away as the east is from the west," and he promises to never bring them up again.[1,2]

The presence of the Holy Spirit became very real to me during this time. I prayed for guidance and accuracy daily before I wrote and frequently during times of writer's block when I could not think of a good way to express the topic at hand. I heard his "voice" many times saying, "Write it this way…" I also came to understand the reality of my physical body being a "temple" of the Holy Spirit.[3]

I gained a new appreciation and love for the Bible. I learned a lot about Bible study methods, which can be much more thorough and efficient with the assistance of technology. I was often reminded of the value of re-reading Scripture at regular intervals because we are not the same persons we were a year or two earlier, and our newly acquired life experiences cause us to make observations and applications we would never have otherwise made. Despite my own inconsistencies in this area, I can see how regular reading and study of the Bible yields much more than just knowledge. It is the most important spiritual discipline in the formation of our spiritual lives and moving us toward maturity. It is powerfully transformative in developing a character that becomes more and more like Christ. It is authoritative in matters of belief and behavior. It tells us about God and ourselves. It presents salvation as the remedy for sin. It gives comfort and hope. It is the handbook for life. It leads us to please God.

I learned a lot about the nature and character of God by gaining an appreciation for what pleases him. The biblical imperatives are a reflection of his mind and heart, an expression of his character and his will for our lives. They are undoubtedly a blueprint for the kingdom of heaven, the hope of every Christian.

Along with the Apostle Paul: "I urge you in the name of Jesus to live your life in a way that pleases God."[4]

1. Ps. 103:12

2. Jer 31:34

3. 1 Cor. 6:19

4. 1 Thess. 4:1

William P. Bunnell

Redlands, CA

DISCUSSION QUESTIONS

ACCOUNTABILITY

Describe someone to whom you have been accountable during some part of your life.

How should knowing that you are accountable to God affect the way you live?

How will you defend your record on the day of God's accounting?

In what ways do you feel accountable to your community?

Discuss ways in which you are accountable to other Christians.

Do you feel accountable to confess your sins to another person?

In what ways do you hold yourself accountable to yourself?

Discuss ways in which you are accountable to your church.

ADULTERY

Do you think this commandment is limited to adultery as we use the term?

What do you think are the primary causes of adultery in our day?

What do you think are best practices to avoid the trap of adultery?

How does breaking of one of God's laws make you guilty of breaking the entire law?

How does lust make you guilty of adultery?

How should you deal with sexual temptation?

Does Jesus really mean you should gouge out your eye? What does he mean?

Discuss the biblical basis for marriage.

Why do you think God hates divorce?

Discuss the biblical examples of spiritual adultery. Give some modern examples.

ALIEN

Can you describe your inner feelings toward others who are not like you?

Why do you think God is so specific about the treatment of aliens (immigrants)?

Contrast God's will for the treatment of immigrants with that of the USA's.

Describe the pathway to citizenship for the kingdom of heaven.

Describe your rights as a citizen of heaven.

How do you manage divided loyalties arising from your dual citizenship?

How would you describe yourself as an alien in this world?

How does being an alien in the world affect your lifestyle?

ANGER

Describe an episode of anger in your life and how the situation ended. Good or bad?

Both God and Jesus have shown anger. Why do you think God calls anger a sin?

How should you deal with feelings of anger and hostility?

What are the effects of uncontrolled anger?

What is the best way to deal with angry or hot-tempered people?

What are the effects of anger in a church congregation?

Why is calling another person a derogatory name such a big deal?

Describe God's anger.

ANXIETY

Define, compare, and contrast anxiety, fear, depression.

Name some of the common causes of anxiety in our society. In Christ-followers.

Discuss the negative effects of anxiety in our society and in Christ-followers.

What are the common secular techniques for managing anxiety?

Name some biblical techniques for anxiety management found in today's text.

In what ways in anxiety a form of "spiritual warfare"?

List some spiritual disciplines useful in dealing with anxiety.

Do you think anxiety is an indicator of spiritual health?

Do you find encouragement in knowing that God cares for birds and flowers?

Share some of the ways you personally deal with anxiety.

APOLOGETICS

What is apologetics and why is it important?

What has been your exposure to or experience with apologetics?

How can you become skilled in apologetics?

What is the role of apologetics in winning others to Christ?

Describe winsome ways to use apologetics in conversation with unbelievers.

How can you convince an unbeliever that the Bible is the ultimate source of truth?

Why are you convinced (if you are) that belief in Christ (Christianity) is the exclusive truth?

Does apologetics help you determine God's will for your life?

Give an example of someone with more zeal than knowledge about Christianity.

ATTITUDE

Describe some bad attitudes you have observed in others or struggled with in your own life.

Describe the attitude of Jesus. How do we develop the same attitude in our own lives?

Write a list of attitudes that are pleasing to God.

Why are these attitudes important?

What is the "joy of the Lord" and how does it affect your overall attitude?

Why is an "attitude of gratitude" so important in the Christian life?

What is contentment and what is its opposite? How do we wind up in either category?

What is the peace of Christ? How do you let it rule your heart?

How do you think being judgmental or a complainer affects your attitude?

Have you ever thought of imitating God? Can you really do that?

AUTHORITY

Describe your attitude toward authority as a teenager.

How has God established his authority over all the universe?

What is the basis of the authority of Jesus Christ?

How does the Holy Spirit express his authority?

How can you be sure that the Bible is authoritative?

How much authority does the church have over your life?

What is your responsibility to the authority of the government?

Discuss human authority structures like family and employment.

Discuss human authority over the environment.

BAPTISM

What are your memories of your own baptism?

What are the requirements of Christian baptism? When should it take place?

Discuss the symbolism of water baptism.

Is baptism required for salvation?

Why is Christian baptism done in the name of the Father, Son, and Holy Spirit?

What does baptism accomplish for a new believer?

BLASPHEMY

What is blasphemy?

In what ways do people blaspheme God?

Why is blasphemy such a serious sin in God's sight?

How do both words and actions constitute blasphemy?

Discuss how Jesus confronted the accusation of blasphemy?

How is it possible to blaspheme the Holy Spirit?

Why is blasphemy of the Holy Spirit the unpardonable sin?

How is it possible to "squelch" the work of the Holy Spirit?

What are the consequences of ignoring the Holy Spirit?

BLESSING

What is a blessing?

Can you think of a person who has given you a special blessing?

Have you given a blessing to someone else?

What are spiritual blessings? Name some of them.

How can you bring yourself to bless those who mistreat you?

Why should we bless rather than curse those who mistreat us as Christians?

Does it seem unusual that you should bless the Lord? How can you do this?

What are some of the things we bless God for?

BODY

What is the relevance of your body to your life in Christ?

What does it mean for your body to be a temple of God?

Does the fact that God formed you in the womb influence your opinion on abortion?

Discuss the importance of Jesus's physical body.

Discuss the spiritual analogy for different parts of the human body.

Do you think harsh treatment of your body can have positive spiritual significance?

Why is sexual sin always presented as the opposite of holiness?

Describe the inner conflict between good intentions and reality in Paul's mind and in ours.

What will ultimately happen to your body?

CHARACTER

What is character? Have you ever known some "characters"?

How can you develop the character traits of a close follower of Jesus?

Contrast the character traits of a close follower of Jesus with those of the world.

What is the importance of joy in the life of a Christian?

Compare the effects of gratitude and greed on someone's life.

Discuss the relationship of faith and works in light of character.

How does a lack of forgiveness affect character?

Discuss the importance of humility in servant leadership.

How can contentment balance the extremes of covetousness and complacency?

What are practical ways to acquire and express a righteous character?

CHARITY

Why do you think the idea of love has been lost in our use of the word charity?

Note some of the admonitions regarding charity toward to the poor.

Discuss wealth in the kingdom of heaven and how to achieve it.

What is "proportional" giving and how does it compare with tithing?

Give examples of sowing generously; sparingly. What are the results?

Discuss the differences between doing your charity publicly and in private.

Explain how giving and doing for the least of society is the same as doing something for Jesus.

In what ways can charity add to the quality of your life?

CHILDREN

Can you think of spiritual lessons you learned by watching children?

Why do you think it is such a serious offense to mislead a child?

Do you think child sacrifice is an ancient practice without modern counterpart?

Have you seen examples of extraordinary childhood wisdom and insight?

Discuss obligations that children have to their parents.

Discuss obligations parents have to their children.

How is a child a model for faith?

Do you think all people are children of God?

What are some of the evidences that you are a child of God?

What are the benefits of being a child of God?

What are the responsibilities of being a child of God?

CHOICES

Tell about a choice you've made that was difficult. What were factors in your decision?

What principles would you use to advise a young person facing a difficult choice?

Describe your process of choosing to follow or not to follow Jesus?

Do you think the choice between following God or following the world is binary?

Describe the narrow pathway that leads to eternal life. Why do so few follow it?

How does one recognize a bad choice (the path of the wicked) and avoid it?

Do you agree that it is better to choose wisdom over wealth?

Why do you think God chooses the poor and simple to confound the rich and wise of the world?

Discuss what it means to choose to do the will of God.

Why is it a bad choice to follow the dictates of your culture?

CHRISTIAN COMMUNITY

How would you define a "community"?

How do you live as a citizen of heaven and a good citizen on earth?

What are the qualifications for leadership in the Christian community?

Describe the differences between "love" in the Christian and worldly communities.

Describe personal interactions between members of the Christian community.

List some practical ways to encourage each other.

How can "freedoms in Christ" lead to controversy in your community?

What happens when knowledge is not translated into action?

Why is favoritism forbidden?

How does this chapter influence your behavior and attitudes in your community?

CHURCH

What is the "Church"?

What have been your best and worst experiences with the church?

Why is the Church important in the world?

What is the main purpose of the Church?

What are the important functional parts of the Church?

What is the role of spiritual gifts in the work of the Church?

What do you see as your role in your church?

Discuss church leadership. Is it ever justified to question their decisions or authority?

Describe your ideal Sunday morning at church.

What are some of the ways churches get into internal conflict and division?

What is your ideal for social outreach for your church?

COMMUNION

Describe the origin of the communion service.

What is your understanding of the significance of communion?

What are the thoughts that go through your head while celebrating communion?

Describe the old covenant that is replaced by the new covenant?

How does the "new covenant" differ from the "old covenant"?

What does it mean to participate in communion in an "unworthy manner"?

What steps are necessary to avoid participation in an "unworthy manner"?

COMPASSION

How would you define compassion?

In what ways has modern society diluted the idea of compassion?

What is the biblical motivation for compassion?

Who are the special objects of the Lord's compassion?

Why does God allow affliction and grief?

Discuss how God's compassion deals with our sins.

Is it a good idea to share our stories of grief and affliction with others? Why?

How should God's compassion for us affect our lives?

CONFESSION

What is your understanding of confession?

How is confession different from repentance?

Name some of the great "confessions" of the Christian church.

In Catholicism, confession includes contrition, naming the sin, and penance. Do you agree?

How does God respond to our confession of sin?

Name some acts and attitudes that should accompany true confession.

Why is it unwise to try to conceal wrongdoing?

Discuss restitution.

What are the benefits of confessing sins to each other?

How does something you say (confess) with your mouth lead to salvation?

Why is obedience to God's will an important outcome of confession?

CONFIDENCE

Describe factors that have contributed to your overall level of confidence.

Do you agree that faith and confidence are basically the same quality? Why?

Do you think it is arrogant to have confidence in your positions of faith?

What gives you confidence that you are right in believing the gospel?

What gives you confidence that you have right standing before God?

In what ways does God continue to do his good work in your life?

What are some of the ways you can increase confidence in your faith?

How can trials and difficulties increase your level of confidence?

How does confidence lead to an upright life?

CONTENTMENT

What is contentment?

Give some reasons why people feel a lack of contentment?

Name individuals whose love for money has ruined their lives.

Why do you think money is listed as the root of all evil?

Why are the things the world has to offer so attractive?

Why do you think greed is mentioned in the same section as contentment?

How is greed like idolatry?

What is the secret of contentment?

How does one maintain contentment in everyday life?

DEVIL

What imagery comes into your mind when you think of the Devil?

Discuss the Devil's history.

Do you think it is possible to make a deal with the Devil?

Discuss the Devil's tactics.

How should you deal with Satan's attacks?

What is your understanding of spiritual warfare?

How is spiritual warfare different from conventional warfare?

How does anger play a role in spiritual warfare?

How does being a victim play a role in spiritual warfare?

In what ways does Satan hold the power of death?

Why is it not up to you to rebuke Satan? What is the proper response to his advances?

DEVOTION

Give an example of great devotion that that you have observed.

What does it mean to be totally devoted to the Lord?

What roles do body, soul, and mind play in devotion to the Lord?

How can you express devotion?

What are some of the benefits of devotion?

Why is it impossible to serve two masters?

How does devotion work out in loving your neighbor?

Why is it important to "keep the main thing the main thing"?

How do you devote yourself to prayer in the digital world?

Name some criteria that would indicate an increasing devotion to God.

DISABLED PERSONS

What is your past experience with persons with physical or mental disability?

What are the biblical imperatives for Christian treatment of persons with disability?

How do they contrast with non-Christian thinking about disabled persons?

Do you think the word "weak" in the NT is a physical or spiritual description?

Describe symptoms of a spiritual disability.

Discuss the "contrarian" God: (the weak and dull of the world confound the strong and clever).

Describe some encounters between Jesus and persons with disability.

What do you think will become of human disability in heaven?

Can you think of any redeeming qualities of human disability?

Have you gained any new insights from this study?

DISCIPLESHIP

What is discipleship? Has someone special guided your journey?

How do you make a disciple?

What do you need to do if you want to be a disciple of Jesus?

What does it mean to bear your own cross?

Discuss the replication process for disciples.

Describe some practical ways to be a more devoted disciple of Jesus.

What does it mean to "give up life as you know it"?

What are some visible evidences that you are a disciple of Jesus?

DISCIPLINE

What is discipline?

Describe appropriate discipline for children.

Why is appropriate discipline important for both you and your children?

Describe different types of discipline God directs towards his children.

Discuss reasons why study of the Scriptures is a key spiritual discipline.

List and define some other classic spiritual disciplines.

In what ways do the spiritual disciplines bring you closer to God?

How can a healthy use of spiritual disciplines keep you out of trouble in life?

DIVORCE

Have you ever observed a "good" divorce?

What are the pros and cons of "no-fault" divorce?

What are some reasons why God hates divorce?

Why is a marriage ceremony important?

What is adultery?

Discuss permissible reasons for divorce.

Do you think that marital unfaithfulness requires divorce?

Do you agree that abuse and abandonment are legitimate grounds for Christians to seek divorce?

In what ways can a believer-spouse bring goodness into an otherwise godless marriage?

How can you reconcile the Old Testament permission for divorce with the NT prohibition?

What are the primary reasons for marriage that are subverted by divorce?

DOUBT

What is doubt? What is its opposite?

How should you handle thoughts of doubt?

How do the Scriptures help alleviate doubt?

Discuss visible evidence that should help remove doubt about Christian belief.

What is an agnostic? Have you ever met one? What were they like?

Do you think belief and doubt can co-exist?

What good work has God started in your heart? Do you think he will complete it? When?

Do you agree that the difficulties of life help to remove doubt?

How do you resolve the issue of questionable lifestyle issues?

Why does God ask us to be merciful to those who doubt when he seems intolerant of it?

DRUNKENNESS

Do you have past experiences with someone who was an alcoholic? What was it like?

Do you believe alcoholism (addiction in general) is a disease or a choice?

Why is alcohol (substance) abuse condemned in the Bible?

Discuss different Christian attitudes toward alcohol consumption.

Why is the "eat, drink, and be merry" philosophy dangerous?

What is the charitable Christian rule in disputable matters?

How is the metaphor of drunkenness applied to the Christian life?

EMPLOYEES

What was your best employee situation ever? What was the worst?

What special obligations do you have as a Christian toward your employer?

Why is it important to be a good employee?

How can you think of Christ as your Boss when you have a difficult one at your job?

What special obligations would/do you have as a Christian employer?

List some proper attitudes of a Christian employee toward work.

Discuss your motivation to be a good employee.

ENEMIES

Have you observed a situation where enemies clashed?

Why is the command to love your enemies so startling?

How can you show love to your enemy?

Why is it important to do so?

Describe how God treats his enemies.

How can you avoid being an enemy of God?

What do you know about the archenemy of God and your personal enemy?

Why is death described as your enemy? Do you think you can defeat it? How?

ENVY

What are some of the things people in general envy the most?

Why are the things we envy dangerous for a Christian?

What is the antidote to envy?

Where does envy come from and where does it lead to?

What other evils accompany envy?

Contrast the evils of envy with the wisdom of God.

Why is greed presented as such a severe sin?

What does the world have to offer that so often inspires greed? Why should we avoid it?

Why do you think the "love of money" is the root of all evil?

How does the expression of love suppress envy?

EVIL

What is evil? What is good? How can you tell the difference?

Since God created all things, did he also create evil? If not, what is the origin of evil?

How has evil affected the human race?

What are actions a Christ-follower should take in the face of evil?

How does evil affect your relationship with God?

Who is the Devil? What are his powers?

Why is the tongue such a dangerous part of your body?

What is a true Christian response to an "evil" attack?

List some ways you can overcome evil with good.

In what ways do you see that the "days are evil"?

FAITH, Part 1

What is faith?

How would you explain Christian faith to someone unfamiliar with it?

Why is faith essential in pleasing God?

Discuss the relationship of faith and works.

What is the role of faith in the life of a Christian?

What is the basis for Christian faith?

What is the object of faith?

What is the source of instruction for your faith?

How does faith help you in your physical and spiritual battles?

How does sharing your faith help you gain a better understanding of your own salvation?

What is "weak faith"? How would you help someone whose faith is weak?

FAITH, Part 2

Can you measure faith (as in someone with "great" faith)?

Why is it important to try to measure faith?

What can you do to increase your faith?

What is the role of faith in fighting spiritual battles?

What are some common things that challenge faith? Why are they important?

Why is it important to share your faith with others?

How would you describe a person with weak faith? How would you help them?

Give examples of disappointment that comes from putting faith in other people.

FAITHFULNESS

Discuss the meaning of faithfulness as a virtue.

Why do you think faithfulness to the Lord is so hard to maintain in good times?

In what ways are we to be faithful to the Lord?

How do you show yourself to be faithful in prayer?

Do you think suffering and adversity tend to drive a person toward or away from God? Why?

In what ways should we be faithful to each other?

Discuss ways in which God demonstrates his faithfulness.

What are ways you should respond to God's faithfulness?

FAMILY

Tell a story about your family origins.

What is the biblical basis for a family? Contrast with alternative definitions.

Why is breakup (divorce) such an affront to God?

What are the husband's responsibilities in a Christian family? What is the model?

Discuss a father's responsibilities in a Christian family. Compare with current social norms.

What are the wife's responsibilities in a Christian family? Compare with current social norms.

Discuss "submission" as viewed Biblically and culturally.

How do traditional family roles change for single parents?

List some children's responsibilities in a Christian family?

How should a Christian family care for each other?

What are your responsibilities to others who are part of your church family?

FASTING

What is fasting?

Describe an experience you have had with fasting. In what way were you affected?

Do you think fasting is a requirement for a deeper Christian life?

What is the purpose of fasting?

In what ways can fasting be about issues other than food?

What is the proper way to fast?

FEAR

What are the similarities and differences between fear, anxiety and worry?

How is "fear of the Lord" different from the fear you have about details in your life?

List some of the common fears of people in general and those at your stage of life.

List some promises of God from the reading that should help dispel fear.

Describe the relationship of fear and faith in your life.

What is the origin of fear?

How does the peace that Jesus offers differ from what the world has to offer?

Why does death cause fear?

As a Christian, how should you handle your fears?

How does a correct understanding of love dispel fear?

FEAR GOD

What does it mean to you to fear God?

How does fearing God differ from fear of God?

Why should you fear God?

List some things you should do that demonstrate that you fear God.

What does fear of the Lord have to do with wisdom and knowledge?

What is God's response to those who fear him?

How does fearing God affect your daily life?

How does nature and creation inspire fear of God?

Why do we need to fear God if he forgives all our sin?

In what way is the fear of the Lord a "fountain of life"?

FORGIVENESS

What is your understanding of forgiveness?

What are the effects of refusing to forgive a wrong?

How does the forgiveness of God compare and differ from human forgiveness?

Why is belief in Jesus essential in obtaining God's forgiveness?

How can you obtain God's forgiveness for your personal sins?

Why is it important to forgive others for wrongs against you?

Do you believe God's forgiveness is unconditional?

What is the unpardonable sin?

FREEDOM

Do you think "freedom" means the absence of all restraint? Why? Give examples.

Many say the idea of personal freedom is incompatible with believing in God. Do you agree?

Describe "freedom in Christ."

How does the "Law of Moses" deny freedom?

Why does freedom from the Law of Moses not free you to ignore its principles?

What is your responsibility toward others with different ideas about personal freedom?

Why is deferring to others important when the issues are disputable?

How will you account to God for your actions in these matters?

GENEROSITY

What is generosity? What is its opposite?

Do you think generosity is a natural quality?

Who does and who does not deserve your generosity?

Why is generosity an important quality of a Christian?

What is the difference between charity and philanthropy?

How can you be anonymous and let others see your good works at the same time?

How should "generosity" help determine your church donations?

Why do you think greed and hoarding are condemned in the Bible?

What are some of the ways you can store up treasure in heaven?

Name some areas other than money where generosity is important.

How can it be more blessed to give than to receive?

GENTLENESS

How would you describe "gentleness" in someone's character? Have you met anyone like this?

How would you "pursue" gentleness?

Do you see gentleness in your church leaders?

Why do you think God values gentleness?

What is the value of gentleness in human relationships?

What role does gentleness play in evangelism?

Why is it important to be gentle with someone caught in a sin?

What are some of the things we can do to hear the gentle whispers of God?

In what ways did Jesus display gentleness?

GOD HATES

If God hates or detests something, what should that say to you?

Can you identify anything on the list that is irrelevant to modern society?

Pick out some of the issues God hates that are the most obvious in our culture.

Name some of the issues God hates that are evident even in the Christian community.

Do you think abortion is the modern equivalent to ancient child sacrifice?

Do you think being transgender is the modern equivalent to simply crossdressing?

Why is idol worship false worship?

How do the biblical ideas of injustice compare with those of the world?

Why do you think "usury" made the list of things God hates?

Discuss violence in our culture as a violation of God's will.

GOD LOVES

Since God loves certain people and qualities, what should that tell you?

What should be your response to God's love for you?

Since God loves the world, why does he tell us not to love the world?

List some personal qualities God loves and the world ignores.

Discuss the biblical view of justice and compare it to current culture.

What is righteousness? How does it appear in our lifestyle issues?

How does humility fit in with the need for confidence, vision, etc. for effective leaders?

How should God's love for Israel and Jerusalem inform our political leaders?

How can God love sinners when he is holy and intolerant of sin?

GOLDEN RULE

Do you think the "Golden Rule" is unique to Christianity?

How does the "Golden Rule" summarize the Old Testament Law?

How does "love your neighbor as yourself" summarize the Law?

What is the only commandment greater than the Golden Rule?

GOSPEL

How would you explain the Christian gospel to a friend?

Discuss the universal mandate of the gospel.

What are the essential elements of the gospel?

What are some of the "requirements" that have been added to the gospel?

What is the source and authority of the gospel?

Describe the "mystery" of the gospel.

Discuss the ministry of reconciliation.

What are the features of a life lived worthy of the gospel?

Why does trying to save your life often end with losing it?

GOSSIP

What is gossip?

What is the difference between gossip and "news"?

Why is gossip so severely condemned in the Bible?

Are gossip and slander the same thing?

Do you agree that gossip is a sign of a depraved mind?

What are some of the effects of gossip?

Why is gossip so easy to enjoy?

How can you participate in discussing neighborhood news without participating in gossip?

GOVERNMENT

What is the origin of human government?

What is "due" our government?

Why are we subject to the will of our government?

What are the responsibilities of government?

How can you pray effectively for your government when you disagree with its policies?

What are the "unseen governments" described in the Bible?

Do you think "unseen governments" affect world governments or just individuals?

How can you let the peace of Christ rule your heart?

What does it mean to consider that your citizenship is in heaven?

GREATEST COMMANDMENTS

What does it mean to you to love the Lord with all your heart?

What does it mean to you to love the Lord with all your soul?

What does it mean to you to love the Lord with all your mind?

What does it mean to you to love the Lord with all your strength?

What does it mean to love your neighbor as yourself?

How does the command to "love one another" differ from the above?

How do these commandments help prove that your faith is genuine?

GREED

Think of some public examples of greed. What were the consequences?

How would you measure the value of your life if not by your net worth?

How does love for the world affect love for God?

Compare the lasting value of what the world offers with that of pleasing God.

Why is money a root of all evil?

Do you agree that you cannot serve both God and money?

Why is the subtle nature of greed such a severe sin?

What is the antidote to greed?

Compare treasure on earth with treasure in heaven.

How do you deposit treasure in heaven?

If you "follow the money", where will you find your affections?

HATE

What is hate?

How have you seen hate affecting other people?

How can you "love" an enemy?

What or who are some things or people that you should hate?

Why do you think Christians around the world are hated for their faith?

What is the effect of hatred on your relationship with God?

Do you agree that hatred is the moral equivalent of murder?

Why can you not love and serve God and money at the same time?

HOLINESS

Have you ever met a holy person? What were their characteristics?

What does it mean to be holy?

Why are you asked to be holy?

How does a sinful person become holy?

What are some of the qualities that demonstrate a holy life?

How can you build yourself up in your faith?

What is sanctification?

How does sanctification take place?

HOLY SPIRIT

How would you explain who the Holy Spirit is to someone who had never heard about him?

What does it mean to quench the Holy Spirit? What are some things that do this?

Make a list of the things the Holy Spirit does in the life of a believer.

What does it mean to be "filled" with the Holy Spirit?

Explain how a human body can be a temple of the Holy Spirit?

What are some things that desecrate this temple-body?

In what way does the Holy Spirit guarantee your salvation?

What does it mean to blaspheme the Holy Spirit? Why is this not forgivable?

In what ways could your heart become "hardened" to the Holy Spirit?

How does the Holy Spirit help you pray?

HONESTY

Do you think it is okay to tell a half truth? A white lie?

Why is honesty such an important characteristic of a Christian?

How do you speak the truth in love?

In what ways are some people not always honest with themselves?

List ways in which some people are deliberately dishonest with others.

How are faith and honesty related?

If dishonesty is so destructive, why is it so prevalent? What is its origin?

How can honesty help you achieve personal freedom?

What role does honesty play in love?

How does honesty advance the gospel? How does dishonesty harm the gospel?

HOPE

Discuss hope as both a noun and a verb.

Compare optimism and hope.

What are the key elements of hope for a Christian?

How does hope affect you as a Christian?

What is the basis of your hope?

How are hope and faith related?

What is the most blessed hope of a Christian?

What is a living hope?

What gives you the most confidence that your hope is well placed?

How does hope change your life?

HUMILITY

Describe a person you have known who exhibited exceptional humility.

What are the personal qualities included in humility?

What is so unworldly about humility in the kingdom of heaven?

What is a servant-leader? Can you point out an example?

In what way(s) is Jesus the perfect example of humility?

Discuss God's attitude towards pride and arrogance and what he will do about it.

List some actions you might take that demonstrate humility.

Describe false humility. Have you ever observed such a person?

What role does humility play in knowing and doing God's will?

How does humility temper your approach to the Devil's advances?

HYPOCRISY

Describe a hypocrite and give an example.

How did Jesus deal with hypocrites?

How should you deal with someone who appears hypocritical?

What do we know about clerical hypocrisy?

Why should you avoid hypocrites?

Do you ever see hypocritical tendencies in yourself? How do you handle them?

Can you link self-righteousness and hypocrisy?

How can you recognize a plank in your eye?

In what ways can you be hypocritical in your observance of the Lord's Day?

In what ways are Christians most hypocritical?

IDOLS

What is an idol?

What are some examples of idols worshipped in our world?

Why does God prohibit idol worship? Does this seem unduly demanding of God?

Why does the human race pursue idol worship even though it is illogical?

Why can God never be considered an idol?

Describe God's attitude towards idols.

How do intelligent people fall into idol worship?

What is the end result of idol worship?

How can you avoid idol worship?

JOY

Compare joy and happiness. How are they similar and how are they different?

How can you be full of joy all the time?

What part does joy play in the worship of God?

Describe the role of Jesus in bringing you true joy.

How can you find joy through prayer?

How do trials bring joy?

How does suffering bring joy?

How does the Holy Spirit produce joy in your life?

How can you create joy for your spiritual leaders?

JUDGMENT

Name several different types of judgment.

Describe the judgment of God unbelievers will face upon their death.

Describe the judgment of Christ, which believers will face upon their death.

In what ways does our current system of justice differ from that which pleases God?

How does being judgmental get us into trouble?

Compare the way we judge others with God's judgments of others.

Discuss judgment as it pertains to disputable issues.

Why is it so easy to see a problem in others that we do not see in ourselves?

Discuss name-calling. Do you think God will excuse it on judgment day?

What does it mean to participate in communion in a worthy or unworthy manner?

How can the Scripture bring judgment to your heart?

JUSTICE

What is justice?

Why do you think justice is so important to God?

List some of the issues that define justice from God's point of view.

Compare the above list with issues mentioned in "social justice" discussions.

Do you agree that "If you see something; say something" is biblical?

Why are multiple witnesses required in matters of justice?

What role do mercy and compassion play in the administration of justice?

Why do you think there is prejudice against the poor and disadvantaged?

List some issues that often pervert justice.

How do our laws sometimes pervert justice?

What is justice for persons living in our country without legal documentation?

KNOWLEDGE

Distinguish between knowledge and wisdom; discernment and discretion.

How does fear of the Lord lead to knowledge?

How does fear of the Lord lead to wisdom?

How does creation lead us to knowledge about God?

Can science lead us to a knowledge of God?

Compare physical light and spiritual light.

What is the relationship of knowledge and faith?

Compare spiritual knowledge with physical knowledge.

In what way(s) is spiritual knowledge expressed?

List some examples of false knowledge prevalent in our society.

What is the danger of zeal without knowledge?

LIFESTYLE, Part 1

How would you best describe the culture and lifestyles of our time?

Read Romans 1:18-32. Describe the process of rejecting God's truth.

Discuss how personal characteristics contribute to lifestyle.

What are some common deceptive and alternative religious views?

Describe some origins of confusion about spiritual truth?

How can you "run the race" for Jesus when you're racing to a soccer game?

What are the characteristics of a Christ-follower? How can you develop them in your own life?

Why can anger be such a drag on your Christian life?

Describe ways you should treat fellow Christians.

Describe a lifestyle worthy of the gospel.

LIFESTYLE, Part 2

How would you as a Christian describe the "good life"?

What is your view of government? Compare it with that of the kingdom of heaven.

Describe a Christian attitude toward a hostile workplace.

Give some guidance to a Christian employer.

Describe the origin and organization of the human family.

What is your understanding of "submission" in the family? In church?

Compare and contrast covetousness and complacency.

Describe contentment in a materialistic society.

Why is the love of money (greed) such a threat to Christian living?

List some practical ways you can show love to your enemies.

In what other ways can you overcome evil with good?

LOVE, Part 1

What is your favorite love story?

How do you love the Lord with all your heart, mind, soul, and strength?

How do you love your neighbor as yourself?

Why is it important to show love to your Christian brothers and sisters?

In what ways does your church community encourage love for each other?

What are the characteristics and features of God's love?

Describe God's love for you specifically? How do you experience it?

Why is love considered the greatest virtue?

How can God's love be reproduced in your life?

How can you love those for whom you do not really feel genuine affection?

LOVE, Part 2

Tell about someone you have known or seen who lived a life of love.

What are some characteristics of a life of love?

How might you demonstrate the real-life characteristics of love to others?

How can love fulfill the requirements of God's law?

Describe ways you can show love to your enemies?

What are some practical ways husbands can show love for their wives?

What are some practical ways wives can show love for their husbands?

In what ways can love of money ruin your life?

What is love for the world?

How can or does love for the world displace love for God in your life?

MARGINAL ISSUES

What do you think are the marginal issues in your church?

Compare the marginal issues of today to those of a decade, a century, and a millennium ago.

What is the overarching principle in dealing with marginal issues?

Discuss the current basis for the various approaches to food and diet.

Why do Jews worship on Sabbath and Christians on Sunday?

How do you decide which issues or practices are acceptable and those that are not?

Discuss the role of doubt and conscience in determining the acceptability of a certain behavior.

How would you resolve conflict between those who accept and reject a certain behavior?

What is your responsibility toward immature believers?

What does it mean to make someone else stumble?

Why is causing someone to stumble in their faith a sin against Christ?

MARRIAGE

What do you like best about going to weddings?

Imagine and discuss what life might have been like for the "first couple," Adam and Eve.

How does the creation story give insight into marriage?

What are the biblical instructions regarding sex within marriage?

What are the biblical standards regarding adultery and divorce?

What are the responsibilities of a husband in a Christian marriage?

What are the responsibilities of a wife in a Christian marriage?

In what ways is marriage a picture of the relationship of Christ and the Church?

Why is marriage between a believer and an unbeliever prohibited?

MATURITY

Define maturity and give examples.

How do you become spiritually mature since this is God's will for you?

What are some of the barriers to becoming spiritually mature?

What are some of the spiritual characteristics of a mature Christian described here?

What are some of the behavioral characteristics of a mature Christian described here?

Compare "spiritual formation" by conformity to the world and transformation by the gospel.

Describe ways you can let Christ "dwell in your heart."

How can you make knowing Jesus as Lord the goal of your life?

What are some ways you can show the practical application of your salvation?

What is the role of church leaders in bringing people to Christian maturity?

How does God equip his people to do his will?

MEDITATION

Describe your best experiences in meditation.

Compare meditation practices by Eastern religions and those of Christian faith.

Why do you think the highest form of meditation focuses on God?

What are some of the characteristics of Christian meditation?

What do you think about when you meditate on God?

What do you think about when you meditate on Jesus Christ?

How can and does meditation on Scripture change your life?

How can suffering change your meditation?

What are the benefits of meditation during sleepless nights?

What aspects of your meditation would be pleasing to God?

MERCY

What is mercy? Can you think of some examples?

Why do you think God requires you to be merciful?

How can a single-sentence prayer change your life?

How does God's mercy contribute to your salvation?

What should be your response to God's mercy?

What are some practical ways for you to show mercy?

How can you be merciful to someone who doubts?

Do you think there are circumstances in which you should not show mercy?

Do you believe you have the gift of showing mercy?

MISSION

What comes into your mind when you hear the word "mission"?

Describe a significant "mission" of your own.

Describe Jesus's mission. Do you think it has specific relevance to your own?

Compare Jesus's mission with the emphasis of the "social gospel" on justice, economics, race, etc.

How does your personal mission derive from Jesus's mission?

What is the gospel message of the Christian mission?

What are the imperatives and authority for Christian missions?

Do you think "short-term missions" are an important outreach of the church?

Discuss ways you can fulfill your mission in everyday life.

Have you written a personal mission statement (vision, mission, strategy)? Discuss its value to you.

MOTIVATION

What are the things that have motivated your life?

What does it mean to you to offer yourself to God?

What are the implications of wanting to please God?

How would you explain "hope" to a non-Christian friend?

What are the specifics of a Christian's hope?

Do you consider future judgment a promise or a threat?

Does the promise of a reward detract from pure love of God?

Does living your life "worthy" of the Lord introduce the idea of merit?

How do you determine what pleases God?

MURDER

Why has murder been an issue in human society forever?

Do you believe the Old Testament commands for capital punishment apply in the twenty-first century?

Why is capital punishment such an important concept?

Do you think a plea bargain is ever appropriate in a capital murder case?

Why is it important to have multiple witnesses?

Do you agree that hate is the moral equivalent of murder?

How do you explain widespread hate in America?

What practical suggestions would you offer to reverse the increasing expressions of hate?

NEIGHBORS

Who is your neighbor?

What aspects of loving yourself do you need to extend to your neighbor?

How does envy of your neighbor conflict with loving them?

What is your responsibility with respect to found property?

What do you think about belonging to the neighborhood clique?

Distinguish between neighborhood gossip and news; slander and fact.

Why do you think it is a sin to belittle a neighbor?

Why is it important to be a good neighbor?

How should you respond when a neighbor is doing good things for you?

OATH/VOW

Discuss some of the ways "oath" is used in modern society.

Discuss use of "vow" in modern society.

Can you give an example of a vow made under pressure?

What gives an oath or a vow its binding nature?

Should you refuse to swear an oath to tell the truth in court?

What if you never made a vow to God? Will he think less of you for not doing so?

OBEDIENCE

Discuss obedience as it is commonly used in Christian circles.

Which do you think is of more importance; the spirit or the letter of the law?

Discuss the importance of obeying God's commandments.

What are the two greatest commandments given in the Bible? What is the third?

Discuss some practical ways to remind yourself frequently of God's commandments.

How would you explain to a non-believer that you love Jesus?

What are some of the results of obedience to God's commandments?

Discuss obedience to your spiritual leaders.

How would you tie obedience to the great commission?

ONE ANOTHER

Do you think "one another" means the same as "your neighbor"?

Discuss the importance of loving one another.

Why do you think we are instructed to confess our sins to each other?

What is the law of Christ?

Describe the features of humility. How is it related to service?

What is the secret to harmony in the church and Christian community?

Describe some practical ways to encourage and build one another up in the church.

Do the words of Scripture and the music of hymns influence your everyday thinking? How?

Do you think hospitality remains an important outreach to one another in our culture?

How can you equate loving one another with loving God?

PATIENCE

Why is patience an important virtue?

In what ways has God shown his patience with you?

Does the patience of God change your view of evil and human suffering?

What is the connection between patience and hope for a Christian?

How does the promise of the Lord's return at any time affect your daily life?

Can you recall a difficult time when you were patient?

How can you be patient with someone who annoys you?

How would more patience affect your daily life?

PEACE

Discuss peace as used in Christianity.

Why is Jesus called the Prince of Peace?

What is the peace of Christ? How do you let it rule your heart?

Describe the peace of God that passes understanding. How can you obtain it?

How does fixing your mind on God fill your life with peace?

Discuss peace as a character trait.

Why does keeping the peace require so much work?

How does peace guard your heart in times of temptation?

Do you agree that suffering or adversity can produce peace?

What is the peace of Jerusalem?

PERSECUTION

Have you ever felt direct persecution because of your Christian faith?

Can you give a contemporary example of loving your enemy?

In what ways is Jesus's command to love your enemy countercultural?

Why should you as a Christian be happy when you face persecution?

How does your own suffering make you a particiapnt in Jesus's suffering?

How does suffering persecution for Jesus differ from suffering from disease?

What should you be doing during times of persecution?

What are some "faith anchors" to remember during times of persecution?

PERSEVERANCE

Why is perseverance in prayer an important discipline?

If God is not bound by time, why does he make us wait so long before answering our prayers?

How are perseverance and hope related?

Describe the fight of faith and how to win it.

How does perseverance (or lack of it) influence your Christian walk?

Do you think of Christianity as a fight or a race?

How do you prevent fatigue in always doing good works?

How does suffering increase your hope of final salvation?

PLEASING GOD

What is your idea of "pleasing" as it is presented in this book?

How difficult is it to please God?

Discuss the concept that God can do whatever he wants to do.

What is the key to living a life that is pleasing to God?

Discuss ways you can please God: body, mind, soul and spirit.

Does God's demand for worship seem self-serving?

How can you determine what will please the Lord in your own life?

Do you understand how sharing someone else's failures pleases God?

How can children please God?

Explain how faith is an essential part of pleasing God.

POVERTY

Discuss poverty in the world. What are its basic causes?

Discuss current attitudes toward the "homeless." What should be that of a Christian?

Why do you think the Lord seems to favor the poor?

What aspects of "social justice" should apply to the poor?

Name some subgroups of poor people. How could you help meet their needs?

What are the basic needs of poor people? How could you help meet them?

Why is anonymity in charity important to God?

Discuss the spiritual aspects of financial poverty.

Do you recognize such a condition as spiritual poverty?

PRAISE

Discuss praise as you see it in our culture.

Why is praise an essential part of Christian worship?

Do you think praise differs from thanksgiving?

Share ways in which you praise God.

Name some things that should come to mind when praising God.

What is the importance of the "name" of the Lord?

Name some of the "works" of the Lord.

List some of the characteristics of God for which he should be praised.

How can your good works be part of your praise to God?

PRAYER, Part 1

How would you explain prayer to someone who has never had the experience?

How do you think Jesus intended for you to use the Lord's prayer?

Why should you pray when God already knows what you need?

How does sin or an unforgiving spirit hinder your prayers?

What is the way to come near to God?

What do you think is the proper physical positioning for prayer?

Why should you pray "in Jesus's name"?

Describe Jesus's present role in the life of a Christian.

What are some specific things for which to pray?

Do you think God always answers your prayers? If not, why not?

PRAYER, Part 2

How do you decide for whom you should pray?

List some groups of people for whom everyone should pray.

How do you decide what to pray for in others?

What are the prayer responsibilities of the elders of your church?

What is your responsibility toward a wayward Christian?

What are some specifics when you pray for our government?

How do you pray specifically for peace in Jerusalem?

How do you come near to God in prayer?

What is the role of prayer in relieving anxiety?

How does prayer defend you from temptation?

PRIDE

What are some manifestations of pride that you have observed?

What is your reaction to the statement that God detests pride?

How can prosperity lead to pride?

Do you think it is trite or super-religious to preface your remarks with "God willing"?

What are the dangers of pride?

How does pride interfere with personal relationships?

In what ways is pride linked to loving the world?

In what ways is pride linked to resisting the Devil?

Why is pride not a part of true love?

PRIORITIES

How have you gone about establishing priorities in your life?

What are some of the ways you can really make God a priority in your life?

Contrast the priorities of the world with those of the kingdom of God.

What character traits should be evident in a Christian with well-ordered priorities?

How has our culture re-ordered priorities for many families?

How can you prioritize the needs of others when you can barely meet your own?

What should be your major priorities with respect to one another?

How do you balance the demands of work with healthy family priorities?

PRISONERS

What do you know about prisoners' "rights" in modern prisons?

Discuss "prison" and "prisoners" from a theological perspective.

How did Jesus fulfill his mission to set prisoners free?

What are some practical ways to minister to those in prison?

Can you equate doing something for a homeless person with doing it for Jesus?

What kind of reward are you expecting in heaven?

What are some visible evidences that a person is a prisoner of sin?

In what way is a person a "prisoner of the Law"?

List some ways in which Jesus sets you free.

PURITY

Discuss purity. Name some little sins that keep us from being pure.

Name some safeguards that protect us from becoming impure.

Why is purity in all aspects of your life so important?

In what ways do contemporary sexual norms conflict with biblical purity?

How can you maintain purity of thought when media and entertainment discourage it?

What measures can you take to maintain the "innocence" of a child?

How does "pure religion" compare with worldly views of religion?

Discuss examples of how a pure life can be a powerful witness to the grace of God.

How can you be preoccupied with heavenly virtues when you are fully occupied on earth?

What part of purifying your heart is up to God and what part is yours?

RECONCILIATION

Define reconciliation. Give some everyday examples.

Explain how you have been reconciled with God. Why is this important?

What does it mean to be an ambassador for Christ?

How can you bring about the reconciliation of a lost soul to God?

What steps are necessary to bring about reconciliation of two estranged people?

Why is it important to resolve adversarial relationships?

Discuss your reconciled relationship with God and its present and future benefits.

REMINDERS

What visual reminders of God's presence and work in your life do you have in your home?

Do you find them helpful in your Christian walk?

How have you taught your children about God's commandments?

Describe the natural tendency to forget God when things are going well.

Why is it important to remind yourself to do good works?

REPENTANCE

What is repentance? Why do you think the word has disappeared from common use?

What is involved in repentance as outlined in Scripture?

How could God overlook sin in the past in view of his stated hatred for it?

What does it mean to tear up your heart rather than your clothing?

Why is it so difficult to repent and turn to God?

What about someone who thinks they have no need for repentance?

How does God's response to repentance demonstrate his true nature?

What does it mean to "perish"?

Describe the joy in heaven over sinners who have repented?

Why is it important to demonstrate your faith by what you do?

RESPECT

What are some synonyms that help define respect?

Name some areas in our culture where respect is no longer a virtue.

Why are we commanded to respect all human authority? Are there any exceptions?

Widows and old men deserve respect if they meet certain criteria. What if they do not?

Do you think the USA is doing a good job caring for its very old and very young?

Why is it important to respect your parents (and grandparents)?

What is the value of older men and women in the church?

How does a lack of respect for elders affect the functioning of a local church?

How can lack of respect for an employer who is a bully affect the gospel?

How do we know that God is no respecter of persons? Why is it important?

REST

Can you think of a time when you were desperately in need of rest? How did you handle it?

What is rest in the biblical sense?

Why do you think it important that physical rest is commanded in the Bible?

What is the practical and religious importance of a special day of rest?

What are some good activities for your day of rest and what are some that are not beneficial?

Why is rest an important spiritual activity?

How do you respond to Jesus's invitation to go to him when you are tired and frustrated?

Describe the "rest" that God has prepared for his people.

Why is true rest to be found in God alone?

REVENGE

Tell about some examples of revenge you have seen or heard?

What's wrong with a little grudge?

Why are you commanded not to want revenge?

Do you think revenge is ever justified?

What is the alternative to revenge?

Can you think of an example of overcoming evil with good?

SABBATH

What is the meaning and purpose of Sabbath?

What is the origin of the Sabbath?

What is the first mention of Sabbath in the Bible?

Why do most Christians observe Sunday rather than Sabbath?

Do you think observing Sunday acknowledges it as a sign between God and Christians?

What activities would you consider inappropriate for Sunday?

What does it mean to say, "Jesus is Lord of the Sabbath"?

Discuss the Sabbath rest that awaits follows of Jesus.

Can you describe the rest Jesus gives when you unload on him?

SACRIFICE

Discuss ancient and modern concepts of sacrifice.

Tell of a sacrifice made by someone you know about that has impressed you.

What are some things you might consider as a sacrifice to God??

Compare what you might consider a sacrifice with the types of sacrifice that please God.

How does the blood of Christ count as a sacrifice for your sins?

How can your body count as a living sacrifice to God?

SALVATION

What is salvation? From what? For what?

How would you explain salvation to someone who knows nothing about it?

How would you explain the way to put faith in Jesus?

How would you defend the exclusivity of the Christian gospel to an unbeliever?

Do you think the only two choices are to either believe or reject Jesus? Eternal life or death?

What is faith? How can you be sure it is going to be your means of salvation?

In what ways are you a new person after committing to follow Jesus?

What role do works play in God's plan of salvation?

Briefly describe the "gospel." What role does it play in salvation?

How should you "work out" your own salvation?

SANCTIFICATION

What is sanctification?

How does sanctification differ from justification and holiness?

When does the process of sanctification begin and end?

What is the goal of sanctification?

What is God's part in sanctification?

What is your part in sanctification?

Does sanctification lead to a sinless life here on earth?

What is the evidence for sanctification in a person's life?

Why is sexual sin specifically identified in the context of sanctification?

What does it mean to offer your body as a living sacrifice to God?

Give examples of things that defile body, soul, and spirit.

SCRIPTURE

Describe the methods, routines, translations, etc. you have used in reading/studying Scripture.

What are your most important reasons for studying Scripture?

How would you explain "inspiration" of Scripture to someone else?

Describe how the Scripture has been transformational in your daily life situations.

Why do you think the "prophets" take up so much space in the Bible?

What are the essential elements of the gospel? Why are they important?

Describe common spiritual battles. How does Scripture help fight them?

Do you think "knowing and doing" is a good summary of our obligation to Scripture?

What are some of the adverse effects of ignoring Scriptural principles?

What are the implications of God's word "standing forever"?

SERVICE

What comes to mind in thinking of "service?"

Are there only two choices in choosing whom to serve and worship?

How should your service to God be characterized?

How do you understand "Not everyone who says they follow Jesus will enter heaven"?

What are some specific ways you can serve God?

What are some of the ways Jesus taught service?

Characterize greatness in the kingdom of God on earth.

Why is it important for you to be using your gifts in serving the church?

Describe the conflicts in trying to serve two different masters.

How can you be sure you are serving "in the name of Jesus"?

SEXUALITY, Part 1

Give a brief description of your own sex education.

Why is sex education such a difficult topic for parents?

Discuss the origin of sexuality and its implications for modern society.

Discuss the mandate for marriage.

What is adultery? Why is it such a serious sin?

What steps can you take to "guard your heart"?

Why do you think God detests homosexuality?

Why do you think modern society is so accepting of homosexuality?

Describe some of the forms of child abuse.

SEXUALITY, Part 2

Why are married men attracted to an affair? Why women?

Why are sexual sins always at the top of the list ahead of other "lesser" sins?

What practical steps can you take to avoid sexual immorality?

Describe your "earthly and sinful nature."

How can you avoid having your sinful nature take control of your life?

Why is sex such a powerful weapon in marital discord?

How does sex create strong bonding within a faithful marriage?

In what ways can a husband love his wife as much as he loves his own body?

Discuss how marriage is an illustration of a great Christian "mystery."

SIN, Part 1

What is sin? What is its origin?

Explain how all the law of Moses is summed up in two commandments.

Is it fair that breaking even one commandment makes you guilty of breaking the entire law?

Why does ignorance of the law or unintentional infractions make you guilty of breaking God's law?

Why is it humanly impossible to please God by keeping the law?

Why do you think Adam and Eve sinned against God? Imagine the incident.

How do you feel about being declared a sinner before you even made your very first choice?

Discuss the influence of a sinful nature on the average individual. The average Christian.

What is the effect and consequence of deliberate and persistent sin?

In what way is the entire world a prisoner of sin?

SIN, Part 2

What is an advocate? Describe that person if you have had one.

If you believe Jesus is God, how could he be tempted in the same ways you are?

How can God forgive some awful sins and still be just?

Do you believe God will refuse to forgive you if you refuse to forgive others?

How does sin affect your prayers?

How can you resist having your life controlled by your sin nature?

What is sanctification? How does it show in your life?

What is the source of temptation? How can you resist it?

What are some ways children are taught to sin?

How should you treat another believer caught in sin?

Describe some common things that can hinder your Christian walk.

SLANDER

What is slander? Give some examples from your experience.

Why is slander so quickly associated with evil?

What are some of the vices associated with slander?

What are some of God's expectations regarding our speech?

Think of some ways to combat slander?

What are some special considerations in slandering a fellow Christian?

What is the origin of slander?

Is your tongue an evil body organ?

In what ways does slander devalue your Christianity?

What are some things you can do to keep yourself from speaking slander?

SOLITUDE

What is solitude? How would or do you spend this time if you have it?

How would or do you arrange solitude in the midst of a busy life?

Why do you think solitude is considered one of the important disciplines of the Christian life?

How can or does solitude reinforce your faith in God?

In what ways does solitude enhance your relationship with Jesus?

Discuss important aspects of Christian meditation in contrast with Eastern meditation.

What are some of the benefits of solitude?

How can solitude help you grow in your Christian faith?

SPEECH

What do you mean when you refer to "speech"?

What are the common situations where speech often becomes heated?

Discuss characteristics of perverse or corrupted speech.

How would you ideally deal with a mocker?

Describe the good feeling that comes with the downfall of someone you don't like?

What are empty words? Give examples.

What are the dangers of idle chatter?

Describe some characteristics of Christ-like speech.

Why is it so important to control your tongue?

Compare and contrast gentle and harsh words and speech.

SPIRITUAL GIFTS

Describe your understanding of spiritual gifts.

What role does the Holy Spirit play in your spiritual gift(s)?

What are the primary purposes of spiritual gifts to individuals?

Develop a list of spiritual gifts (See Romans 12, 1 Corinthians 12, and 1 Peter 4).

How are spiritual gifts like body parts?

What choice(s) if any do you have regarding your spiritual gift(s)?

What are the primary purposes of spiritual gifts to the Church?

Why is love an indispensable part of exercising your spiritual gift(s)?

How would you describe God's "indescribable" gift?

SPIRITUAL WARFARE

What is your understanding of spiritual warfare?

Who started this war?

Give specific examples of this warfare found in Scripture.

What are the consequences of this warfare?

How does this war differ from human warfare?

How do you fight this war and what is your objective?

Contrast the armor of a spiritual warrior with that of a human warrior.

Is the outcome of this war pre-determined? If so, why do we have to fight it?

Give examples of spiritual warfare that you have observed in yourself or other people's lives.

SUBMISSION

Discuss the meaning of submission in the Christian context.

What does it mean to submit to God?

Are there instances where you should resist rather than submit to your government?

Are there legitimate reasons to challenge your church leaders?

How should submission to each other be worked out in daily life?

Are there legitimate situations in which a wife is "alpha" in a family and the husband is "beta"?

What does spousal love have to do with submission?

Why is it important for employees to submit to employers?

SUFFERING

What are the various types of suffering that you have seen or experienced?

In what ways is suffering a discipline in the Christian life?

How can you stay positive and be joyful when you are suffering and feeling poorly?

How does suffering test your faith?

What are the desired outcomes of suffering?

How does personal suffering connect you with the suffering of Christ?

What is your understanding of Philippians 3:10?

Discuss the kinds of suffering that are imposed on Christians in the USA and worldwide.

What is the "law of Christ"?

In what ways does suffering force us to focus on knowing and doing God's will?

TEACHING

What characteristics attracted you to your favorite teacher?

Discuss the things that are necessary to become a great teacher.

Describe guidance given in Scripture for teaching your children about your faith.

Why are parents' instructions critical in shaping the lives of their children?

How can you be taught by God?

What obligations fall on you when you become a student of Jesus and his teachings?

Name some qualifications for someone who wants to teach in the church.

How can you let the message of Christ fill your life?

Why should teachers be held to a higher standard of accountability?

TEMPTATION

What is temptation?

What are some healthy ways to deal with temptation?

Since God is Creator of all things, is he not responsible for temptation?

If Satan is the source of temptation, can you not plead innocence if you fall?

Should you really gouge out your eye if what you see is a serious temptation?

How is it possible to tempt the Lord?

What are some Scriptural ways to deal with temptation?

If you believe that Jesus is God, do you believe he was really subject to temptation?

How can God help you deal with temptation?

How should you deal with Satan, the Tempter?

Describe appropriate attitudes and actions toward someone who has fallen into temptation.

THANKSGIVING

Describe some of your Thanksgiving traditions.

What is your understanding of thanksgiving?

How can you tie thanksgiving together with bad circumstances?

What is the difference between thanksgiving and praise?

List some practical ways to show thanksgiving to God by the way you live.

What are some of the things noted in the reading for which to be thankful to God?

What are some practical ways to develop a thankful heart?

What is the role of thanksgiving in prayer?

What is the role of thanksgiving in work?

What is the role of thanksgiving in assessing possessions?

THEFT

Can you tell about a famous theft in history?

How does the theory of evolution support theft?

Why do you think the idea of restitution is such a small part of our laws?

Give some examples of ill-gotten gain.

Discuss the social and spiritual aspects of wealth inequality.

What are some of the ways employees steal from their employers?

If loving your neighbor sums up all the commandments, why are we given so many of them?

In what ways can you store up treasure in heaven?

What are some important reasons to have treasure in heaven?

TIME

Can you quote some of the world's wisdom about time?

In what ways do you try to make the best use of your time? Why is this important?

How do you try to understand the times in which we live?

What resources do you use in interpreting the "signs of the times"?

How is God a foundation for your times? How does this work when times are rapidly changing?

Do you ever feel conflicted about talking to God only in the bad times?

Why do you think God makes us wait for him to answer our prayers?

Illustrate "a time for everything" in a modern lifespan.

What is the meaning of "set eternity in your heart"?

Discuss the timeline of the timeless God.

Do you think time as we know it will ever end?

TRUST

Discuss the modern use of the word "trust."

What does it mean to put your trust in Jesus?

What does it mean to put your trust in God and lean on him?

Why should you put your trust in God?

Discuss the roles of faith and good works in your salvation.

Point out the benefits of trusting God.

What are the alternative places to put your trust?

Discuss the role of trust in love.

TRUTH, Part 1

What is truth? How can you be sure that what you think you know is true?

Why is it important to tell the truth?

How can you be sure that God is true?

God wants you to be saved and know the truth. What is this truth?

Explain the wrath of God to someone who only sees him as loving and compassionate?

How do you make your worship of God "spiritual and true"?

How do you communicate spiritual truth? (Also see 1 Corinthians 2:1-16)

How does knowing and obeying the truth affect your inner life?

How does denying the truth affect your inner life?

What are some practical implications of being truthful?

TRUTH, Part 2

How do you react when someone says, "I'm not going to lie to you"?

How do you react when you read Jesus's words, "I'm going to tell you the truth"?

Read each of the "I tell you the truth" statements and be prepared to comment.

Pick a couple of the statements and discuss in detail.

Why is truth in general so important in a well-functioning society?

What is God's attitude about lying? How should that influence us?

UNITY

What is unity? Contrast unity and diversity.

How is unity portrayed in the Holy Trinity?

Describe unity within the Christian faith.

What is the basis for unity in the church?

In what ways is marriage an illustration of unity?

What is the importance of unity in the normal function of the human body?

How does a properly functioning church demonstrate unity?

What are the hallmarks of unity in the local church?

Discuss how love is the perfect bonding together of all other virtues.

WAITING

Can you remember a time of intense waiting? What was the outcome?

What does it mean to wait "intensely" and "in expectation"?

In what ways should waiting be an active, not a passive process?

What are the rewards for waiting for God?

What is the primary object of our waiting?

Why is it important to get prepared for the object of your wait?

Discuss time expectations when waiting for God to answer.

In what ways can waiting be a time of renewal?

WEALTH

Discuss the problems of income and wealth inequality.

List some of the financial advice available in the Bible.

What are the dangers of financial success?

Why is greed considered such a grave sin?

If the quantity of possessions is not a good measure of your life, what is?

How can you store up treasure in heaven?

What are the risks of storing up treasure on earth?

How can contentment be the happy medium between covetousness and complacency?

In what ways are love for God and love for the world incompatible?

Can you see ways God uses both wealth and ability disparity in the church?

How should the church handle visible wealth disparity in its members?

WILL OF GOD

What is or has been your understanding of "the will of God"?

Do you think the will of God is general for everyone or specific for each person?

What are the specifics of God's will with regard to salvation?

How does the will of God affect your understanding of the relationship of faith and works?

What is sanctification and why is it a priority with God?

How can you learn to understand the will of God?

Explain how God's will relates to the Church.

How completely must you know and do the will of God to enter the kingdom of heaven?

What does being thankful have to do with the will of God?

What are the important principles in determining the will of God for your life?

WISDOM

Compare and contrast knowledge, understanding, and wisdom.

Describe the wisdom of a person influential in your life.

Describe the experiences of life that contributed the most to your wisdom.

Who is "Wisdom" in Proverbs chapter 8?

How does fear of the Lord lead to wisdom and understanding?

How would you explain the wisdom of God to someone who does not know him?

Compare the wisdom of the world to the wisdom of God.

How does one acquire the wisdom of God?

Does being wise have anything to do with faith?

How would other people know that you are wise?

How do/did you teach wisdom to your children?

WITNESS

Discuss the meanings of the term, "witness."

How would you go about becoming a witness for Jesus?

What is the core message of the gospel?

What is the exclusive claim of the gospel? Why do you or do you not believe it?

Why do you think so many find it difficult to witness for Christ and the gospel?

Trace the mandate and history of Christian world missions.

Discuss the many parts of a global mission organization and how you can play a role.

How can you prepare yourself to be a better witness for Christ?

How does sharing your personal faith help you better understand what you have in Christ?

What are the rewards for being a good witness for Jesus?

WORK

What is work?

Why do most people take great pride in their work?

How can you feel like you are working for the Lord when you have a menial, repetitive job?

How does work and the creative process reflect the nature and image of God?

Why is idleness (sloth) considered by many to be a sin?

What are or should be the objectives of work?

Give some good reasons for observing a day of rest each week.

Discuss good habits to be followed on your day of rest and worship.

What are the spiritual benefits of observing the Sabbath?

How can you reconcile your belief in the Sabbath with a job that requires you to work on that day?

WORKS

What are "works"? Give some examples of good works.

Define the terms salvation, grace, faith, forgiveness, justification, eternal life.

What role do works play in salvation?

Discuss the relationship of faith and works in salvation.

What are the purposes of works in the kingdom of God?

Should your good works be limited to other believers?

Why are "thankless jobs" important in God's work?

What are some of the works God has done in your life?

How is belief in Jesus accurately described as work?

WORLDLINESS

What is the "world"? What is worldliness?

How have the ideas of worldliness changed in your lifetime? Is the term purely cultural?

What is love for the world? How does it displace love for God?

Compare and contrast conformity to the world and transformation by God.

Describe some of the "empty philosophies" of the world. What is their origin and ending?

How can you determine truth?

Give some guidance for living in the world of today.

Discuss worldliness as a spiritual battle.

Describe a healthy Christian view of wealth.

Why do you think there is such hostility to Christians in the world?

WORSHIP

What is worship? Can you tell about a special worship experience you may have had?

Why is worship such an important Christian activity?

List some of the things for which we worship God.

Contrast true and false worship.

Why is joy and its expression an important part of worship?

What are some ways we can delight in the Lord?

Discuss meditation and its part in worship.

What roles do thanksgiving and praise play in worship?

Discuss the role of music in worship.

Describe some physical aspects of worship? Are they meaningful to you?

How does offering your body to God become an act of worship?

YOU ARE...

How would you describe your own uniqueness in all of creation?

Compare Jesus's statements of "I AM" with his statements of "You are..."

What does it mean to be the light of the world?

What does it mean to be the salt of the earth?

Compare the "blessed" situations in the kingdom of God with those of the world.

In what ways do you see yourself as part of the body of Christ?

Have you ever thought of yourself as a temple of God? Or a letter from God?

What are your duties as a "royal priest"?

Describe the benefits of membership in God's family.

As an ambassador for Christ, how do you go about "reconciling" people to God?

ACKNOWLEDGMENTS

Marilyn Bunnell: my wife who gave me love, time, space, and encouragement.

Jennifer Crosswhite: editor and consultant who guided production of this book.

John Powell: vacuum cleaner salesman and faithful pastor who led me to Christ.

Wilbur McCullough: pastor during my high school years who taught me Bible content.

Gary Bradley: Navigator who taught me inductive Bible study.

Bo Matthews and Larry Poland: creative pastors who sparked my imagination.

Gary Inrig: pastor for twenty years, whose preaching encouraged me to dig deeper.

APPENDIX A

BIBLE TRANSLATIONS

NEW INTERNATIONAL VERSION Holy Bible, New International Version®, NIV® Copyright ©1973, 1978, 1984, 2011 by Biblica, Inc.® Used by permission. All rights reserved worldwide.

KING JAMES VERSION Public Domain

ENGLISH STANDARD VERSION The Holy Bible, English Standard Version. ESV® Text Edition: 2016. Copyright © 2001 by Crossway Bibles, a publishing ministry of Good News Publishers.

NEW LIVING TRANSLATION Holy Bible, New Living Translation, copyright © 1996, 2004, 2015 by Tyndale House Foundation. Used by permission of Tyndale House Publishers, Inc., Carol Stream, Illinois 60188. All rights reserved.

THE MESSAGE Copyright © 1993, 2002, 2018 by Eugene H. Peterson

NEW AMERICAN STANDARD VERSION Copyright © 1960, 1962, 1963, 1968, 1971, 1972, 1973, 1975, 1977, 1995 by The Lockman Foundation

NEW REVISED STANDARD VERSION New Revised Standard Version Bible, copyright © 1989 the Division of Christian Education of the National Council of the Churches of Christ in the United States of America. Used by permission. All rights reserved.

NEW ENGLISH TRANSLATION. NET Bible® copyright ©1996-2017 by Biblical Studies Press, L.L.C. http://netbible.com All rights reserved.

WORLD ENGLISH BIBLE by Public Domain. The name "World English Bible" is trademarked.

BIBLE IN BASIC ENGLISH Copyrighted in the United States of America by E.P. Dutton & Co,. New York.

APPENDIX B

WEBSITES

BIBLE.ORG

BIBLEGATEWAY.ORG

BIBLEHUB.COM

BIBLESTUDYTOOLS.COM

BIBLIA.COM

CARM.ORG

CROSSWALK.COM

CROSSWAY.ORG

DESIRINGGOD.ORG

GOSPELCOALITION.ORG

GOSPELWAY.COM

GOTQUESTIONS.ORG

GRACELIFE.ORG

KINGJAMESBIBLEONLINE.ORG

OPENBIBLE.INFO

PROBE.ORG

STUDIESINTHEBOOK.COM

APPENDIX C: BOOKS OF THE BIBLE AND ABBREVIATIONS

OLD TESTAMENT

Genesis	Gen.	Amos	Amos	Philemon	Philem.
Exodus	Ex.	Obadiah	Obad.	Hebrews	Heb.
Leviticus	Lev.	Jonah	Jonah	James	James
Numbers	Num.	Micah	Mic.	1 Peter	1 Peter
Deuteronomy	Deut.	Nahum	Nah.	2 Peter	2 Peter
Joshua	Josh.	Habakkuk	Hab.	1 John	1 John
Judges	Judg.	Zephaniah	Zeph.	2 John	2 John
Ruth	Ruth	Haggai	Hag.	3 John	3 John
1 Samuel	1 Sam.	Zechariah	Zech.	Jude	Jude
2 Samuel	2 Sam.	Malachi	Mal.	Revelation	Rev.
1 Kings	1 Kings				
2 Kings	2 Kings	**NEW TESTAMENT**			
1 Chronicles	1 Chron.	Matthew	Matt.		
2 Chronicles	2 Chron.	Mark	Mark		
Ezra	Ezra	Luke	Luke		
Nehemiah	Neh.	John	John		
Esther	Est.	Acts	Acts		
Job	Job	Romans	Rom.		
Psalm	Ps.	1 Corinthians	1 Cor.		
Proverbs	Prov.	2 Corinthians	2 Cor.		
Ecclesiastes	Eccl.	Galatians	Gal.		
Song of Solomon	Song	Ephesians	Eph.		
Isaiah	Isa.	Philippians	Phil.		
Jeremiah	Jer.	Colossians	Col.		
Lamentations	Lam.	1 Thessalonians	1 Thess.		
Ezekiel	Ezek.	2 Thessalonians	2 Thess.		
Daniel	Dan.	1 Timothy	1 Tim.		
Hosea	Hos.	2 Timothy	2 Tim.		
Joel	Joel	Titus	Titus		

ABOUT THE AUTHOR

Dr. Bunnell is a semi-retired pediatric orthopaedic surgeon. A native of Pennsylvania, he is a graduate of Houghton College and Temple University School of Medicine. He completed an orthopaedic residency in Syracuse, NY followed by fellowships in pediatric orthopaedics and adult foot and ankle surgery. He has held attending staff and faculty positions at SUNY Upstate Medical Center, Alfred I. Dupont Institute, Thomas Jefferson University, and Loma Linda University where he also served as Professor of Orthopaedic Surgery and Pediatrics, Orthopaedic Residency Program Director, and Chairman of the Department of Orthopaedic Surgery.

He has been active in several professional societies and on several editorial boards. He has published numerous peer-reviewed journal articles and patented the Scoliometer, a device for detecting scoliosis. He has served his church as elder and small-group leader. His hobbies include photography, woodturning, gardening, and cooking. He and his wife, Marilyn, live in Southern California. They have four daughters and nine grandchildren.

You can reach him at bunnellwp@gmail.com.

CPSIA information can be obtained
at www.ICGtesting.com
Printed in the USA
LVHW060423200221
679363LV00005B/222